Alte   es

... exploring such fun-
and subjectivity, the volume
... mple, unified object of study called
that in its place we must define and contest a
... of alternative 'Shakespeares'.

Today, the volume's author list reads like a 'who's who' of modern Shakespeare studies, and a new afterword by Robert Weimann outlines the extraordinary impact of *Alternative Shakespeares* upon its field. No doubt the Shakespeare myth lives on, not only as the source of many a high-revenue business venture, but also in education. But this only ensures that *Alternative Shakespeares* remains as relevant, powerful and crucially important as it was upon publication.

The Editor, **John Drakakis**, is Professor of English Studies at the University of Stirling. Contributing authors include Francis Barker, Catherine Belsey, Jonathan Dollimore, John Drakakis, Keir Elam, Malcolm Evans, Terence Hawkes, Peter Hulme, James Kavanagh, Christopher Norris, Jacqueline Rose, Alessandro Serpieri, Alan Sinfield and Robert Weimann.

IN THE SAME SERIES

John
Drakakis

Alternative Shakespeares

Routledge
Taylor & Francis Group

LONDON AND NEW YORK

First published 1985 by Methuen & Co. Ltd
Reprinted 1986

Reprinted 1988, 1990, 1991, 1992, 1996, 2001
by Routledge
11 New Fetter Lane, London EC4P 4EE

Simultaneously published in the USA and Canada
by Routledge
29 West 35th Street, New York, NY 10001

Second edition first published 2002

Routledge is an imprint of the Taylor & Francis Group

Typeset in Joanna by RefineCatch Limited, Bungay, Suffolk
Printed and bound in Great Britain by
TJ International Ltd, Padstow, Cornwall

British Library Cataloguing in Publication Data
A catalogue record for this book is available from the British Library

Library of Congress Cataloging in Publication Data
A catalog record for this book has been requested

ISBN 0–415–28723–5 (Pbk)
ISBN 0–415–28722–7 (Hbk)

CONTENTS

GENERAL EDITOR'S PREFACE

No doubt a third General Editor's Preface to New Accents seems hard to justify. What is there left to say? Twenty-five years ago, the series began with a very clear purpose. Its major concern was the newly perplexed world of academic literary studies, where hectic monsters called 'Theory', 'Linguistics' and 'Politics' ranged. In particular, it aimed itself at those undergraduates or beginning postgraduate students who were either learning to come to terms with the new developments or were being sternly warned against them.

New Accents deliberately took sides. Thus the first Preface spoke darkly, in 1977, of 'a time of rapid and radical social change', of the 'erosion of the assumptions and presuppositions' central to the study of literature. 'Modes and categories inherited from the past' it announced, 'no longer seem to fit the reality experienced by a new generation'. The aim of each volume would be to 'encourage rather than resist the process of change' by combining nuts-and-bolts exposition of new ideas with clear and detailed explanation of related conceptual developments. If mystification (or downright demonisation) was the enemy, lucidity (with a nod to the compromises inevitably at stake there) became a friend. If a 'distinctive discourse of the future' beckoned, we wanted at least to be able to understand it.

With the apocalypse duly noted, the second Preface proceeded piously to fret over the nature of whatever rough beast might stagger portentously from the rubble. 'How can we recognise or deal with the new?', it complained, reporting nevertheless the dismaying advance of 'a host of barely respectable activities for which we have no reassuring names' and promising a programme of wary surveillance at 'the boundaries of the precedented and at the limit of the thinkable'. Its conclusion, 'the unthinkable, after all, is that which covertly shapes our thoughts' may rank as a truism. But in so far as it offered some sort of useable purchase on a world of crumbling certainties, it is not to be blushed for.

In the circumstances, any subsequent, and surely final, effort can only modestly look back, marvelling that the series is still here, and not unreasonably congratulating itself on having provided an initial outlet for what turned, over the years, into some of the distinctive voices and topics in literary studies. But the volumes now re-presented have more than a mere historical interest. As their authors indicate, the issues they raised are still potent, the arguments with which they engaged are still disturbing. In short, we weren't wrong. Academic study did change rapidly and radically to match, even to help to generate, wide reaching social changes. A new set of discourses was developed to negotiate those upheavals. Nor has the process ceased. In our deliquescent world, what was unthinkable inside and outside the academy all those years ago now seems regularly to come to pass.

Whether the *New Accents* volumes provided adequate warning of, maps for, guides to, or nudges in the direction of this new terrain is scarcely for me to say. Perhaps our best achievement lay in cultivating the sense that it was there. The only justification for a reluctant third attempt at a Preface is the belief that it still is.

TERENCE HAWKES

LIST OF ILLUSTRATIONS

CONTRIBUTORS

Francis Barker: Professor in English, University of Essex
Catherine Belsey: Professor in English, University College, Cardiff
Jonathan Dollimore: Professor in English, University of York
John Drakakis: Professor in English, University of Stirling
Keir Elam: Professor, University of Florence
Malcolm Evans: Senior Lecturer in English Studies, North London
  Polytechnic
Terence Hawkes: Professor of English, University College, Cardiff
Peter Hulme: Professor in English, University of Essex
James Kavanagh: Associate Professor of English, University of Princeton
Christopher Norris: Professor in English, University of Wales Institute
  of Science and Technology, Cardiff
Jacqueline Rose: Professor in English, Queen Mary and Westfield
  College, University of London
Alessandro Serpieri: Professor of English, University of Florence
Alan Sinfield: Professor of English, University of Sussex

Acknowledgements

It is of the nature of a collection of essays such as this one that an editor will incur many debts of gratitude. My first is to Catherine Belsey whose help and advice in the early stages of planning this volume were invaluable. To my fellow contributors I owe thanks for their co-operation in what might otherwise have proved to be an intractable task, and to the general editor, Terence Hawkes, my debt is of a long-standing nature and goes well beyond the encouragement of this volume. Finally, thanks are due to Miss Yvonne McClymont whose sterling skills at the keyboard made the task of editing less of a chore and more of a pleasure than it might otherwise have been.

J.D.

NOTE

References to Shakespeare's texts throughout are to the Arden editions of individual plays unless otherwise stated.

References to works mentioned throughout the volume are given in full in a consolidated bibliography at the end.

1

INTRODUCTION

John Drakakis

I

> It may well be that Shakespeare idolatry is drawing strength from
> something other than its roots in the past. Having lost their anchor-
> age in the faith of their fathers, many are seeking a substitute in
> secular literature, and perhaps, in a materialistic age, any form of
> idealism has something to be said for it. But for some forms very little
> can be said – specifically, any that cannot be judged on their own
> merits, and cannot stand on their own feet, rather than on Shake-
> speare's. Besides, faith should begin when we reach the limits of
> knowledge.
>
> (Harbage 1966, p. 38)

Since the publication of *Re-reading English* (Widdowson 1982) it has
become commonplace to speak of 'a crisis in English Studies' (p. 7).
That crisis, in evidence long before 1981, and generated by the assault
on established critical practice from a variety of carefully formulated
theoretical positions, has resulted in a series of radical shifts of
emphasis within the institution of English Studies. Criticism is now an

openly pluralist activity, with proponents of particular positions contesting vigorously the intellectual space which it has occupied. Raymond Williams has recently argued that what is in crisis is 'the existing dominant paradigm of literary studies' (R. Williams 1984, p. 192) as it confronts serious challenges from a diverse variety of alternatives. What is surprising in this situation is the extent to which the study of Shakespeare has remained largely untouched by these concerns, a still point with a seemingly infinite capacity to absorb and domesticate the most hostile of challenges. But what ardent admirers are disposed fanatically to regard as the plenitude of Shakespearean texts is no longer adequate as a means of fighting off or neutralizing the force of alternative accounts, and the time has now come to challenge from a number of positions this last bastion of the 'existing dominant paradigm'.

In the past attempts at a kind of revisionism have been made, but they have almost invariably become prisoners of a history which has proved too strong for them. Alfred Harbage chose the quadricentenary celebration of Shakespeare's birth in 1964 to investigate what he called 'the effect of *mythos* upon current Shakespeare criticism' (Harbage, 1966, p. 25). Some twenty years later the mythos persists, resisting the exposure of its assumptions by a deflection of attention onto Shakespearean texts as the repositories of eternal wisdom. The difficulty encountered by attempts to challenge this heavily fortified tradition resides in their ultimate failure to break decisively with those discourses which covertly permeate the critical argument. It is worth considering Harbage's timely attempt to 'demystify' Shakespeare as a paradigm case whose strategy is finally undermined by a refusal to examine its own epistemological assumptions. Harbage's conclusion to what he called 'The Myth of Perfection' proposed an uncomfortable connection between the implied political concerns of 'a materialistic age' and a form of quasi-religious idealism which may be readily traced back to Arnold's conception of the function of literature. In pointing out the discrepancy between the phenomenological existence of Shakespeare's texts and the ways in which they have subsequently been used, the veneration of the dramatist himself can be shown to be not an act of simple idolatry so much as a process of transubstantiation. The view that would substitute the Shakespeare canon for a fully operative theology constitutes, as Harbage mischievously proposes, a search for faith.

Harbage's project aims not at the denigration of Shakespeare but at his rehabilitation, and his preoccupation is with the distorting potential of the process of mythmaking. But he argues that what he calls the persistence of 'the afterimage' of Shakespeare may not be wholly perverse since: 'if the mind's eye of our kind once stares intently at greatness it will continue to see greatness whatever the new coloration' (Harbage 1966, p. vi). While we may have no reason to doubt that his case 'has not been composed in a mood of bitter reproof', it is clear from these opening remarks that a discontinuity exists between the framework which Harbage constructs for his argument and the potentially subversive implications of some of the individual insights themselves. Indeed, a contradiction exists between the notion of an *essential* Shakespeare capable of surviving the distorting potential of any afterimage and the warning against the recuperation of the Shakespeare canon for a secular theology. The problem which this discourse does little to disturb concerns the question of 'greatness' and those values which contribute to its definition.

In fact, it is surprising to encounter in the opening essay of *Conceptions of Shakespeare* a perspective hardly different from that implicit in the quasi-theological stance which Harbage questions. Following Keats, he proposes that 'Shakespeare's significant life' transcends the world of 'specific personal experience', compelling us to think of him as 'the abstract of what makes men men'. The texts themselves, it is asserted, provide a flattering glass, permitting us to see reflected 'one of our selves at our best' (p. 22). Thus Shakespeare can be divested of his historical particularity, becoming an 'Everyman' whose 'important episodes in that life's journey were not his experiences as self but his experiences as Man' (ibid.). As a result the Bard becomes a 'Culture Hero', and:

> The idea suggests itself that what has actually happened in the case of Shakespeare is that his high repute for wisdom has triggered a myth-making process such as has operated many times before in human cultures and that the solution to the puzzling aspects of the Shakespeare controversy lies in works which have nothing to do with

> Shakespeare. . . . We must enquire into the general process of myth-making, and its basis in human psychology. When we do this, the Shakespearean case reveals so many points of kinship with recognized examples of the process that we wonder why the cultural anthropologists have not hit upon it.
>
> (Harbage 1966, p. 104)

Mythmaking, as Roland Barthes has observed, is 'a type of speech' (Barthes 1972, p. 109) involving the imposition upon a given object of additional layers of signification. But while this may account for the ascription of talismanic qualities to Shakespeare, it does little in Harbage's case to prevent the texts themselves from becoming divorced from the historical conditions of their own production.

The eradication of historical pressures, allied with the uncritical acceptance of a non-political, universal 'humanity' is itself, as Barthes rightly indicates, a function of ideology. 'Eternal Man' or 'Everyman' is thus created, and then drained of history. In the case of Shakespeare's plays, the world which they are said to imitate is reduced to a unified a-historical cipher divested of all contradiction. In this way, Harbage's project of demystifying Shakespeare, valid though it undoubtedly is at one level, falls prey to the very process of mythmaking against which it consciously inveighs. Shakespeare as universal and eternal Man, and the body of the texts which he produced under determinate historical conditions as the repository of human wisdom, function together to encourage both the eradication of the memory 'that they were once made' (Barthes 1972, p. 142), and to disguise the ideological process of reconstruction to which they are constantly subjected by the societies in which they now exist as manifestations of 'high culture'.

II

The elision of critical perspective and object of enquiry has always provided the foundation for an empiricist-romantic view of Shakespeare. From Maurice Morgann's *Essay on the Dramatic Character of Sir John Falstaff* (1777) onwards, the combined admiration of Shakespeare's 'poetry' and characterization has prevailed. Writing in 1817 William Hazlitt observed: 'our idolatry of Shakespeare (not to say our admiration) ceases with his plays' (Hazlitt 1906, p. 263), and he added that only when the chameleon dramatist resorted to self-expression in his non-dramatic poetry was his artistic stature reduced: 'In expressing the thoughts of others he seemed inspired; in expressing his own he was a mechanic' (ibid.). This judgement – misleading though it undoubtedly is – sits uncomfortably at odds with the no less romantic conception of Shakespearean genius which Hazlitt extolled in opposition to the dogged classicism of Dr Johnson. Moreover, behind Hazlitt's proselytizing but distinctly partial enthusiasm lies a national pride offended that an outsider should provide 'reasons for the faith which we English have in Shakespeare' (p. xiv).

It is to Coleridge, however, that we look for the most comprehensive account of a thoroughly romanticized Shakespeare. The Coleridgean synthesis, which Alfred Harbage has described as 'organic not mechanic thinking' (Coleridge 1969, p. 22), draws together a number of critical concepts which, taken separately, have profoundly influenced twentieth-century Shakespeare criticism. At the centre of Coleridge's own poetics was a notion of the poet 'described in ideal perfection' as someone who was able to bring 'the whole soul of man into activity with the subordination of its faculties to each other according to their relative worth and dignity', and whose function was to diffuse 'a tone and spirit of unity that blends, and (as it were) fuses, each into each by the synthetic and magical power to which I would exclusively appropriate the name of Imagination' (1969, p. 40). This combination of idealism and literary formalism could, without apparent difficulty, disengage the poet from any historical context, thus rendering ineffectual any form of materialist interrogation of the work itself. In the case of Shakespeare the 'historical' elements of his texts could be pared away to reveal an essential irreducible 'oceanic mind' subject to no historical pressures or imperatives whatsoever:

> I believe that Shakespeare was not a whit more intelligible in his own day than he is now to an educated man, except for a few local allusions of no consequence. As I said, he is of no age – nor, I may add, of any religion, or party or profession. The body and substance of his works came out of the unfathomable depths of his oceanic mind: his

observation and reading, which was considerable, supplied him with
the drapery of his figures.

(Coleridge 1969, p. 122)

This is a Shakespeare perfectly familiar to modern criticism; a
chameleon figure whose work resists in its very essence any dogged
questions that would tie it to time and place.

Coleridge abstracted from Shakespearean texts an aesthetic harmony
which reflected what he thought of as the omniscience of the artist. For
him Shakespeare was 'the Spinozistic deity – an omnipresent creative-
ness' (1969, p. 107) and the implications of this observation for the
study of the poet's 'mind' and 'art' were not lost on nineteenth-
century critics. But it is to A. C. Bradley that we look for a thorough
domestication of the Coleridgean position, and for that eclectic drawing of critical boundaries which has determined the agenda for much
twentieth-century Shakespeare criticism. Romantic 'pan-poetism', to
use Lukács's term (Lukács 1974, p. 47), becomes for Bradley part of an
economy of literary pleasure – 'Poetry for Poetry's sake' (Cooke 1972,
p. 49) – while his dilution of Hegelian categories fuses the romantic
preoccupation with philosophical themes with an essentialist concept
of characterization. Also, through Bradley comes a re-affirmation of the
narrowing of critical focus onto particular exemplary texts, and the
restatement of the view that tragedy, because of its philosophical
content, is the most superior of all dramatic forms.

In his essay, on 'Hegel's theory of tragedy' (Bradley 1909), Bradley
abstracts from Hegel what he takes to be the essence of dramatic conflict: 'a conflict . . . between powers that rule the world of man's will
and action – his "ethical substance"' (p. 71). Later, in *Shakespearean Tragedy*
(1904), this conflict of spirit, essentially idealistic in its trajectory,
could be reduced to the formula: 'character in action' (p. 7), although
Bradley includes as part of his definition a principle of 'waste' which,
he argues, is inherent in the tragic catastrophe itself. But in addition to
his reduction of Hegelian dialectic, Bradley also broke with Victorian
moralizing, preferring a more pragmatic formulation, although he was
unable to develop some of the theoretical implications of his position:

The family and the state, the bond of father and son, the bond of mother and son, the bond of citizenship, these are each and all, one as much as another, powers rightfully claiming human allegiance. It is tragic that observance of one should involve violation of another.

(Bradley 1909, p. 75)

This stance presupposes the autonomy of each individual character, while at the same time insisting that the tragic protagonist is a representative of the deeply divided human spirit. The demands of family and state – essentially political demands involving questions and relations of power – are placed in an anterior relation to the autonomous consciousness of the tragic protagonist. This allows Bradley to effect a uniting of the principle of universality with that of the specific individual traits of character. If throughout *Shakespearean Tragedy* he falls prey to speculation about the extra-dramatic lives of Shakespeare's characters, then this is nothing more than a logical extension of the basic premisses of his argument. That the family, the state, and all those cultural and social institutions in which human beings are necessarily involved might conceivably *determine* character, or that the notion of character so produced may be anything but unified, is well beyond the problematic that Bradley fashions from Hegel, as is his argument that we are moved by the conflict of family and state 'because we set a high value on family and state' (Bradley 1909, p. 86).

The emphasis which Bradley places upon the 'affirmative' as well as the 'negative' aspects of tragedy, and his definition of the catastrophe itself as 'the violent self-restitution of the divided spiritual unity' (ibid., p. 91) delineates the strictly *internal* nature of the dramatic struggle and concentrates for us the contradiction in his own position. He clearly has some difficulty in resolving the opposed impulses inherent in the tragic catastrophe, but he refuses to break with the metaphysical conception of order and harmony. Indeed, the only way in which he can resolve his difficulties is to propose that tragedy itself is beyond rational analysis and is a formal affirmation of the mystery of life:

We seem to have before us a type of the mystery of the whole world, the tragic fact which extends far beyond the limits of tragedy. . . . Tragedy is the typical form of this mystery, because the greatness of soul which it exhibits oppressed, conflicting and destroyed, is the highest

> existence in our view. It forces the mystery upon us, and it makes us realize so vividly the worth of that which is wasted that we cannot possibly seek comfort in the reflection that all is vanity.
>
> (Bradley 1904, p. 16)

Underwriting this concern with the elements of dramatic form is both an acceptance of the romantic conception of authorial intention, and a theory of reading. For Bradley the mystified first cause must constitute the intention of the author, while the object of reading and interpretation is to enable the reader to enact in his or her own imagination the process of artistic creation itself:

> Our one object will be, what again in a restricted sense, may be called dramatic appreciation; to increase our understanding and enjoyment of these works as dramas; to learn to apprehend the action of some of the personages of each with a somewhat greater truth and intensity, so that they may assume in our imagination a shape a little less unlike the shape they wove in the imagination of their creator.
>
> (Bradley 1904, p. xiii)

Indeed, as the analysis unfolds, it becomes increasingly clear that Bradley's formulation of 'the centre of tragedy' as 'action issuing from character, or character issuing in action' (1904, p. 7) may with equal force be taken also to imply that each play is thoroughly expressive of its author. On these grounds excluded plays, such as Titus Andronicus, can be summarily dismissed as having been written before Shakespeare 'had either a style of his own or any characteristic tragic conception' (p. xv; my italics). But notwithstanding the emphasis upon 'centre', 'mystery', 'soul', and 'imagination', all keywords in Bradley's lexicon, he senses a danger in the process of reading itself. For example, his desire to make the experience of reading 'true to Shakespeare' (p. 17) is, he argues, constantly frustrated by the conflicting desire to reduce this truth to a conventionalized response. The result is that reading then becomes akin to misrecognition or self-alienation, where what is at stake is the location of an essential reality which social convention somehow distorts:

And the consequence is not only mistaken theories; it is that a man will declare that he feels in reading a tragedy what he never really felt while he fails to recognize what he actually did feel.

(Bradley 1904, p. 17)

Thus a recognizably Hegelian drama is displaced from the site of the text itself, to become enacted in the reader's own responses as a separation of 'spirit' (the work's 'true' content) from those conventions (unspecified, but clearly social) which would alienate the reader from him/herself. Clearly, Bradley fails here to theorize clearly the relation between text and reader which recent debate has rendered so problematical. And yet the assumptions upon which this misrecognition of the problem is based have continually dominated the study of Shakespeare.

III

To assert a monolithic development of Shakespeare criticism after Bradley, however, would be to falsify its history. Indeed, it could well be argued that different priorities and considerations have demanded attention at different times in response to particular, though not always overtly connected, questions. At one level each area of the study of Shakespeare, whether it be the study of the bibliographical characteristics of the texts, the theatre, the audiences for the plays, or the society whose pressures they mediate, has evolved in accordance with its own internal dynamics. They have encountered each other synchronically at particular historical conjunctures, have individually reverted to positions held at earlier stages of their own history, and have often revealed in oblique ways the effects of external historical pressures. Also, especially during the first half of the twentieth century, Shakespeare criticism felt with some force the effects of the debates which were being conducted within the area of literary criticism generally.

But the Bradleian conception of dramatic character has remained very much at the centre of critical concern. Ernest Jones' Hamlet and Oedipus (1949) for example, seeks to provide a psychoanalytical justification for character and begins from the assumption that 'No dramatic criticism of the personae in a play is possible except under the pretence that they are living people' (Jones 1949, p. 20). In a play such as Hamlet, the hero's 'state of profound melancholy' (Bradley 1904, p. 86) is given a Freudian gloss while at the same time Jones imports into his analysis a large number of concepts which can be traced back to Coleridge. Generally, however, it has been normal to treat the question of Shakespearean dramatic character at this level of naive empiricism. Where psychological accounts have been used to support critical argument then they have tended to vulgarize Freud, as in the case of J. I. M. Stewart's explanation of Leontes's behaviour in the opening scene of The Winter's Tale (Stewart 1949, p. 49). Here Stewart argues that Leontes suffers from 'delusional jealousy' and that his attitude to Hermione is 'an attempt at defence against an unduly strong homosexual impulse' whereby 'an earlier fixation of his affections upon his friend (Polixenes), long dormant, is re-awakened in him'. At a less fanciful but ultimately no less romantic level, Kenneth Muir asserts that 'the intense reality of Shakespeare's principal characters' is such that 'we are made to feel we know them more intimately than we do our own friends' (Muir 1977, p. 49). Muir's renewed enthusiasm for Morgann's Essay on The Dramatic Character of Sir John Falstaff (1777), which seems subsequently to have become contagious, leads him to the conclusion that 'the subtlety of his [Shakespeare's] characterization survives the process of translation, the transplanting into alien cultures, and the erosion of time' (ibid., p. 136). More recently, John Bayley has sought to equate what he takes to be Morgann's keyword 'impression' with 'the modern conception of code' (Bayley 1981, p. 3), but this only leads him back, via a weak existentialism, to the notion of the transcendence of the consciousness of dramatic character:

> But with Shakespeare the mere fact and story of consciousness replaces both action and ideal. It is the imminence of action which brings that consciousness into prominence, but it remains independent of action.
>
> (Bayley 1981, p. 6)

This represents little more than a minor adjustment to Bradley, although it is also in some ways reminiscent of Frank Kermode's definition of 'the classic' (Kermode 1975, p. 134) in so far as it locates in 'consciousness' that excess of signification which remains after any monolithic reading of the text has been completed. Although there have been minor changes of emphasis from time to time, this line of Shakespeare criticism remains firmly committed to the idealistic assertion that 'consciousness' precedes action, and that dramatic character constitutes axiomatically a unified subject of consciousness. As spectators or readers we experience that consciousness in terms of the infinite plenitude of individual character. In short, the philosophical position underpinning this kind of criticism is that of liberal humanism, with its attendant predisposition of philosophical idealism.

Of course, humanism and idealism do not openly advertise their philosophical assumptions within the discourses of Shakespeare criticism. Rather, they seek to co-exist at an empirical level with other more formalistic concerns. Few readers of M. C. Bradbrook's *Themes and Conventions in Elizabethan Tragedy* (1935) would deny the argument that Shakespeare and his fellow dramatists availed themselves of dramatic and theatrical conventions. The difficulty arises when the question is posed of precisely what relationship these conventions bore to the social, economic, psychological and cultural life of writers and theatre audiences. In his concern to free Shakespeare from the restrictions of classicism, E. E. Stoll proposed, alongside the study of conventions, a picture of the dramatist as an untutored genius instinctively mediating custom, social outlook and cultural disposition:

> Such, I suppose, are the ideal conditions for the making of art – the supremely gifted genius, master of his medium and immediate heir to an artistic tradition, throwing himself into the undertaking prodigally and exuberantly, ignorant or regardless of esthetic rules or principles, guided and guarded by the healthy instincts and customs of his race, his temperament and his day.
>
> (Stoll 1960, p. 32)

Stoll's critical discourse is a disturbing mixture of elements of romanticism, nineteenth-century naturalism, and conventionalism, with no clear theoretical awareness of what it might involve or where it might lead. He is only prepared to contemplate Literature and History as separate entities, and he asserts that the one is an escape from the other:

> Literature is, of course, not life, neither history nor material for history, but a scroll whereon are traced and charactered the unfettered thoughts of writer and reader – a life within a life, fancy somewhat at odds with fact.
>
> (Stoll 1960, pp. 39–40)

Indeed, Stoll's separation of 'Literature' and 'History' involves ascribing to the writer a mental freedom (which he labels 'fancy') which is ultimately meaningless.

The strategic function of such remarks is, obviously, to clear the ground for formalistic analysis. Of itself, the investigation of dramatic convention and theatrical practice is, as many subsequent studies have demonstrated, valuable. The problem has always been that the investigation of detail rests upon a whole series of unstated assumptions about authorial presence, the practice of writing, the relationship between artist and society, and the very structure of the relations within society itself. The retreat into formalism, though ostensibly a response to textual anomaly and a desire to analyse internal structure, may also sometimes be seen as a rejection of unfamiliar or unpalatable forms of social analysis. On the other hand, a selective revitalization of the past may be shown to represent an affirmation of values which in cultural terms are either dominant or desirable. Many would resist instinctively the profoundly political suggestion that the study of Shakespeare reflects on a number of levels the larger ideological pre-occupations of our own culture, yet this essentially dialectical relationship between drama and society has always operated in specifically historical terms. Indeed, some of the seminal work which emerged during the period of the Second World War can be shown to rest upon assumptions which are deeply ideological, though they are invariably presented as either 'natural' or desirable.

To take a specific example, Alfred Harbage's judicious study, *Shakespeare's Audience* (1941) shaped for the modern scholarly imagination a vision of the Elizabethan theatre as 'a democratic institution in an intensely undemocratic age' (p. 11), in which 'the rights and privileges of class melted before the magical process of dropping pennies into a box' (p. 12). He argued that Shakespeare's audience was 'a cross-section of the London population of his day', and that because of 'the great numerical superiority of the working class in the London area' theatre prices were designed primarily for them (p. 90). Having constructed this populist view of Shakespeare's audience, Harbage was then faced with the difficulty of equating it with the view that the plays could only be fully understood by an intelligentsia. The arguments that result range from anticipations of the positions subsequently advanced by cultural anthropologists, to naive adducements of the relevance of childhood experience to the question of audience behaviour. Although the evidence Harbage mobilizes did not admit to harmonious integration, he clung to a picture of the Elizabethan theatre as an institution in which different social groups relinquished their mutual antagonisms in favour of a corporate activity that was both festive and anticipated the modern spirit of democracy. What this account emphasizes is the principle of unity and its application to a distant historical phenomenon at a time when 'the globe' in a more literal and local sense of the term was in a state of political turmoil.

The remarkable achievement of Harbage's analysis is that, far from being seriously challenged, it effectively laid down the parameters within which subsequent debate about Shakespeare's audience proceeded. Certain of the populist assumptions underpinning Harbage's thesis emerge in S. L. Bethell's *Shakespeare and the Popular Dramatic Tradition* (1944) which began ostensibly by raising again the question of conventionalism v. naturalism that had previously preoccupied Stoll and Schücking. Bethell's argument focused initially upon the ways in which the demands of the theatre shaped the materials which Shakespeare used in his plays, and this practical emphasis on performance was what T. S. Eliot, in a preface to the first edition, found of value. It seems likely that what also appealed to Eliot in Bethell's thesis was the account it provided of cultural history. To explain 'the growth of naturalism' as the direct result of 'far-reaching changes in philosophical outlook' may be, Bethell argued, 'unnecessarily high-flown', while the suggestion that the barriers to naturalism were merely technical ones to be overcome in the desire 'to represent life more naturalistically upon the stage' is regarded as having 'an alluring appearance of common sense, but suffers from the same sort of over-simplification which characterizes the Marxian materialist interpretation of history' (p. 17). What Bethell seems to be fighting here, in a displaced form, is the claim of a socialist realism, but although he wishes to preserve an organic theory of culture he is perfectly prepared to entertain the prospect of a historical relativism:

> It is, of course, possible that, so far as they thought about it at all, the Elizabethans did aim consciously at what they conceived to be dramatic naturalism; but if so, their conception of naturalism must have differed so widely from our own, as still to demand the explanation I have already given in terms of a changing 'climate of thought'.
>
> (Bethell 1944, p. 19)

Bethell's analysis is valuable in so far as it draws explicit attention to the nature of 'dramatic illusion', and to the formal mechanisms whereby it is sustained. But he does reject out of hand even the most straightforward of reflectionist models of realism, preferring to collapse any potentially dialectical explanation of the production of meaning into the notion of Christian 'paradox': 'Christianity, however, is founded upon the tension of opposites: God and man, nature and supernature; its doctrines define a union without confusion, between the spiritual and the material. Indeed any profound reading of experience calls *naturally* for paradoxical statement' (p. 22; my italics). It is within this dualistic framework of opposition that Bethell situates the concept of multi-consciousness, a facility demanded of an audience by 'the mixture of conventionalism and naturalism' and which produces 'the dual awareness of play world and real world' (p. 23). What Eliot had regarded as the impurity of Elizabethan dramatic art Bethell preferred to regard as 'an unconscious and organic outgrowth of playhouse psychology; a body of traditional assumptions held in common by playwright and audience' (p. 25). This view of unity-in-diversity provides a more plausible social model than that of Harbage, though it clings doggedly to an organicist view of culture and of the human unconscious which has served to facilitate the appropriation of Shakespeare for ideological purposes, particularly in times of national and political crisis.

In certain crucial respects works such as Theodore Spencer's *Shakespeare and the Nature of Man* (1942), and E. M. W. Tillyard's *The Elizabethan World Picture* (1943) and *Shakespeare's History Plays* (1944), and indeed, Sir

Laurence Olivier's film of *Henry V* (1945), fall within the purview of this argument. J. W. Lever has sought to trace the line of Tillyard's critical thinking back to the Eliotean 'recoil from debased values of bourgeois society', arguing that 'fearful of radical change, many took refuge in scholastic visions of an ideal hierarchical order' (Lever 1976, p. 80). It is not difficult to see how such a position could be appropriated for political purposes, or rather, that it could be made to accord with a particular political mood. For Lever, Tillyard's thesis was a displacement of a medieval heritage with its 'manifestation of universal *caritas*, bound by infinite links of duty and interdependence' which became 'a symmetrical design whose natural or metaphysical aspects served mainly to justify the social-political *status quo*' (Lever 1976, p. 85). Interestingly, Tillyard was groping towards the concept of an ideological apparatus, but he did not perceive in the analogy a strategy of coercion, nor could he comment on the mechanisms whereby this coercion might be internalized psychologically as a system of rules governing behaviour. Rather, Tillyard's 'picture' of culture, though now discredited, is tacitly regarded as a desirable objective coterminous in his own time with an aesthetic which is offered as its natural manifestation.

Missing from Tillyard's account of what can, retrospectively, be termed Elizabethan 'ideology' is any clear theoretical sense of how power functions. Subsequent attempts to revise Tillyard's thesis, such as Wilbur Sanders's *The Dramatist and the Received Idea* (1968) proffered a secular reworking of Tillyard's theocentric conception but they did little to disturb the epistemological foundations which he had laid down in the 1940s. The pressure for significant change has, however, begun to emerge from other quarters. For example, the excavatory social demographic work of Lawrence Stone in his *The Crisis of the Aristocracy, 1558–1641* (1965), *The Causes of the English Revolution 1529–1642* (1972) and *The Family, Sex and Marriage in England 1500–1800* (1977), Peter Laslett in *The World We Have Lost* (1965), and the work of the historian Christopher Hill, have provided considerable information for a historical revaluation of the period, and this has inevitably begun to have its effects on the study of Shakespearean drama.

The nature of the relationship between drama and society has usually been treated eclectically by Shakespearean scholars, alternating between empirical and idealistic approaches to the problem. More recently, and in connection with the larger issues raised by a consideration of Tillyard, attention has turned to the difficult concept of 'mimesis' but from a more openly materialist standpoint. In this respect Robert Weimann's *Shakespeare and the Popular Tradition in the Theatre* (1978) and A. D. Nuttall's *A New Mimesis: Shakespeare and the Representation of Reality* (1983) stand at virtually opposite ends of the epistemological spectrum. Weimann concerns himself not with 'idealistic methodologies' (1978, p. xxi) but with the material historical conditions of performance, representation and reception, all of which are shown to be related dialectically to each other, while Nuttall espouses a positivistic conservative materialism which rejects the specificity of history for the '*eterne mutabilitie* of human nature, perennial, unhistorical variations of temperament' (1983, p. 167) which Shakespeare's plays are said to reflect unproblematically.

Alongside this the call has been for a radical departure based upon an extrapolation of certain of the theoretical implications of Saussurian linguistics, especially those areas concerned with the differential mechanisms of sign production, along with new developments in cultural materialism, psychoanalysis, marxist social analysis and latterly, feminism. In an ambitious attempt to locate the conditions for the production of cultural unity and individual subjectivity, Stephen Greenblatt in his *Renaissance Self-Fashioning from More to Shakespeare* (1980) has called for 'a poetics of culture' in which both the social aspects of language and the dialectic between 'world' and 'text' become the basis of an analysis of the construction of a renaissance subjectivity:

> Language like other sign systems, is a collective construction; our interpretative task must be to grasp more sensitively the consequence of this fact by investigating both the social presence of the world of the literary text and the social presence of the world in the text.
>
> (Greenblatt 1980, pp. 4–5)

Greenblatt's focusing upon the dialectical mechanisms of signification raises fundamental questions about the concept of a unified renaissance literary text, as indeed it does about any notion of 'a single history of the self' as being anything other than an enabling fiction both for its producer and the modern reader. The general questions of power and ideology exposed by this form of analysis have led to the re-thinking of a whole range of problems posed by the drama of Shakespeare and his contemporaries, as evidenced in works such as Alan Sinfield's *Literature in Protestant England 1550–1660* (1983) and Jonathan Dollimore's *Radical Tragedy: Religion, Ideology and Power in the Drama of Shakespeare and his Contemporaries* (1984).

IV

Although these accounts fall under what may loosely be termed a 'new historicism', they have yet to displace the conservative tradition of history within which Shakespeare's texts have been so often inscribed. In fact, that tradition itself has proved a flexible weapon mobilized against change. Indeed 'historical' and, in certain cases, historicist, accounts of Shakespearean texts, pluralist in emphasis and liberal in their capacity to assimilate revisionist, or even radical, challenges, have become a staple of Shakespeare criticism. At their methodological worst, traditional historical approaches can become little more than extensions of existing social relations, as evidenced in Helen Gardner's astonishing defence of historical method against what, during the years 1953–6, she regarded as the excesses of New Criticism:

> The counterpoise to the necessity of 'examining the genius of his age and the opinions of his contemporaries' if we are to arrive at 'a just estimate' of a writer's quality and to understand his meaning, is the necessity of learning the author's own personal language, the idiom of his thought. The discipline of imaginative intercourse is now wholly different from the discipline of social intercourse. We learn to know our friends so that we do not misunderstand them or put a wrong construction on their actions. We can say with certainty 'He can't have meant that', because we know the kind of person 'he' is. In the same way we can arrive at a similar conviction about a poem because we know the habit of the author's mind and are familiar with his associations of ideas and have come to sympathize with his moral temper. It is possible, in the light of this knowledge, to check our own habits and

> associations and feel some assurance that one interpretation is better, because more characteristic than another.
>
> (Gardner 1959, p. 52)

Gardner's *reductio ad absurdum* of empirical historical and critical practice, which presupposes that meaning is a question of extracting the essence from any utterance, is the prologue to an attack upon Cleanth Brooks's account of *Macbeth* proposed in 'The naked babe and the cloak of manliness' (1947). This short essay, a model of the methods of 'New Criticism', effectively separated the formal aspects of literary study from those moral and ethical preoccupations which had begun with Matthew Arnold and which reached their fullest expression in the *Scrutiny* school of criticism. Gardner's response to Brooks's elimination of history was to propose a sub-textual narrative which would itself be reduced to a history of the transcendent individual. Thus one form of essentialism could replace another while at the same time claiming to be ostensibly opposed to it on fundamental grounds. Indeed, both seemingly opposed positions rested upon the existence of some irreducible master narrative which lay beneath the surface of the text, which in Brooks's case was simply assumed to exist, but which in Gardner's case was actually the quarry to be stalked.

Brooks's essay represents the logical culmination of a movement in Shakespeare criticism which grew out of the concern with 'practical criticism', and which revealed itself initially in the early 1930s as a reaction against A. C. Bradley's preoccupation with 'character' and 'plot'. The move to displace characterization from the centre of critical concern crystallized in the work of G. Wilson Knight, whose book *The wheel of Fire* (1930), like Bethell's some fourteen years later, contained a preface by T. S. Eliot. Eliot applauded the break from what he called the 'hypostasizing of "character" and "plot"' (p. xix) and concentrated his approval of Wilson Knight's project upon the latter's concern with the poetic elements of the plays themselves, in so far as they yielded a sense of the whole design, and of the individual work's 'subterrene or submarine music' (ibid.). Eliot approved strongly of Wilson Knight's stated wish 'to rely upon his sense of power and accomplishment in language to guide him' (p. xiv), although he demurred over the question of interpretation, suggesting that this activity was necessary 'only insofar as one is passive, not creative oneself' (p. xviii). Wilson Knight eschewed evaluation, what he called 'the judgement of vision', preferring 'interpretation, a reconstruction of vision' (p. 1), and arguing that each play was 'a visionary whole, close-knit in personification, atmospheric suggestion, and direct poetic-symbolism: three modes of transmission equal in their importance' (p. 11). The result was not a critique of mystification, but rather a celebration of it, removing from the text itself any traces of a concrete history – 'when such a divergence occurs the commentator must be true to his artistic, not his normal ethic' (p. 9) – insisting that response to certain Shakespearean characters and what they stand for will be 'natural', and culminating in a hymn to the 'divine worth' of Shakespeare:

> The soul-life of a Shakespearean play is, indeed, a thing of divine worth. Its perennial fire is as mysterious, as near and yet as far, as that of the sun, and like the sun it burns while generations pass.
>
> (Knight 1930, p. 14)

Wilson Knight's free-ranging responsiveness produces, he argues, 'certain conclusions which may seem somewhat revolutionary', and it is certainly the case that his reading of the Last Plays as 'mystical representations of a mystical vision' (p. 16) replaces the Victorian image of Shakespeare as a tired artist with one of a more actively engaged allegorizing poetic consciousness. But such a responsiveness, relying upon the moment of the text's impact upon the reader, could also be misled, as evidenced in the eccentricities of his first two essays on *Hamlet*. Moreover, it is clear from Wilson Knight's own, often stimulating, analyses that the image-clusters and thematic patterns which he discerned and then responded to were products of an evaluative reading, though it was one which sought to efface its own role as structuring agent. Reading, as Eliot seems to have hinted in his preface to *The Wheel of Fire*, is not a simple replication of the process whereby the work receives its initial structure, although both he and Wilson Knight assumed that interpretation was 'passive' in its receipt of impressions.

Such theoretical inconsistency, though grounded in a recognizable 'metaphysics of the text' was desperately in need of a more rigorous justification, and from within the purview of the Scrutiny school L. C. Knights undertook the task of reformulating the anti-Bradleian position in his seminal essay in Explorations (1933) 'How many children had Lady Macbeth? An essay on the theory and practice of Shakespeare criticism'. Knights combined the close-reading techniques of I. A. Richards and William Empson with a shrewd, if at times opportunistic, deployment of historical evidence in support of his arguments, but his main objective was to define the activity of reading in such a way as to account for 'the unique arrangement of words' on the page (p. 28). The imposition of a textual stability allied to a unitary, if complex, meaning, permitted the overriding of historical consideration to the point where the de-materialized readerly intelligence could be said to eavesdrop directly upon the authoritarian text: 'Read with attention the plays themselves will tell us how they should be read' (p. 17). This notion of text-as-authority contains within it the notion of an idealized audience, worthy, like the critic himself, of those claims to intelligence and sensitivity demanded by the poetry. Thus Knights could infer from the texts an Elizabethan audience in possession of 'an educated interest in words, a passionate concern for the possibilities of language and the subtleties of poetry' (p. 17), capacities which allowed it, along with the critic, to share 'the speech idiom that is the basis of Shakespeare's poetry' (p. 18).

For Knights the activity of reading, determined and controlled by an essential, unchanging text whose own constituents are irreducible and therefore untheoretically 'given', is crucial. But this turns the responsive reader into a site of contradiction, at one extreme exercising 'the razor-edge of sensibility' by which a Shakespearean text can be possessed (p. 28), while at the same time receiving passively the imprint of the structure laid down by the authoritative artist whose fullness of utterance resides exclusively in 'the exact words of the poem concerned' (p. 29). Clearly, what is at issue here is the fundamental question concerning the immanence of literary structure, the role of the reader, and the extent to which a theoretical 'knowledge' of the text and its processes is possible given the unstated assumptions of Knights's argument. Nor is the position clarified by his enlistment of a vocabulary of violence in his description of the critic's activity as being one designed to 'force the subject to expose itself' (p. 29). Indeed, if anything, this is the mailed fist of coercion inside the velvet glove of a submissive intelligence.

Knights's definition of the 'good critic' as someone who points 'to something that is actually contained in the work of art' as opposed to 'the bad critic' who 'points away from the work in question' (p. 29) effectively sidesteps the problems of meaning, while at the same time marginalizing contextual study in favour of a dominant metaphysics of the text. Investigations of the processes of the making of the text, and of its reconstitution in criticism, which, inevitably, point away from the phenomeno-logical texture of its surface, are condemned summarily as bad criticism. But ironically, despite his inveighing against Bradley, Knights's extolling of what at first sight might seem to be a crude textual positivism while at the same time pointing directly to a category of transcendent truth, effectively leaves the door open for the readmission of categories such as 'character' which can be shown to exist in an empirical sense in the text. The reading discipline which Knights advocates is one which reduces the text to a quintessential 'experience'; thus *Macbeth* is 'a statement of evil' although this is to be understood as 'a statement not of a philosophy but of ordered emotion' (p. 41), while two of the play's 'main themes' are the suitably universal 'reversal of values and of unnatural disorder' (p. 29). The detail of the text is harmonized with a general centripetal impulse of which each element is a manifestation, so that universal principles located by the critic can only be discussed 'in terms of the poet's concrete realization of certain emotions and attitudes' (p. 41). At best this is a positivism devoid of any clear theoretical underpinning.

This isolation and privileging of poetic discourse – 'the essential structure of *Macbeth*, as of the other tragedies, is to be sought in the poetry' (Knights 1959, p. 102) – looks back to Coleridge, but also points forward to those studies of imagery and wordplay which have been more or less loosely allied to assumptions about the mental development of Shakespeare as man and artist. Indeed, in the interval between *Explorations* (1933) and the later *Some Shakespearean Themes* (1959) the two issues became gradually fused together, though in a pragmatic rather than in a systematic way. It is significant that the L. C. Knights of *Drama and Society in the Age of Jonson* (1937), who mobilized historical data as a backcloth to a series of moral arguments about Jonson and his fellow dramatists, and their attitudes towards an encroaching economic materialism, has never really mingled seriously with the Shakespearean critic of *Explorations* and *Some Shakespearean Themes* at the theoretical level, although what unites all these projects is the desire to abstract 'feeling' as the basis for a definition of an even more abstract 'life'. In *Some Shakespearean Themes* the earlier position of *Explorations* is tempered by a seemingly more pragmatic approach to questions of authorial intention, but, sophisticated though Knights's responses undoubtedly are, his search is still for universal patterns tinged this time with vague psychological implications. The essential quarry now appears to be, not so much the meaning of 'life', though in his treatment of individual plays this quest is not in any sense abandoned, but rather 'the urgent personal themes that not only shape the poetic-dramatic structure of each play, but form the figure in the carpet of the canon as a whole' (Knights 1959, p. 14). Surprisingly, what surfaces here is the Bradleian notion of 'a characteristic . . . conception' but translated into formalistic terms reminiscent of New Criticism.

The history of modern Shakespeare criticism is full of such contradictions, apparent movements forward which surrender to a ubiquitous tradition the very ground which they seek to occupy. Thus, some forty years after Knights's essay, and with the emphasis having shifted nominally from 'poetry' to 'performance', a critic such as John Russell Brown can argue for the immanence of structure in 'the action': 'Although unfixed by detailed rehearsal and direction, the drama would be held together by the structure of its action' (Brown 1974, p. 85). Aesthetic unity remains, but the reader, now transformed into a spectator, experiences a 'loss of self-consciousness' (p. 95) which is somehow the condition of 'freedom' for which Brown argues on the assumption that a 'free' text, i.e. one which is 'open to almost any interpretation' (p. 62), produces an equally free spectator. What begins as a plea for an anti-authoritarian Shakespeare ends by extolling a verbal score which aspires to the condition of music (pp. 86–7), encouraging in these 'free' spectators an instinctual response and culminating in a vaguely romantic erotics of performance. The mechanism involved in these apparent shifts, and there have been a very large number of them in recent years, represents an attenuation of that process described by Raymond Williams as 'an intentionally selective version of a shaping past and a pre-shaped present, which is then powerfully operative in the process of social and cultural definition and identification' (R. Williams 1977, p. 115). But as part of the same argument Williams goes on to suggest that the pressure mediated as 'tradition' is powerful because it is the mechanism whereby 'active selective connections' are made, but also vulnerable because 'the real record is effectively recoverable, and many of the alternative or opposing practical continuities are still available' (pp. 116–17). At one level the continuities of Shakespeare criticism and textual and historical scholarship all exert a powerful institutional brake upon any attempt to diverge from the order of concepts and methods they have sought to establish for themselves, either by occlusion, or, more commonly, by seeking to neutralize their oppositional content through a process of domestication. But, conversely, the very process of selection opens itself to analysis, making possible both the recovery of the historical conditions of artistic production on the one hand, while at the same time exposing its methods of reconstructing both the past, and the text.

In the case of Shakespearean texts generally, the power and the vulnerability of which Williams speaks have co-existed with an increasing sense of unease in recent years, and yet the dominant critical discourses which hold these texts in place remain committed to idealist constructions. However, the massive influx of theoretical writing from the European continent, as evidenced in the availability in translation of the major writings of Roland Barthes, Michel Foucault, Louis Althusser, Antonio Gramsci, Bertold Brecht, Jacques Derrida, Walter Benjamin, Julia Kristeva, Pierre Macherey and Jacques Lacan, among others, the burgeoning of semiotics with its detailed investigative procedures for the analysis of signifying practices, and the revised estimate of such post-formalist Russian writers as Mikhail Bakhtin, have all served to provide a rich and heterogeneous foundation for the development of radically alternative strategies and objectives. This, combined with the more specific historiographical work being undertaken in Britain and America, threatens to break the dominant paradigm of Shakespeare studies.

The present volume of essays seeks to accelerate the break with established canons of Shakespeare criticism. What follows firmly resists those strategies habitually mobilized by liberal humanism to draw into its a-historical aegis an infinite variety of interpretations generated by individual sensibilities, which it then permits to circulate around a stable and unchanging text. Inevitably, all of these essays address themselves to questions of 'reading', but they all reject the notion that reading is itself an exclusive effect of the text. Rather, what is proposed in a number of very different ways is a series of explorations of the ways in which historically specific readings are generated, and which acknowledge the existence of structures within the text as devices for exclusion and repression, while at the same time insisting that the process of 'making sense' of a Shakespearean text is itself determined by a multiplicity of forces.

General questions of a theoretical nature are raised throughout, but they are firmly linked to distinct critical practices. Moreover, the overall objective has been to eschew coverage of all of those texts which are generally thought to occupy pride of place in the Shakespeare canon, since what is being challenged here, on a very broad front, is the concept of a distinct 'canon' itself. The volume opens with an examination of certain of the ways in which Shakespeare has been used at particularly important moments in academic and national history, and proceeds from there to offer a variety of perspectives upon Shakespeare and the criticism which sustains his reputation, through new work in post-structuralism, deconstruction, psychoanalytic criticism, continental semiotics, structural marxism, feminism, the analysis of discursive practices, and cultural materialism.

The 'alternative' Shakespeares which emerge resist, by virtue of a collective commitment to the principle of contestation of meaning, assimilation into any of the dominant traditions of Shakespeare criticism. That contestation takes place both in relation to established views and *between* individual contributions, each of which is written within a position which engages critically with specific areas of theoretical concern. It has not, and never has been, the case simply of applying new methods to old texts. The following pages offer, across a wide spectrum, a series of radical transformations of the questions that can be asked of texts, a problematizing of the concept of the text itself, and a sustained critique of those critical discourses that have claimed for themselves the role of transparent mediators of the text. The objective common to all of these essays is the demystification of the 'myth' of Shakespeare.

Human and critical history have proved right the Jonsonian eulogizing of Shakespeare as being 'not of an age but for all time' in a very perverse sense indeed. In concrete historical terms Shakespeare can never be 'our contemporary' except by the strategy of appropriation, yet the protean values which subsequent generations of critics have discovered in the texts themselves can be demonstrated to be in large part the projections of their own externally applied values. The resounding failure of successive traditions of humanist criticism to articulate critically the ensemble of assumptions upon which their perceptions rest makes it clear that what is now needed as a matter of extreme urgency are new kinds of Shakespeare criticism which are thoroughly self-aware and which actively resist those traditions whose main strategy for dealing with the threat they pose is one of domestication. Such forms of criticism will, in the final analysis, liberate these texts from the straitjacket of unexamined assumptions and traditions. When the record is scrupulously and disinterestedly examined these traditions will not be found to contain covert radical sensibilities waiting for post-structuralism, deconstruction, psychoanalytical criticism, feminism or marxism to give their disparate perceptions a local habitation and a name. Indeed, methodologies which naively favour plural 'approaches' or a multiplicity of 'readings' generated from within the essentialist individual critical consciousness as a form of 'unbridled subjectivity' (Anderson 1983, p. 54) are wholly inadequate as responses to the challenges now proposed by theoretically informed modes of criticism. These challenges provide the solid basis for the essays that follow.

2

SWISSER-SWATTER

Making a man of English letters

Terence Hawkes

I MAN OF IND

'What have we here? A man or a fish?' It is Trinculo's question, and it is a disturbing one, arising from a confusing encounter. All cultures find themselves impelled to divide the world into the fundamental categories of human and non-human, and when the division between these becomes blurred or uncertain, the effect is undoubtedly troubling.

Trinculo is particularly troubled. His question focuses exactly on that vexing boundary and from the perspective of a European signifying system, the lineaments of an exotic, aboriginal or Indian culture are bound to smell fishy. The problem centres precisely on that major cultural question. On which side of the necessary, defining boundary does the creature Caliban fall? Is he a man, or is he something else?

Despite an initial and reassuring location of Caliban as some kind of fishy monster, the possibility that he might at some time and in some place creep worryingly close to the category of 'man' is discussed at some length by Trinculo. It is worrying, of course, because, should Caliban cross that boundary, it would mean that the category of 'man' is not the closed, finished and well-defined entity that sustains and is sustained by a European taxonomy. Even more disturbing, a sly deictic turn of the text suddenly thrusts this possibility down the throat of the play's first, English audience:

> A strange fish! Were I in England now, as once I was, and had but this fish painted, not a holiday fool there but would give a piece of silver: there would this monster make a man; any strange beast there makes a man.
>
> (II. ii. 27 ff)

There is, as all editors note, a slippery quality to the term 'make' here which the text carefully exploits, imposing an economic dimension on an act of cultural taxonomy, and inviting us to see the one through, and thus in terms of, the other. To 'make a man' means to achieve the status of a man, to be ranked in a particular category. But the verb 'make' here also carries the implication of making money for, or making the fortune of, its subject. The monster may become ranked as a man or, alternatively, a man can be 'made' (i.e. made rich) by means of the monster. The two sentences 'There would this monster make a man. Any strange beast there makes a man' offer in themselves no clues as to which meaning of 'make' is to be preferred in each case. The one is always clearly discernible through the other and the slippage between signifier and signified proves as difficult to control here as it does in the case of the terms 'man' and 'monster'. If any strange beast can make a man, the distinction between these is no simple matter. In the arena of meanings opened up by the text here, classifications which we assume to be settled, objective and definitive appear to fluctuate with the tides of the 'making' market-place: to be determined, at least in England, by the exchange of money.

There are of course a number of reasons why a confusion about the relation of monsters to men should be an aspect of English ideology at the time when *The Tempest* was initially performed. First amongst these must be the impingement on the popular consciousness of the adventures of various groups of settlers on the American continent, particularly their encounter with Indian cultures. Indeed, the making of money by the display of Indians in Elizabethan London was not uncommon and Trinculo's subsequent words refer directly to the practice (see Lee 1929). The citizens proved regrettably curious, in fact:

> when they will not give a doit to relieve a lame beggar, they will lay out ten to see a dead Indian.
>
> (II. ii. 32–4)

Caliban's status as 'Indian' can be said to be partly confirmed by this, the more so when, moments later, Stephano sees him as part of the armoury of 'tricks' played upon him by the 'devils' of the island:

> What's the matter? Have we devils here? Do you put tricks upon's with salvages and men of Ind, ha?
>
> (II. ii. 58–9)

In respect of western society, Indians are indeed tricky: they do not make sense. As innumerable Hollywood films inform us, they make trouble. Their presence thus requires an ideological adjustment of a major kind. And as the Elizabethans, that society which initially, for practical purposes, began to make contact with Indian cultures, discovered, the challenge is fundamental. The Indian's meaning undoes our meaning. The Indian's world denies the order and coherence we discover in our world. Only when the disorder and incoherence which the Indian represents is subdued to our own and made to serve it, can we make sense/order/money – not of him, so much as out of him.

And of course, whether as inhabitants of the eastern or western peripheries of our civilization (it was, says Lee, a 'common habit' amongst the Elizabethans and Jacobeans to designate the Far West, like the Far East, by the one word 'Ind') such creatures offered a troubling challenge to a settled European notion of 'manhood'. If Caliban is an Indian, eastern or western, then the question of whether he is a man or not is indeed problematical.

A further dimension of the problem has recently been probed by Peter Hulme, who argues that Caliban's status as a 'man of Ind' in the discourse of Jacobean England falls between, and thus indicates that culture's engagement with, two competing polarities of the exotic, aboriginal challenge to the settled notion of a 'man': the European concept of the 'salvage' or 'wild' man on the one hand, and the newer Caribbean or American concept of the sun-worshipping 'cannibal' on the other.[1] In these terms, Caliban is a figure of considerable ambiguity: an anomaly, a 'compromise formation' of discourses whose figure mediates between two different sets of connotations. Produced in discourse, Caliban proves to be an aspect of a particular struggle carried out in terms of discourse between Europe and America.

To all this, we now have to add one finally confusing feature: Caliban's indeterminate status is irrevocably and ultimately muddled by the fact that, at the height of his interrogation by the egregious representatives of European culture, he emits the major and undeniable signal of genuine manhood: he speaks English. This confuses his discoverers utterly: 'Where the devil should he learn our language?' (II. ii. 67–8) – and it adds the final, undermining touch of ambiguity which then proceeds to permeate the body of the play.

For this short, pivotal scene, right at its centre, starts disconcertingly to unravel an apparently straightforward distinction between monster and man which has seemed thus far to be one of the play's central commitments. Caliban stands, in Frank Kermode's words, as 'the core of the play' (Shakespeare 1954, p. xxiv). Yet this scene offers us, as Peter Hulme demonstrates, a notion of 'monster' which somehow hovers between contradictory European and American concepts of the outlandish. And it also suggests, in Trinculo's affectionate reference to English habits, the possibility of an alternative to the prevailing European notion of what a 'man' might be. Two possible concepts of 'monster' confront two alternative notions of 'man' here. When the monster then speaks English the inherited opposition between the categories is fundamentally undermined. European notions both of monster and of man, and of the distinctions that may be negotiated between these, confront a challenge – not to say a refusal – in the form of an alternative which is both American and English-speaking. In the monster's own words, the effect is shattering and apparently liberating:

'Ban, 'Ban, Cacaliban
Has a new master: – get a new man.

(II. ii. 184–5)

But clearly, this array of competing meanings has dimensions which are not inappropriate to a culture which, for profound historical reasons, had by now turned its back on Europe and was looking to the west as a sphere where its own way of life might be re-established, even re-born, in a gigantic exploitative venture.

It is in this sense that *The Tempest* can be said to establish itself as a text whose plurality makes it an arena for the sifting of the immense issue: what makes a man? It is a vitally important question and as a result must surely become the site of the most bitter economic and political competition. Whatever makes a man stands as a major and controlling principle of coherence, both in terms of the present and the past, in any society. To make a man is to make sense. And who makes sense, makes history.

II MAN OF LETTERS

Making history, that is making sense of the past in terms of the exigencies of the present, is a necessary concern of all societies. It was never more necessary in England than in the late nineteenth and early twentieth centuries, particularly in that period which followed the second Reform Bill of 1867. The extension of the franchise was a disturbing prospect, a massive 'leap in the dark'. To meet it implied an equally massive effort of incorporation, inclusion and accommodation; of asserted continuity and of willed coherence in the name of national cultural identity. The example of Germany earlier in the century suggested Education as an obvious means by which English Prosperos might domesticate their own Calibans. Thus having new masters, getting new men, meant, to the prescient, a project whose slogan would urge, as one Minister put it, that 'We must educate our masters.' As a result, with Forster's Education Act of 1870, Britain embarked on a system of compulsory primary education which effectively constituted a drive towards universal literacy. In the next twenty years the average school attendance rose from one and a quarter million to four and a half million and the money spent on each child for the purposes of education was doubled (Trevelyan 1942, p. 581).

It was a revolution, so to speak, by letters. And so it is hardly surprising that the enshrining, embalming and even the prophylaxis of the national culture took the form so often of monumental literary undertakings whose purpose was the creation, reinforcement and maintenance of a national English heritage through the medium of what might be delicately termed English letters. This is the era of *The New English Dictionary* (later to become the *Oxford English Dictionary*), of the ninth edition of the *Encyclopedia Britannica*, of the *Victoria County History* and of that astonishing project the *Dictionary of National Biography*. (see Murray 1977, p. 340). By June 1894, the University of Oxford had established its first chair of English Literature (though it remained unfilled until 1904) and in February 1903 the British Academy was founded.[2]

It was also the era which saw the beginning, in 1878, of a collection of biographical and critical works called *English Men of Letters*. Published by Macmillan, edited by John, later Lord Morley, the series found its title only after a certain amount of dithering between revealing alternatives such as *Studies of English Authors*, *Sketches of Great English Authors*, *Lives of English Authors*, *Great English Authors*, *Great Men of Letters*, *Masters of Literature*, and ignobly, *Short Books on English Authors* (Nowell-Smith 1967, pp. 164–5). However, *English Men of Letters* eventually and significantly triumphed and the series proved an immediate, penetrative and lasting success. In the words of John Gross, 'Right from the start it was accorded semi-official status, and for a couple of generations it remained an unfailing standby for harassed teachers and conscientious students. No comparable series had ever come so close to attaining the rank of a traditional British institution' (Gross 1973, pp. 122–3). Making men of English Letters was clearly a powerful way of making British sense and of making world history. Propelled by the immense, formative power of an expanding educational system, the series thus quickly reinforced and became part of the dominant discourse of British ideology.

The fact that, as the volumes succeeded one another, a number of their subjects turned out to be neither English (there was Burns, Burke, Sterne, etc.) nor Men (there was Fanny Burney, Maria Edgeworth), nor writers of 'letters' except in an expanded sense of that term (Morley found himself becoming 'more and more averse' to it: 'To call Bunyan or Burns. . . by that title is certainly not good' (Nowell-Smith 1967, p. 163)) indicates the anaesthetic power that all discourses possess. They neither disguise nor reveal the truth. The monumentalizing, coherence-generating, sense- and history-making activity of *English Men of Letters* simply *constitutes* the truth: the truth that the true heritage of British culture is written down, and in English, and by Men.

III SUPERMAN

One of the great pinnacles of the enterprise, the jewel in its crown, was bound, of course, to be the volume on Shakespeare, and the Bard was duly constituted an English Man of Letters in 1907. An appropriate author for this exalted project had not proved easy to find: Matthew Arnold had turned the task down, and in 1877 so had George Eliot, even in the face of a greatly increased fee, thus adding another title to the list of the world's great unwritten books. But at the end of the summer of 1903, man, moment, and monument came together. The project was offered to, and accepted by, Walter Alexander Raleigh, then professor of English at the University of Glasgow. He was effusive. 'Two days ago', he writes to Macmillan on 30 August,

> I should have said, with emphasis, that I would never write for a series. But I could not guess that I should be given the opportunity of designing a monument for the poet I love best, in the national cathedral church. The *English Men of Letters* is not as other series are.
>
> (Nowell-Smith 1967, p. 250)

In the event, the consequences of having what, in a less formal letter, he termed 'a fling at Bill' were perhaps to justify that last statement. Within a year of beginning work in the national cathedral church, preferment in one of its central parishes had come his way. So fundamental and formative a fling could not be flung in the far North, and Bill's chronicler was appointed to be first holder of the newly established chair in English literature at the University of Oxford.[3]

At its unveiling, then, in 1907, the monument could hardly have been more solidly based, or centrally placed. Focusing on the figure which, for over a hundred years, had been growing to the stature of cultural superman, obviously designed to become the lynch-pin of a series which was almost a 'traditional British institution', at a time when the national drive towards universal literacy was creating a mass audience for it, authored by a man whose very name – Walter Raleigh – carried inevitable and appropriate connotations of reassuring contemporaneity, special knowledge, buccaneering glory and a fine literary style, and who was, by then, the first Professor of English Literature appointed by the most ideologically central educational institution in the country, the *English Men of Letters Shakespeare* arrived with an aura available to few other volumes before or since. Small wonder that, within four years, the maker of Shakespeare as a Man of Letters was himself 'made'. Recommended by both Asquith and Balfour in the 1911 Coronation Honours list, he became Sir Walter Raleigh.

'So', this astonishing volume's opening chapter announces with what must be judged a paradoxical air of finality, 'So Shakespeare has come to his own, as an English man of letters.' And in so far as any book is susceptible of a tersely discursive account of its contents, that is what this one single-mindedly sets out to demonstrate. Shakespeare is constructed here precisely in those terms, and to the rigorous exclusion of others that might modify them. Rarely can the manufacturing process of a culture's presuppositions have been so nakedly made visible.

That Shakespeare is English is held to be readily demonstrable, but significantly only in terms of a reduced geographical and racial model which of course sidesteps the thorny, and over the years thornier, question of in what precisely the genuine 'Englishness' of an imperial power (at this time ruling roughly a quarter of the world's population) consists. Raleigh, who had spent two years in India at the beginning of his career, must have known of the cultural complications at stake – the Boer War which raised some of them had continued till 1902 – but his book takes a simpler, narrower and more consoling view, endorsing the opinion of 'that excellent antiquary Mrs. Stopes' in her conclusion that Shakespeare's pedigree 'can be traced straight back to Guy of Warwick and the good King Alfred' and that this 'noble ancestry' played 'no small part in the making of the poet' (p. 31). That the first sign of this enviable lineage is the Bard's 'unerringly sure touch with the character of his highborn ladies' will prove reassuring to those who persist in finding Lady Macbeth's capacities as wife and mother a cause of some concern.

Shakespeare's engagement with *letters*, i.e. with language in its written form, is less easily demonstrable of course, and for a variety of reasons. In a far from wholly literate age, he produced plays: a form of art committed to and involved in language's *oral* form and its visual concomitants. He showed very little interest in preserving his major works in a stable written form, and indeed few absolutely certain examples of his sustained handwriting are known to have survived. However, Raleigh's argument here reaches the heroic pitch appropriate to a wholesale commitment to literacy. Shakespeare cannot be fully appreciated until he is read. Consequently the Folio edition of his plays in 1623, addressed to 'the great variety of readers', marks the beginning of his real fame. From that time onwards (like the race itself perhaps) it 'steadily advanced to the conquest of the world' (p. 2). Milton considers him, rightly and simply, as 'the author of a marvellous book' and 'The readers of Shakespeare took over from the fickle players the trust and inheritance of his fame.' As a result 'his continued vogue upon the stage is the smallest part of his immortality' (p. 2), and his true genius is enshrined in the fixed certainties which words apparently acquire when they are written down. It is a matter of demonstrable and inevitable progress to the present: 'While the Restoration theatre mangled and parodied the tragic masterpieces, a new generation of readers kept alive the knowledge and heightened the renown of the written word' (p. 2). And the result is that, in the twentieth century, just, by chance, as literacy is about to become universal, so the realization dawns: 'The truth is', Raleigh solemnly assures us, 'that his best things are not very effective on the stage' (p. 146). As a result, as English syllabuses begin to be constructed following the growth of that subject which Raleigh so successfully professed, it is Shakespeare's 'book' (p. 25) that becomes so centrally, so prodigously – in all its manifold implications – the ultimate 'set' text. Rather like Prospero's 'book', it offered power.

Raleigh, it should be said, was always ready to assume the role of Magus in that professional respect. Certainly, more than a trace of Prospero's megalomania –

> graves at my command
> Have wak'd their sleepers, op'd, and let 'em forth
> By my so potent Art.
>
> (V. i. 48–50)

inhabits his view of the function of criticism:

> the main business of Criticism, after all is not to legislate, not to classify, but to raise the dead. Graves, at its command, have waked their sleepers, oped, and let them forth. It is by the creative power of this art that the living man is reconstructed from the litter of blurred and fragmentary paper documents that he has left to posterity.
>
> (Raleigh 1926, I, pp. 128–9)

Finally, the English writer of Letters must be seen to be a Man. I have already discussed the notoriously complex issues this raises for most cultures, not least the one of which Shakespeare himself was (if you'll pardon the expression) a male member. But I'm happy to report that Raleigh's highly potent critical art proves able to cut through these with the dispatch of one to whom maleness is evidently a crucial touchstone of manliness. Shakespeare's standing as an English Man of Letters is vested not in a-sexual social intercourse with its sentimentalized rural décor: the 'dear inanities of ordinary idle conversation' set against the 'lazy ease of the village green' – but in a much more assertive, even aggressive mode of existence where a horny-handed Bard who is 'the greatest of artisans' manifests the starkest kind of maleness, not to say membership,

> when he collects his might and stands dilated, his imagination aflame, the thick-coming thoughts and fancies shaping themselves, under the stress of the central will, into a thing of life.
>
> (Raleigh 1907, p. 7)

Shakespeare as Phallus of the Golden Age – Phallus in Wonderland – is of course no more peculiar a formulation than many. That he should be thus presented in a context where his potency is diverted and channelled to a national educational drive to universal literacy may seem unduly restrictive, but, again, it is no more peculiar a formulation than many. The pressures and compulsions of ideology are at work here. These are what seek to control the alarming plurality of all texts, and clearly there could be no more effective instrument for such a controlling, prophylactic function in Britain than the aptly named edifice of English letters.

IV GERMAN

Eleven years later a particularly apt instance of this process took place. We can even be quite precise about the date: Thursday, 4 July 1918 – a point in time which has its own resonances, no doubt, but of which, perhaps surprisingly, the Archbishop of York was prepared at the time to say 'The Fourth of July 1918 will surely be known in after days as one of the great landmarks of history' (*The Times*, 4 July 1918).

The reasons for such a claim are not far to seek. Four years previously, the First World War had plunged Europe into a vast disintegrating crisis, and the resolution of that conflict was obviously a central concern. In April of 1917, a major and ultimately decisive event had occurred: the United States of America had entered the War on the British (and French) side.

The truly momentous nature of the entry of America onto the world stage could of course hardly have been perceived by the Allies. It was, hindsight confirms, a turning point in world history of massive proportions. The open involvement of a foreign power from three thousand miles away in the affairs of Europe – the mirror-image if you like of America's own history – needed a kind of ideological adjustment, or digestion, of some magnitude.

So far as Britain was concerned, the path of adjustment was clear. Americans were not savages. They were not Indians. They spoke our language.

And so, amidst much talk of 'Anglo-Saxon unity'; with messages of greeting involving 'a new and special heartiness' announced by Mr Winston Churchill from the people of Britain to the President of the United States; with the King, no less, scheduled to attend a special baseball match arranged in London between the US Army and Navy; with a meeting of the Anglo-Saxon Fellowship at Central Hall,

Westminster (organized by the Minister of Information) graced by a 'short special prayer' from the Bishop of London, together with a long thundering editorial in *The Times* in support of what it called 'the old Anglo-Saxon "world idea"', the preparations for the celebration of American Independence Day ground out, in 1918, an unmistakable message. As Anglo-Saxons, speakers of English, freely embracing what amounted to their cultural destiny, if not duty, our fellow-men, the Americans, would join us in combating the genuine savages, that race whose unspeakable activities and ineffable deformities marked them indelibly as men of Ind.

All nations execrate their enemies, and the discourse of denigration has a long and monotonous history in Europe, on all sides, and towards all cultural groups. But what is of interest at this turning point in European history is the mode and implication of a particular piece of vilification at a particular time. Academics, we could all profitably remember, are not exempt from this activity, and in fact are often rather good at it. Certainly the first Professor of English at Oxford University proved equal to the challenge. In the Preface to a volume of lectures called *England and the War* published in 1918, Sir Walter Raleigh had observed that:

> The character of Germany and the Germans is a riddle. . . . There is the same difficulty with the lower animals; our description of them tends to be a description of nothing but our own loves and hates. Who has ever fathomed the mind of a rhinoceros . . .?
>
> (Raleigh, 1918, pp. 7–8)

and in a lecture delivered on 14 March 1918 the same theme emerges:

> That is what makes the Germans so like the animals. Their wisdom is all cunning. . . . You could talk to them about food, and they responded easily. It was all very restful and pleasant, like talking to an intelligent dog.
>
> (Raleigh 1918, p. 107)

Less than men, the behaviour of the Germans is readily identifiable, and the Professor speaks at length about 'The filthiness that the

Germans use, their deliberate befouling of all that is elegant and gracious and antique . . . their defiling with ordure the sacred vessels in the churches . . . a solemn ritual of filth, religiously practised, by officers no less than men' (Raleigh 1918, pp. 9–10). Such animality in apparent human beings can only indicate savagery, and 'The waves of emotional exaltation which from time to time pass over the whole people have the same character, the character of savage religion' (p. 10). Germans are thus 'alien to civilization' and so to civilization's token, language: 'It is as if they despised language and made use of it only because they believe that it is an instrument of deceit' (p. 10). And as for the noises which amongst such sub-human creatures might have passed for language, here the Professor feels clearly called upon to make a dispassionate and objective professional assessment:

> The Germans poisoned the wells in South-West Africa; in Europe they did all they could to poison the wells of mutual trust and mutual understanding among civilized men. Do they think that these things will make a good advertisement for the explosive guttural sounds and the huddled deformed syntax of the speech in which they express their arrogance and their hate?
>
> (Raleigh 1918, p. 93)

On 4 July, 1918, then, the truth-bearing, civilizing and English-speaking representatives of humanity celebrated its confrontation with and certain defeat of its opposite, the savage, deformed, less than human representatives of the bestial and the depraved. Genuine men confronted creatures whose status was a matter of obvious dispute. English speakers, to change only the terms of the metaphor, confronted those whose animality was confirmed by their being deprived of that language.

Amongst the celebrations marking the day was an auspicious occasion all the more interesting since it wasn't formally part of the official celebrations. It was the occasion of the annual Shakespeare lecture of the British Academy. And that august body had chosen no less a person to address it than the Professor of English at Oxford University.

When of all people the Professor of English at Oxford University addresses of all bodies the British Academy on of all topics the subject of Shakespeare, then an audience might well feel that truths of cardinal, possibly superlative, and certainly ultimate importance are likely to be delivered. Sir Walter Raleigh again proved equal to the occasion. Taking as his title 'Shakespeare and England', he produced, within that enormous range, a piece of ideological processing as perfectly fitted to the occasion as could be hoped. And at its centre, there is a reading of the scene from *The Tempest* with which this discussion began:

> A small British expeditionary force, bound on an international mission, finds itself stranded in an unknown country. The force is composed of men very various in rank and profession. Two of them whom we may call a non-commissioned officer and a private, go exploring by themselves, and take one of the natives of the place prisoner. This native is an ugly low-born creature, of great physical strength and violent criminal tendencies, a liar, and ready at any time for theft, rape, and murder. He is a child of Nature, a lover of music, slavish in his devotion to power and rank, and very easily imposed upon by authority. His captors do not fear him, and which is more, they do not dislike him. They found him lying out in a kind of no-man's land, drenched to the skin, so they determine to keep him as a souvenir, and to take him home with them. They nickname him, in friendly fashion, the monster, and the mooncalf, as who should say Fritz, or the Boche. But their first care is to give him a drink, and to make him swear allegiance upon the bottle. 'Where the devil should he learn our language?' says the non-commissioned officer, . . .
>
> (*Proceedings of the British Academy 1917–18*, pp. 407–8)

It is important that we should try to focus clearly on whatever is going on at this moment. In my view it has crucial implications, and it should not go unnoticed that Raleigh's sense of the occasion's importance is reflected in his subsequent printing of this lecture as the final item in the volume *England and the War*: a collection of which he said that if any of his books were to survive him, he believed that none had a better chance (Raleigh 1926, I, p. xvii).

Raleigh's aim – no cruder a project than that of many another critic – is, as I have said, to reinforce a particular ideological position at a vitally important historical conjuncture. The specificity of his reading at this point can be highlighted if we set it against a previous reading made by him some fourteen years earlier, in September 1904, just after he had accepted the Oxford chair. Writing then about *The Tempest* as a 'fantasy of the New World', he sees Trinculo not as a sturdy, good-natured 'non-commissioned officer', but quite the reverse: 'The drunken butler, accepting the worship and allegiance of Caliban, and swearing him in by making him kiss the bottle, is a fair representative of the idle and dissolute men who were shipped to the Virginian colony.' Similarly Caliban, far from being 'an ugly low-born creature, of great physical strength and violent criminal tendencies, a liar and ready at any time for theft, rape, and murder', is seen as a 'wonderfully accurate' composition with 'his affectionate loyalty to the drunkard, his adoration of valour, his love of natural beauty and feeling for music and poetry' giving a clear manifestation of Shakespeare's 'sympathetic understanding' of uncivilized man (Raleigh 1905, pp. 112–13).

Both readings are of course partial, harshly reducing what we have readily recognized as the text's plurality to the dimensions of a single, coherent statement. But in the later, wartime one the ideological pressures work rather more obviously and their effects lie closer to the surface. In 1918, Caliban has to become less than a man in quite specific terms. He turns into a German, 'Fritz' or 'the Boche', a bestial, savage and deformed slave in a precisely European dimension. Wholly determined, thus, as a European 'wild man', as Peter Hulme's analysis has it, there is clearly no room left in this reading of Caliban for any 'American' potential. On 4 July 1918, this is self-evidently a good idea.

But more than that, the un-manning, the 'Germanizing' of Caliban irons out any ambiguity that might accrue from his later speaking of English. Any language that Caliban learns, is learned for the purpose of cursing: the 'explosive guttural sounds and the huddled deformed syntax of the speech' expressive of his nature. What surfaces in this reading is something of genuine concern to a Prospero-like professor of English who is far more aware of what is finally at stake than some of his later detractors have been prepared to give him credit for.

For what Raleigh clearly sees is that the war involves a historic clash in terms of linguistic hegemony, and that victory in the struggle would settle what, at that time, was a major issue: which was to be the dominant world language, German or English? In a letter to John Sampson on 6 July 1917, he had made his prophecies crudely enough:

> The War is going to be All Right, my son. The English Language is safe to be the world language. The very Germans will treat their own tongue as a dialect. Goethe will be like Dunbar, or perhaps Burns. Scandinavians and Latins will cultivate English. German is a shotten herring. It's all right. . . . Their only chance was to bully their language up to a cock position, and they have failed. On its own merits it hasn't a chance.
>
> (Raleigh 1926, II, p. 468)

The entry of America into the war was portentous for this reason. The 'special relationship' between Britain and the United States was and is based on a common language, representing the full flowering of the linguistic seeds planted by the Elizabethan colonizers: a massive adventure in cultural re-creation to which The Tempest stands as a lasting monument. By the time he delivered a lecture entitled 'Some Gains of the War' to the Royal Colonial Institute in February 1918, Raleigh was making it clear that the major gain of American involvement in Europe would surely be the subsequent dominance of Prospero's English over Caliban's German: 'After the War the English language will have such a position as it has never had before. It will be established in world-wide security'. 'The future', it clearly follows, 'does not belong to the German tongue' and it seems reasonable to announce that 'the greatest gain of all, the entry of America into the War assures the triumph of our common language'. English, and English men, will obviously be 'made' by such a victory – and the ambiguities lurking in that English verb gently surface as a curious fiscal metaphor seeps through the pseudo-philology:

> This gain, which I make bold to predict for the English language, is a real gain, apart from all patriotic bias. The English language is incomparably richer, more fluid, and more vital than the German language. Where the German has but one way of saying a thing, we have two or three, each with its distinctions and its subtleties of usage. Our capital wealth is greater, and so are our powers of borrowing.
>
> (Raleigh 1918, pp. 93–5)

English, one might conclude, has scarcely ever been better served by those who profess it. It will become the gold standard, the sterling mark of civilization, the currency of sense, the mint of history, the hallmark of that which sets Prospero above Caliban, the common coin, in short, of genuine manhood.

V SCARMAN

Happily, Sir Walter's account of the status of Germans proved open to a different audit. In his lecture 'The War and the Press' he goes on to make the sensible point that whatever the true nature of our enemies might be, it does not help the Allied cause if the newspapers persist in depicting *all* Germans as Calibans:

> Is it feared that we should have no heart for the War if once we are convinced that among the Germans there are some human beings? Is it believed that our people can be heroic on one condition only, that they shall be asked to fight no one but orang-outangs?
>
> (Raleigh 1918, p. 118)

This rather canny assessment of the function of propaganda was originally delivered to another bastion of the English establishment at Eton College on 14 March, 1918. However, when Raleigh repeated it four months later at Mill Hill School in London, on 5 July, the day after the celebration of the American festivities, it was given a particular prominence in the next day's *Times*. It is an excellent indication of how constitutive contexts are of meaning that the lecture is now read by *The Times* reporter as outrageously extolling the virtues of our enemies. We cannot 'deny nobility', Raleigh is made to say, to the simple German soldier fighting for his country. Unfortunately, that is exactly what the discourse of the press was currently seeking to deny. The result, Raleigh tells us, was 'shoals of abusive letters by every post'; one of the worst from a working man who concluded by denying his manhood (Raleigh 1926, II, p. 488). Worse was to follow. On 7 August, *The Times* reported a piece written in the German press by Raleigh's former colleague at Liverpool University, the 'notorious Professor Kuno Meyer'. Meyer (a scholar of Celtic) cleverly raised the spectre of

Further Calibans beyond the English pale by congratulating his old friend on the reported Mill Hill speech, and saying that his insight into the true nature of the German people undoubtedly came from the fact that Raleigh himself was not English, that Scottish blood ran in his veins, and that awareness of the Celtic dimension should undoubtedly make him applaud what Meyer, twisting the knife, calls the 'splendid behaviour' of the Irish rebels in Dublin in the rising of Easter, 1916.

For the truth, revealed by these alternative readings, is that the world is not, shockingly, unitary or English in its meanings and does not always agree to be read as if it were. No doubt Kuno Meyer's ghost could find plenty of examples of subsequent 'splendid behaviour' in Ireland with which to undermine the current English reading of that particular tragic text.

Nor should we allow any notion of an 'essential' or 'stable' Shakespearean text, which can only be read in a particular way, to mock Sir Walter's shade. My point is not that he was engaged in any illicit importation into Shakespeare of extraneous political considerations in that, beyond those, there lies a comforting, unchanging, permanent Shakespearean play to which we can finally turn. Shakespeare's texts always yield to, though they can never be reduced to, the readings we give them: their plurality makes Walter Raleighs of us all. As a result, his 1918 'politicized' reading of The Tempest is no isolated aberration. We should remind ourselves of the propaganda function of Olivier's film reading of Henry V (financed by government sources) which served as a prolegomenon to the D-Day landings in Normandy in 1944. We should remember E. M. W. Tillyard's Shakespeare's History Plays of the same period. And indeed, we can extend the process to the present day. One of the bizarre by-products of the Falklands campaign in 1982 was a book entitled Authors Take Sides on the Falklands. In it, the Shakespearean critic G. Wilson Knight delivers himself of the following:

> Britain's response to the Falklands crisis was ratified by all three parties in Parliament, and I accordingly would not presume to register any complaint. . . . I can only assess our prospects by stating my own convictions. I have for long accepted the validity of our country's historic contribution, seeing the British Empire as a precursor, or prototype, of world-order. I have relied always on the Shakespearian vision

> as set forth in my war-time production *This Sceptred Isle* at the West-minster Theatre in 1941 (described in *Shakespearian Production*, 1964). The theme I also discuss in various writings collected under the title *The Sovereign Flower* in 1958. Our key throughout is Cranmer's royal prophecy at the conclusion of Shakespeare's last play, *Henry VIII*, Shakespeare's final words to his countrymen. This I still hold to be our one authoritative statement, every word deeply significant, as forecast of the world-order at which we should aim.
>
> (Woolf and Moorcroft-Wilson 1982, pp. 66–7)

Shakespeare is a powerful ideological weapon, always available in periods of crisis, and used according to the exigencies of the time to resolve crucial areas of indeterminacy. As a central feature of the discipline we call 'English', his plays form part of that discipline's commitment – since 1870 in a national system of education – to the preservation and reinforcement of what is seen as a 'natural' order of things. To talk of a 'natural' order of things is of course to accept the limits imposed by the contours of a specific discourse. Such a discourse or 'knowledge' posits certain sets of differences or oppositions, presenting these as 'natural' and offering them for a variety of uses in response to historical pressures. My point is that the discourse forged by and for the Elizabethan colonial adventure offered a Prospero/Caliban, man/monster, non-Indian/Indian opposition of this sort which, since 1918 and Sir Walter Raleigh's astonishing reading of it, has made 'English-speaking/non-English speaking' a feasible extension of its range. It involves the notion of one sort of English as the carrier and transmitter of the 'real' and the 'natural': the basis of that 'world-order' at which Wilson Knight chillingly urges us to aim. That English is the saving grace which is always denied to Caliban, but which must, in charity, always be offered to him. And it follows that those who reject, challenge or refuse that offer will find Caliban's mantle and fate ready and waiting for them.

Between 10 and 12 April 1981, it seemed to some in Britain as if Caliban had begun to take over the island. In the London district of Brixton, a series of violent incidents occurred which subsequently escalated to the level of a full-scale riot. Major participants were the Metropolitan police and those West Indian residents of the area whose presence perhaps represents one of the most ironic consequences of the Elizabethan encounter with the New World. After the event, the Government ordered an inquiry into the affair to be conducted by the Right Hon. the Lord Scarman, OBE, a High Court judge. His report is a model of what most people consider to be the essence of justice and good sense, and its 'reading' of the disorders seems to have won general acceptance. Yet the basis of it is by now familiar: of the factors making the incorporation of the black community into the larger one extremely difficult, 'trouble with the English language' is seen as 'most important of all' (Scarman 1981, p. 10). Not surprisingly, the central role of the study of English language and culture in promoting coherence and continuity becomes a constant theme:

> The problems which have to be solved, if deprivation and alienation are to be overcome, have been identified – namely, teaching a command of the English language, a broad education in the humanities . . . etc.
>
> (Scarman 1981, p. 9)

More than a hundred years on, the spirit of the 1870 Education Act, mediated by Sir Walter Raleigh, glints purposefully through the text. 'While it is right', says Lord Scarman, speaking of the education of the immigrants' children,

> that the curriculum should fully recognize the value of different cultural traditions, I echo the Home Affairs Committee's view that the primary object of schooling must be to prepare all our children, whatever their colour, for life in Britain. It is essential therefore, that children should leave school able to speak, read and write effectively in the language of British society, i.e. English.
>
> (Scarman 1981, p. 105)

It is a minor, though not a carping point that the language of British society has never been, and is not now, simply English, and it is difficult to believe that a humane and learned British judge is genuinely unaware of that as a straightforward historical and social – not to say economic – fact. But then, in the face of what the report terms 'scenes of violence and disorder . . . the like of which had not previously been seen in this century in Britain' (p. 1); indeed, watching the flames spread with the outrageous symbolism Brixton affords, down Atlantic Road, into Chaucer Road, along Spenser Road, up Milton Road, ultimately to lick at the borders of Shakespeare Road itself, it becomes clear that the 'straightforward facts' can never be straightforwardly available to us, and that they present themselves only in the terms which a specific discourse permits, by routes which it lays down, streets which it names.

I have offered Sir Walter Raleigh's reading of The Tempest in support of this view, and it is only an extension of the same case to suggest that a version of the Prospero–Caliban conflict finds itself also located, indistinctly, intermittently, but nevertheless palpably, at a very deep level in the report of Lord Scarman.

Sir Walter's subsequent career manifests the rich rewards awaiting those whose readings, like those of Lord Scarman, find public favour. In the same month in which he gave his British Academy lecture, the Professor of English at Oxford found himself almost overtly 'made' in political terms: he was offered a seat in Parliament by the Liberal prime minister, Asquith. Rejecting that dubious honour, he was nevertheless delighted to accept – in the same month – an appointment as official historian of the Royal Air Force and, devoting the rest of his life to the task, managed to complete the first volume before his premature death in 1922.

As an example of another 'reading' and perhaps of a career which ended rather less auspiciously, I turn at last to Sir Walter Raleigh's illustrious namesake, who peers challengingly at us through the text of their common nomenclature. Since this intertextuality provides the only point of connection between the two (although the Elizabethan Sir Walter knew quite a lot about America, about Indians, and, on one famous occasion involving his cloak, the Queen and a muddy puddle, about prophylaxis), I offer a famous anecdote (that most revealing of texts) as a perfect instance of how, under the pressures of 'making', any use of language proves capable of disintegration. John Aubrey tells the story:

He loved a wench well; and one time getting one of the Maids of

Honour up against a tree in a wood ('twas his first lady) who seemed at first boarding to be something fearful of her honour, and modest, she cried, 'Sweet Sir Walter, what do you me ask? Will you undo me? Nay, sweet Sir Walter! Sweet Sir Walter! Sir Walter!' At last, as the danger and the pleasure at the same time grew higher, she cried in the ecstasy, 'Swisser Swatter, Swisser Swatter!'

It remains a matter of only minor interest to record that the wench turned out eventually to be with child, that she was subsequently delivered of a son, and that a man was thus 'made' to the sound of this creative deconstruction of English letters. His father, it may be recalled, had the good sense to appoint Ben Jonson as his tutor.

3

POST-STRUCTURALIST SHAKESPEARE

Text and ideology

Christopher Norris

I

For Shakespeare criticism, as for current post-structuralist theory, a good deal hinges on the crucial ambiguity of Derrida's cryptic statement: 'there is no "outside" to the text' ('*il n'y a pas de hors-texte*'). On the one hand this can be taken to signify a literary formalism pushed to the extreme, a last-ditch retreat from 'reality' into the solipsistic pleasures of textual freeplay. Such is the reading widely canvassed by those who reject post-structuralist theory in the name of a common-sense or humanist tradition founded on the doctrines of mimetic realism. But Derrida's statement is capable of a different reading, one which answers more precisely to the context and logic of its appearance in *Of Grammatology* (Derrida 1976, p. 73). This would bring out the reverse implication of a radically 'textualist' argument. If reality is structured through and through by the meanings we conventionally assign to it, then the act of suspending ('deconstructing') those conventions has a pertinence and force beyond the usual bounds of textual (or 'literary') interpretation. Maintaining those bounds is the business of a common-sense philosophy which stakes its authority on a stable relation between world and text, the real and the written, object and representation. This mimetic economy is argued out between Plato and Aristotle and becomes, in effect, the grounding rationale of western philosophic tradition. It is questioned only at moments of stress when the *texts* of that tradition appear to threaten its otherwise self-regulating norms.

This point deserves emphasis in view of certain current polemical attacks on post-structuralist and deconstructive theory. Such ideas, it is argued, amount to a merely delusive and self-indulgent 'radicalism', a fetishistic cult of the text which can only end up severing all connection between literature (or criticism) and practical reality. These arguments are employed both by Marxists (see Eagleton 1981) and by critics who conceive themselves as speaking up for plain common-sense truth against all the varieties of bother-headed theory, marxist versions included. What these opponents have to ignore – in line with the traditional prejudice which unites them – is the fact that such arguments are challenged *at root* by the extended, non-reductive sense of 'textuality' that Derrida brings into play. There are powerful institutional forces at work in the assumption that texts are mimetic or second-order constructs, referring back always – by whatever kind of mediating process – to a first-order realm of empirical reality. To deconstruct that assumption, in all its manifold forms, is to turn back the logic of common-sense discourse at precisely the point where it thinks to challenge the activity of deconstruction. The 'question of the text' is not to be so lightly dismissed by a tradition which – of internal necessity – has failed to think through its effects and implications.

In his latest writings Derrida has laid increasing stress on this power of deconstruction to breach and subvert the instituted orders of discourse. Text 'overruns all the limits assigned to it', refusing the conventional protocols of genre, method or answerable style. It embraces, in Derrida's words, 'everything that was to be set up in opposition to writing (speech, life, the world, the real, history . . .)' (Derrida 1979a, p. 84). And this not by way of reducing such activities to an undifferentiated signifying flux, but by challenging the systems of discursive propriety which hold them each within clearly marked bounds. Hence Derrida's reiterated stress on the wider (pedagogical and ultimately political) effects of deconstruction. What 'the institution' cannot tolerate, he writes,

> is for anyone to tamper with language, meaning both the *national* language and, paradoxically, an ideal of translatability that neutralizes this national language. Nationalism and universalism . . . It can bear more readily the most apparently revolutionary ideological sorts of 'content', if only that content does not touch the borders of language and of all the juridico-political contracts that it guarantees
>
> (Derrida 1979a, pp. 94–5)

Among such institutions, I shall argue, is that of literary criticism at large, and more specifically the history of Shakespeare studies as inscribed within the national culture. The question of the text and its 'juridical' limits is nowhere posed with more insistent (and problematic) force.

The link between Shakespeare and ideas of 'the national language' is one that hardly needs documenting here. From Dr Johnson to F. R. Leavis, critics have looked to Shakespeare for linguistic intimations of an 'Englishness' identified with true native vigour and unforced, spontaneous creativity. Johnson, of course, ran into all kinds of difficulty when he tried to square this idea with the practical business of editing Shakespeare. 'Nationalism and universalism' – to recall Derrida's formulation – turn out to have sharply paradoxical consequences for Johnson's project. On the one hand Shakespeare has to be accommodated to the eighteenth-century idea of a proper, self-regulating discourse which would finally create a rational correspondence between words and things, language and reality. From this point of view Johnson can only deprecate the tiresome 'quibbles' and redundant wordplay which so flagrantly transgress the stylistic norm. On the other hand, allowances have to be made for the luxuriant native wildness of Shakespeare's genius, its refusal to brook the 'rules' laid down by more decorous traditions like that of French neo-classicism. This clash of priorities in turn creates all the manifest twists and contradictions of Johnson's argument in the *Preface* to his edition (Johnson 1969). Patriotic self-interest – the idea of a 'national language' and of

Shakespeare as its chief exemplar – comes up against a powerful universalist creed which effectively consigns such interests to the status of provincial special pleading.

What is at stake here is the question of the text as posed by two conflicting ideologies, each with a prepossessing claim upon eighteenth-century 'taste' and reason. Propriety of style is a matter of observing the economy of reference which ideally should relate words and things in a one-to-one system of disambiguated usage. In this respect Johnson stands squarely within the Lockian tradition of positivist thinking about language, logic and epistemology. Shakespeare's unfortunate proclivities of style – his 'quibbles', 'clinches', 'idle conceits' and so forth – represent a constant threat to the civilized consensus which works to maintain this proper economy. But tugging against Johnson's rationalist creed is an equal and opposite determination to hold Shakespeare up as the naturalized voice of a peculiarly *English* character and style. And where is this genius to be located if not in the very excesses of temperament and language that Johnson is constrained to criticize?

The following passage from the *Preface* brings out the deep-lying rationalist assumptions in Johnson's dealing with Shakespearean style.

> Not that always where the language is intricate the thought is subtle, or the image always great where the line is bulky; the equality of words to things is very often neglected, and trivial sentiments and vulgar ideas disappoint the attention, to which they are recommended by sonorous epithets and swelling figures.
>
> (Johnson 1969, pp. 67–8)

What Johnson expressly objects to here is the disturbing non-coincidence of 'language' and 'thought', and the corresponding failure to observe a due proportion (or 'equality') between words and things. Such delinquencies of style present a twofold danger to the stable currency of meaning. They threaten both the *expressive* relationship which holds between word and idea, and the *representational* function which consists in an adequate matching-up of language and the world. Disorders of reference – brought about by figural excess – are simultaneously felt as disorders of identity, breaking or suspending the privileged tie between words and expressive intent. This amounts to an implicit morality of style, an assumption that language should properly say what it means and mean what it says. Unbridled figuration – where words, in Wittgenstein's phrase, threaten to 'go on holiday' – leaves the interpreter uncomfortably bereft of such assurance. Shakespeare's equivocal style refuses, as it were, to *take responsibility* for the 'sonorous epithets' and 'swelling figures' that compose its own discourse.

This ethical charge is rarely far from the surface in Johnson's denunciatory strain. A quibble to Shakespeare, most famously,

> is what luminous vapours are to the traveller; he follows it at all adventures, it is sure to lead him out of his way. . . . It has some malignant power over his mind, and its fascinations are irresistible . . . . A quibble was to him the fatal *Cleopatra* for which he lost the world, and was content to lose it.
>
> (Johnson 1969, p. 68)

The question of style here takes on a whole strange dimension of associated myth and metaphor. Ironically, the passage might be seen to exemplify the very linguistic vices that Johnson treats with such contempt. He is most in danger of yielding to the power of seductive multiplied metaphor precisely when criticizing Shakespeare for the selfsame fault. One recalls, in this connection, Derrida's copious examples of how figurative language invades the discourse of philosophy even where attempts are made – as by Locke – to expunge its insidious effects. To adapt Bacon's saying: 'drive metaphor out with a pitchfork, yet she will return'. A perverse compulsion seems to operate here, turning language back against its own self-regulating ordinance.

In Johnson, this phenomenon is all the more disturbing for the sexual overtones – of yielding, seduction, abandoned self-mastery – which mark its emergence. The metaphor of word-play as a 'fatal Cleopatra' is just one of many suggestions, in the *Preface* and elsewhere, that work to associate feminine wiles with the mischiefs created by unbridled linguistic figuration. The straightforward virtues of a 'manly' style – vigorous, commonsensical, unembellished, plain-dealing – are opposed to the weaknesses attendant upon metaphor and other such womanish devices. Rationality demands that the seductive

ornaments of language be kept within bounds by a firm sense of masculine propriety and discipline. Otherwise, as Johnson repeatedly
complains, good sense is all too often overwhelmed by the blandish-
ments of figural language. Such distractions are evidently not to be
borne by a critic and editor so intent upon distinguishing the virtues
from the vices in Shakespeare's plays.

'It is impossible to dissociate the questions of art, style and truth
from the question of the woman' (Derrida 1979b, p. 71). Thus Derrida, in a reading of Nietzschean metaphor which seeks to deconstruct
– or turn back against itself – the 'phallocentric' discourse of male
mastery and power. Derrida traces a strange concatenation of themes
beyond the explicit message of Nietzsche's virulent anti-feminism.
Woman is the very antithesis of philosophic truth, she whose 'seductive distance' and 'dissimulating ways' are traps set on purpose to lure
the philosopher out of his appointed path. Truth-seeking discourse is
deflected from its aim by an 'abyssal divergence' which 'engulfs and
distorts all vestige of essentiality, of identity, of property'. If woman is
'but one name for that untruth of truth', then the other names are
'style', 'metaphor' and 'writing' – temptations which likewise beckon
to philosophy from the distance of an unmasterable charm and provocation. The question 'what is woman?' founders on the rock of this
dissimulating non-identity.

So much, one might say, for the standing provocation which instigated Nietzsche's well-known rabid antifeminism. Yet within those
same texts, as Derrida reads them, there also emerges the outline of a
counter-interpretation, one which would affirm the undoing of truth by
stratagems of 'feminine' style. Thus Derrida quotes a passage from 'The
History of an Error' where Nietzsche, tracing the symptoms of intellectual decadence, seizes on the point at which 'it becomes female' ('sie
wird Weib'). Yet it is precisely the case that Nietzsche's own writings
exploit those very symptoms of decline as a tactical resource against the
truth-claims of philosophy from Socrates to Hegel. By his practice of a
'literary', aphoristic style, Nietzsche sets out to undermine all the
system-building constructs of traditional thought. What he writes
about the intellect's 'becoming-female' could just as well be applied,
point for point, to Nietzsche's 'dissimulating' strategies.

This might seem all very remote from Dr Johnson and the major issues of eighteenth-century Shakespeare scholarship. Yet there is, after all, a similar paradoxical strain about Johnson's contemptuous yet fascinated dealing with Shakespeare's seductive wordplay. That his own critical language, like Nietzsche's, shows signs of the same infectious malaise would suggest that the analogy is not so far-fetched. What we read in the Preface are the twists and blind-spots of an argument pressed beyond the limits of consistent sense by its own contradictory commitments. Johnson, as I have argued, is caught between two opposing ideologies, each with its attendant structure of linguistic and critical presupposition. Was Shakespeare a wild, untutored genius or one who transcended (and effectively transformed) the dictates of conventional propriety? Can his plays survive the test of rational judgement, or must reason itself come to terms with the signal fact of his achievement? And above all, the matter of Shakespearean style: can such excesses be justified despite their offence against reason, dignity and truth?

Johnson returns contradictory answers to each of these questions. As regards Shakespeare's language, his talk of 'luminous vapours' and 'malignant powers' may be set alongside the confident claim that

> he who has mazed his imagination in following the phantoms which other writers raise up before him, may here be cured of his delirious ecstasies by reading human sentiments in human language.
>
> (Johnson 1969, p. 61)

Such manifest inconsistencies are commonly put down to Johnson's last-minute haste in composing the Preface, or – more charitably – his judicious habit of weighing up alternative viewpoints. What is overlooked by such generalized accounts is the way that Johnson's text both stages and evades a more specific conflict of ideological motives. The signs of that tension are there to be read in the aberrant figural swerves and complications which conventional eighteenth-century wisdom would confine to the margins of sense.

II

'Marginal' is precisely the term Johnson uses by way of modestly playing down the significance of textual commentary vis-à-vis the text. 'I have confined my imagination to the margin', he writes, unlike – presumably – those overweening editors who allow their emendations to disfigure the text, instead of decently recording them in footnotes. The *Preface* winds up on a curious note of ironic diffidence mixed with defensive self-esteem. Textual criticism is a thankless labour, its efforts at best a humble contribution and at worst a monument to misguided scholarly ingenuity. And yet, Johnson writes, it is an art which, properly performed, 'demands more than humanity possesses', so that 'he who exercises it with most praise has very frequent need of indulgence' (Johnson 1969, p. 84). The licence which Johnson elsewhere extends to Shakespeare is in this case applied to his own present labours. On the one hand the editor-critic is cast as a harmless drudge whose activities are strictly *subservient* and *marginal* to the text he would faithfully transmit. On the other, textual scholarship becomes a kind of surrogate creative act, requiring a well-nigh superhuman measure of moral and imaginative strength. 'Let us now be told no more of the dull duty of an editor.'

And yet, as the *Preface* repeatedly insists, Johnson counts himself a foe to 'conjecture', or to textual emendations which cross the line between self-effacing scholarship and creative licence. Such speculative ventures on the critic's part are a hazard which common sense wisely avoids. It is, Johnson warns,

> an unhappy state, in which danger is hid under pleasure. The allurements of emendation are scarcely resistible. Conjecture has all the joy and all the pride of invention, and he that has once started a happy change is too much delighted to consider what objections may rise against it.
>
> (Johnson 1969, p. 96)

Figures of allurement, seduction, dangerous pleasure: the passage can hardly fail to recall Johnson's strictures on the 'fatal Cleopatra' of Shakespearean wordplay. For the critic to indulge in speculative fancy is a weakness complicit with the dramatist's worst excesses. It offends, that is to say, against the principled economy of logic and sense which insists on a proper correspondence between signifier and signified, word and concept. In his redaction of previous editorial efforts,

Johnson recollects how he encountered 'in every page Wit struggling with its own sophistry, and Learning confused by the multiplicity of its views' (Johnson 1969, p. 95). Confusion worse confounded is the only result of allowing conjecture to practise its arts upon such powerfully seductive and bewildering material.

Yet of course it is that very confusion in the sources – textual corruption as well as the aggravating wordplay – which called forth the editors' unhappy labours in the first place. Criticism may be deluded if it thinks that mere ingenuity ('wit') can point the way back to plain good sense. But with Shakespeare – as Johnson has often perforce to admit – the sense may lie so far beyond the common bounds of 'propriety' and 'truth' as to render such distinctions untenable. Sober scholarship is no better placed than speculative fancy when it tries to bring order to such resistant material. Editorial surmise becomes lost in the labyrinths of figural undecidability. How can one distinguish, on scholarly grounds, between the malign genius of Shakespearean wordplay and the multiplied errors and confusions attendant on the process of textual transmission? Johnson's desire for stability and the permanence of truth demands that he cling to some vestigial faith in the authority of origins, in the text as providing sufficient guidance to its own most authentic form. Common sense might then at least hope to unravel the worst of those super-induced perplexities created by the muddle-headed copyists and critics. Yet even this chastened ambition seems wildly optimistic in the face of such intractable problems. That the commentator should so often turn out to be mistaken 'cannot be wonderful, either to himself or others, if it be considered that in his art there is no system, no principal and axiomatical truth that regulates subordinate positions' (Johnson 1969, pp. 95–6).

This throws a whole series of paradoxes into Johnson's express editorial creed. How can speculation be 'confined to the margin' where texts are perceived as standing in need of such elaborate restorative treatment? How can criticism aim at any kind of settled or consensual reading where the vagaries of textual transmission are compounded by the lawlessness of Shakespeare's equivocating style? Commentary becomes, in Johnson's words, a self-acknowledged 'art', rather than a matter of regulative 'system' or 'axiomatical truth'. It is bound to transgress the prescriptive line between creation and criticism, text and context, meaning and the margins of meaning. And this touches directly on those areas of sensitive concern that Derrida associates with language in its 'juridical' or legislative aspect. Common sense requires that the peculiar licence extended to a poet like Shakespeare should at least be prevented from working its mischief on the efforts of rational prose commentary. Yet this transaction is not achieved on such amicable terms as might be suggested by a simple parcelling-out of different linguistic domains. 'Where any passage appeared inextricably perplexed', Johnson writes, 'I have endeavoured to discover how it may be recalled to sense with least violence' (Johnson 1969, p. 93). Thus the restoration of tolerable 'sense' may involve a certain *violence, a* willed imposition of common-sense juridical norms. If reason is in danger of being contaminated by Shakespeare's sophistical language, the opposite is also the case: that Shakespeare may be literally *disfigured* by the rational sense-making efforts of the scholar.

I have pressed rather hard on these problematic aspects of Johnson's text because they point symptomatically to larger questions about the practice and tradition of Shakespearean criticism. These may be summarized as follows. Firstly, there is the matter of textual scholarship, its relation to 'the text' on the one hand and to problems of interpretation on the other. That these distinctions may be blurred, as in Johnson, is an index of their artificial character, their obedience to certain specific laws of discursive economy. Any notion of the sacrosanct literary text – whether as an object of scholarly or critical attention – is rendered problematic by the instance of Shakespeare. And this leads on, secondly, to the question of how Shakespeare's significance, as a *textual* phenomenon, is processed and maintained within the constraints of a dominant ideology. These constraints may be far from monolithic or logically consistent. They may indeed give rise to obvious internal contradictions, as with Johnson's facing-about between an abstract universalism and a nationalist ideology of language. As a result, his role is constantly shifting: from self-effacing editor to speculative critic and then, beyond that, to those weighty moralizing passages which effectively *re-write* Shakespeare on their own preferred terms of imaginative 'truth'.

And it is here that we find the central and continuing paradox of Shakespeare criticism, from Johnson's day to the present. Outside theological tradition, no body of writings has been subjected to more in the way of interpretative comment and textual scholarship. Yet the upshot of this activity – visible already in Johnson's edition – is to cast increasing doubt on the power of criticism to distinguish between the two. No doubt this is partly a matter of contingent historical circumstance. Criticism, as Johnson so often complains, rushes in with manifold fictions of its own to redress the delinquent carelessness of Shakespeare and his copyists. But there is also a more general lesson to be drawn, one which returns us to the question of the text as raised in post-structuralist theory. Shakespeare is an extreme but representative case of the way in which commentary works to erase all the firm, juridical limits surrounding that privileged entity, the literary text. Even textual scholarship, with its self-denying ordinances, finds itself repeatedly *crossing over* from a strictly ancillary to a kind of rival-imaginative role.

It may be the case – as Raymond Williams has argued (R. Williams 1977) – that this distinction between 'literature' and other kinds of writing was not yet an issue for Johnson and his contemporaries. It was only in terms of the nineteenth-century 'culture and society' debate that such ideas took on a definite and complex ideological character. 'Literature' – like 'culture' itself – came to connote a whole alternative order of human aspirations and values, an imaginative creed set firmly against the grim utilitarian outlook of 'society' at large. Dr Johnson, as Williams remarks, gets along with a generalized notion of literary activity which includes many kinds of writing – poetry, history, criticism – and has no need, as yet, for such charged ideological distinctions. But the absence of 'literature' as a key term in Johnson's lexicon doesn't at all signify a lack of concern with those issues which were later to emerge in more sharply contested form. With Johnson we witness the beginning of that powerful ideology within English criticism which sets up 'literature' as a paradigm of healthy creativity, and Shakespeare in turn as the test-case and touchstone of literary values at large. This despite the fact that Johnson, of course, judges Shakespeare by his own 'eighteenth-century' standards, and often finds him wanting. What is more significant, as I have argued, is the encounter thus staged between an as yet ill-defined ideology of literature and an answering (but deeply confused) critical practice.

'Nationalism and universalism' – Derrida's terms are still very pertinent here. Since Johnson, critics have ceased by and large (with a few exceptions, like Tolstoy and Shaw) to lament Shakespeare's 'barbarous' language and corresponding lack of stern moral fibre. The problem is no longer posed in such overtly ideological terms. But they have still had to acknowledge, in various ways, what is felt as the *exorbitant* character of Shakespearean English, its resistance to rational or common-sense accounting. On the one hand the plays are held up, by critics from Coleridge to Leavis, as the central and definitive achievement of literary language at full creative stretch. Of literary *English*, that is, although there is often a larger (and vaguer) claim in the background: that Shakespearean English embodies an ideal of co-operative thought and sensibility transcending all rootedness in time and place. By such means has criticism managed to reconcile the otherwise contradictory demands of 'nationalism' and 'universalism'. But there remains, on the other hand, a persistent problem in accommodating Shakespeare's language to any kind of moral or prescriptive norm. The rhetorical *excess* which so troubled Johnson continues to vex a critic like Leavis, though the anxiety issues in a typically displaced and indirect form. To watch this displacement at work is to see how criticism repeatedly falls into traps and contradictions of its own ideological creating.

III

Leavis's essay on *Othello* (Leavis 1952) is a typically combative and charged piece of writing. It sets out not only to interpret the play but to treat it as a primer for criticism, a test-case of what responsive reading ought to be when measured against the vital complexity of Shakespeare's language. It also carries on a running polemic against A. C. Bradley and his idea of 'character' as the primary, psychological reality of Shakespearean drama. More specifically, Leavis pours scorn on Bradley's portrayal of Iago as a villain of near-superhuman resourceful cunning, and of Othello as his nobly-suffering idealized counterpart. Leavis's arguments are sufficiently well known to require no detailed summary here. Sufficient to say that he views Othello as laid open to Iago's insinuating wiles by a fatal combination of weaknesses in his own temperament. The Bradleian account is a falsification of the play resulting from the naive assumption that Othello's opinion of himself is also the opinion that we, as audience or readers, are supposed to entertain. In fact, Leavis argues, the contrary signs are unmistakeably there in Othello's strain of grandiloquent rhetoric, his indulgence in manic alternating moods of heroic projection and plangent self-pity. Othello falls victim to flaws in his own make-up which are merely obscured by viewing him, like Bradley, as the noble dupe of a devilishly complex and interesting Iago.

'Like Bradley' has a pointed ambiguity here. Bradley's account of *Othello* is branded by Leavis as 'naive', 'sentimental' and 'idealizing' – as sharing, in short, precisely that complex of temperamental flaws that Leavis detects in Othello himself. This is in keeping with the logic of Leavis's argument, and gives rise to some neatly turned jokes at Bradley's expense. Thus 'Iago's knowledge of Othello's character amounts pretty much to Bradley's knowledge of it (except, of course, that Iago cannot realise Othello's nobility quite to the full)' (Leavis 1952, p. 137). Or again, with more heavy-handed irony: 'to equate Bradley's knowledge of Othello with Othello's own was perhaps unfair to Othello'. Every detail of the Bradleian account can be held up to ridicule as yet another instance of patent simple-mindedness and sentimentality. The difference of views between Bradley and Leavis becomes oddly intertwined with the drama played out between Othello and Iago. Leavis conceives himself as speaking up for a tough-minded realist assessment of the play inherently at odds with Bradley's 'idealizing' approach. One desirable result, as Leavis sees it, is to undermine the romantic fascination with Iago as a character of baffling complexity and sinister appeal. Leavis's counter-idealist reading is at any rate 'a fit reply to the view of Othello as necessary material and provocation for a display of Iago's fiendish intellectual superiority' (p. 138).

Leavis can therefore claim support for his reading in the fact that this is, after all, *Othello*'s and not *Iago*'s tragedy. Bradley's account has the absurd upshot of reducing the play to 'Iago's character in action'. Nor is he alone in this, since the Bradleian reading – as Leavis ruefully observes – has been current, even prevalent, at least since Coleridge. It thus remains for Leavis, writing in the face of this 'sustained and sanctioned perversity', to cut through the layers of sentimental falsehood and restore the play to its rightful interpretation.

> The plain fact that has to be asserted ... is that in Shakespeare's tragedy *of Othello* Othello is the chief personage – the chief personage in such a sense that the tragedy may fairly be said to be Othello's character in action.
>
> (Leavis 1952, p. 138)

Yet there is clearly a sense in which the logic of Leavis's argument tends to undercut this confidently orthodox assertion. His attitude of prosecuting zeal toward Bradley cannot help but carry over into his treatment of Othello, just as – conversely – Othello's romanticized self-image finds an echo and analogue (according to Leavis) in Bradley's reading. And there is, furthermore, a touch of Iago's corrosive or deflationary cynicism in the way that Leavis sets out to confound those twin representatives of virtuous self-ignorance, Othello and Bradley. The latter, 'his knowledge of Othello coinciding virtually with Othello's', sees nothing but doomed nobility and pathos. By a further twist of the same interpretative logic one can see how Leavis plays a Iago-like role in destroying the illusion of Othello's nobly suffering innocence. If Bradley's blinkered idealism is, as Leavis says, 'invincible', so also is Leavis's ruthlessly debunking approach.

It is not uncommon for critics to become thus involved in curious patterns of compulsive repetition which take rise from their resolutely *partial* understanding of a literary text. Criticism belongs to what Freud called the work of 'secondary revision', a process aimed at achieving some consistency of 'fit' between manifest and latent sense, but also producing all manner of disguise, repression and 'uncanny' repetition of themes. This compulsion is most in evidence where critics deal with an overtly ambiguous narrative like Henry James's *The Turn of the Screw*. The text seems to support two opposite interpretations – the 'psychological' and 'supernatural' – and to offer no consistent means of deciding between them. Recent deconstructionist readings have shown how critics mostly espouse one side or the other, and are thus forced to suppress or unconsciously distort any textual evidence which controverts their reading (see Felman 1977 and Brooke-Rose 1981). If the story turns – as the 'naturalists' would have it – on neurotic delusions suffered by James's governess-narrator, then her symptoms are oddly reproduced in the gaps and obsessional lapses of argument displayed by the critics. Such 'Freudian' readings are crudely reductive in their wholesale, unmediated use of psychoanalytic terminology and method. On the other hand, the 'supernatural' version of James's tale requires that the interpreter pass over some striking indications of neurosis and paranoid delusion on the part of the governess. In both cases there is an inbuilt bias of approach which unconsciously produces its own tell-tale symptoms of thematic displacement and reworking.

Post-structuralism is perhaps best characterized by its willingness to acknowledge this predicament, rather than set itself up as a 'meta-language' ideally exempt from the puzzles and perplexities of literary texts. The structuralist enterprise aimed at precisely this ideal: that criticism should aspire to a 'science' of the text which would finally uncover its invariant 'grammars' of structure and style. This approach laid down a firm disciplinary line between literature and the systematic discourse of knowledge which sought to comprehend it. But such ambitions soon gave way as critics like Roland Barthes came to recognize the inadequacy of formalistic methods and the way in which textual signification exceeds all merely heuristic limits. Barthes's S/Z (1970) marked a turning point in this passage from structuralist to post-structuralist thinking. At the same time Jacques Derrida was developing his powerful deconstructive critique of traditional epistemic categories, including that conservative notion of 'structure' which he found implicit in Saussure, Lévi-Strauss and others (see especially Derrida 1978). Textuality was recognized as breaking all the bounds of a conceptual regime which had striven to hold it in check. And this betokened a corresponding shift in the relations between literature, criticism and textual theory. As the latter relinquished its claim to sovereign knowledge, so it took on something of the complex, contradictory character normally attributed to 'literary' language.

Shoshana Felman (1977) reveals the extraordinary lengths to which this process can be carried in her reading of various critics on *The Turn of the Screw*. Interpretation can only repeat, in compulsive fashion, the acts of misreading exemplified by various, more or less deluded characters *within the tale*. Any attempt to provide an omniscient critical reading is always foredoomed to this chronic partiality of viewpoint. As Felman puts it:

> In seeking to 'explain' and *master* literature, in refusing, that is, to become a *dupe* of literature . . . the psychoanalytic reading, ironically enough, turns out to be a reading which *represses the unconscious*, which represses, paradoxically, the unconscious which it purports to be 'explaining'.
>
> (Felman 1977, p. 193)

This applies as much to self-styled 'theoretical' criticism as to essays of a more traditional interpretative cast. Such distinctions break down against the 'uncanny' transference which carries across from the narrative to its various symptomatic partial readings. The tale is *contagious* in the sense that it creates a frustrated desire for coherence, one which can never be satisfied except by certain self-defeating acts of textual repression.

Leavis's essay on *Othello* bears all the marks of this obscure compulsion at work. It is to Iago that Leavis attributes a 'deflating, unbeglamouring, brutally realistic mode of speech' (Leavis 1952, p. 144). But the same description could equally be applied to Leavis's essay, working as it does to 'deflate' and 'unbeglamour' the nobility of character mistakenly imputed to Othello. At times this curious transference of roles comes close to the surface in Leavis's prose:

> Iago's power, in fact, in the temptation-scene is that he represents something that is in Othello . . . the essential traitor is within the gates. For if Shakespeare's Othello too is simple-minded, he is nevertheless more complex than Bradley's. Bradley's Othello is, rather, Othello's; it being an essential datum regarding the Shakespearian Othello that he has an ideal conception of himself.
>
> (Leavis 1952, pp. 140–1)

What makes Othello more rewardingly 'complex' than Bradley can show is the fact that his character (as Leavis reads it) partakes somewhat of Iago's destructive nature. And by the same odd logic it is Leavis's account of *Othello* which raises the play to a level of dramatic complexity undreamt of in Bradley's naive philosophy. The undoing of simple-minded virtue takes place not so much 'in' the play – since Othello is already thus tainted – but in the contest of readings between a tough-minded Leavis and a feebly romanticizing Bradley. As with James's tale, so here: interpretation is drawn into a scene of displaced re-enactment where critics have no choice but to occupy positions already taken up by characters within the play.

This lends an added resonance to Leavis's metaphor of the 'traitor within the gates'. A certain curious logic of host-and-parasite is insistently at work in Leavis's essay. It operates by a series of thematic reversals, substituting 'maturity' for 'innocence' ('Bradley, that is, in his comically innocent way'), 'realism' for 'idealism' and – ultimately – 'Leavis' for 'Bradley'. In each case the second (dominant) term has a Iago-like ambivalence, exposing simple-minded virtue to the trials of an undeceiving, rock-bottom worldly knowledge. Leavis attacks the sentimental reading which prefers to see the play 'through Othello's eyes rather than Shakespeare's'. His own account is designed to correct this romantic bias by focusing attention on those qualities of Othello's *language* – in particular, his rhetoric of nobly-suffering pathos – which supposedly should lead us to a proper 'Shakespearean' reading. In fact it is quite obvious that Leavis is simply substituting one interpretation for another, his own drastically 'deflating' account for Bradley's idealizing version. The claim that his approach enables us to see Othello 'through Shakespeare's eyes' is merely an enabling fiction, though one that few critics seem prepared to forgo. Othello's great flaw – like Bradley's after him – consists very largely in a failure to grasp the Leavisite criteria of poetic health and vitality.

Leavis makes the point plainly enough in objecting to Bradley's description of Othello as 'the greatest poet' among Shakespeare's tragic heroes. For Leavis, this provides just one more example of Bradley's inveterate romanticism, his habit of seeing Othello through Othello's own self-deluding eyes.

> If the impression made by Othello's own utterance is often poetical as well as poetic, that is Shakespeare's way, not of representing him as a poet, but of conveying the romantic glamour that, for Othello himself and others, invests Othello and what he stands for.
>
> (Leavis 1952, p. 143)

Those 'others' include Bradley but not, of course, Leavis – or indeed

Iago, who makes some very effective points of his own about Othello's 'romantic glamour'. All the same it is hard to see that Leavis's case rests on anything more than his predisposed view of what constitutes 'the Shakespearean use of language'. And that view rests in turn, as I have argued, on a complex of deeply ideological assumptions about language, thought and sensibility. Poetry is conceived as expressing the truth of a vital and properly self-critical response to the realities of lived experience. 'Intelligence', 'maturity' and 'life' are the fixed co-ordinates around which Leavis constructs his highly selective 'tradition' of English poetry. It is a view of literary history which locates its main high-point in the early seventeenth century (Shakespeare and Donne), and which judges later poets – especially the Romantics – against that mythical ideal of a 'unified sensibility' belonging to a long-lost 'organic' culture. If Milton and Shelley, among others, are tried by this standard and found sadly wanting, so also is Shakespeare's Othello.

Leavis set out his main criteria in a number of early Scrutiny pieces (reprinted in Leavis 1975). Among other critical touchstones (like 'thought' and 'judgement'), he offered close readings of several short poems intended to emphasize the difference between 'emotion' and 'sentimentality'. The hallmark of sentimental poetry, Leavis argued, was its surrender to a mood of plangent, self-regarding pathos unchecked by any sense of 'mature' critical restraint. Such is the standard that Leavis applies to Othello's characteristic strain. It involves, Leavis writes, 'an attitude *towards* the emotion expressed – an attitude of a kind we are familiar with in the analysis of sentimentality' (Leavis 1952, p. 143). Which of course presupposes that Othello's rhetoric is *placed*, or shown up for what it is, by the implicit contrast with Shakespeare's most vital ('creative-exploratory') style. Leavis would have it that this contrast is self-evident, at least to any reader 'not protected (like Bradley) by a very obstinate preconception'. Romantic misconceptions should be easy to rebut 'because there, to point to, is the text, plain and unequivocal'. This would make it odd, to say the least, that critics have differed so widely over the play's interpretation, and that Leavis should feel summoned to redeem such a history of multiplied error and delusion. But this is to ignore the more likely explanation: that Leavis has invented his own *Othello* in pursuit of an imaginary coherence required by certain pressing ideological imperatives.

These motives are evident in the curious shifts of argumentation which Leavis adopts in the course of his essay. The central appeal is to a normative idea of human 'character' and 'experience', closely related to the virtues of 'mature', self-critical intelligence which Leavis finds at work in all great poetry. Shakespeare's genius has to consist in this consummate union of truth-to-experience and language raised to its highest creative power. Othello, says Leavis, 'is (as we have all been) cruelly and tragically wronged', so that 'the invitation to identify one-self with him is indeed hardly resistible' (Leavis 1952, p. 153). There is irony here at Bradley's expense, but also a measure of acceptance, necessary if Othello is to retain any remnant of genuine 'tragic' dignity. For it is the nature of Shakespeare's genius, as Leavis goes on to argue, that it 'carries with it a large facility in imposing conviction locally'. Othello's self-deceiving rhetoric must be taken to possess at least a certain moving force if the play is to achieve its effect. 'He is (as we have all been) cruelly and tragically wronged' – the essay founders on this quite undecidable mixture of Iago-like irony and generalized 'human' pathos. Such are the conflicts engendered by a reading which stakes its authority on presupposed absolute values of language, moral-ity and truth. At the close, Leavis writes, 'he is still the same Othello in whose essential make-up the tragedy lay'. It is on this notion of 'essen-tial' human nature – both as norm and as measure of 'tragic' deviation – that Leavis's essay splinters into so many diverse and conflicting claims.

IV

From Johnson to Leavis there occurs a marked shift in the ideological values sustaining the project of Shakespearean criticism. For Johnson the prime imperative is to stabilize the text by application of common-sense criteria, and to reach a corresponding measure of agreement on issues of interpretative truth. Underlying this approach is a generalized assurance that language, though forced against its natural grain by Shakespeare's deplorable excesses, can yet be restored to something like a rational, perspicuous order of sense. Johnson's praise for the universality of Shakespearean drama ('his story requires Romans or kings, but he thinks only on men') goes along with his faith – however sorely tried – in the joint accountability of language, reason and truth. With Leavis, this appeal to common-sense universals has given way to a more embattled ideology, one which pits the truth of individual experience against all forms of abstract generalization. There is, so Leavis argues, a close and exemplary relation between Shakespeare's 'creative-exploratory' language and the process of anguished discovery through which his protagonists attain to authentic self-knowledge. This becomes the measure of Othello's characterizing weakness, his rhetorical evasion of the truths borne home by his own tragic predicament.

Johnson stands near the beginning, Leavis near the end of a certain dominant cultural formation in the history of Shakespeare studies. It is an effort of ideological containment, an attempt to harness the unruly energies of the text to a stable order of significance. With Johnson this takes the form of a conservative textual-editorial policy allied to an overt moralizing bent which very often issues in flat contradictions of precept and practice. With Leavis, it produces a reading of Othello ruptured by striking inconsistencies of statement, logic and intent. Beneath them runs the reassuring persuasion that dramatic 'character' has its own coherence, and that language must properly be always in the service of authentic human experience. What Leavis so forcefully rejects in Bradley – the idea of 'character' as a simple, real-life analogue – takes a different but related shape in his own appeal to the characterizing force of Shakespearean language. Thus Othello in Act V is 'still the same Othello', while Iago represents 'a not uncommon kind of grudging, cynical malice' (p. 154). In the end Leavis can only reduplicate Bradley's cardinal error in a form of displaced but none the less naive and reductive moralizing judgement.

Post-structuralism affords an understanding of the ideological compulsions at work in this persistent allegory of errors. It provides, most importantly, an argued theoretical perspective on that effort to recuperate Shakespeare's text in the name of autonomous subjectivity and universal human experience. From Johnson to Leavis, a tradition grows up in which the plays are subjected to a powerful normative bias, an imposition of meanings and values as conceived by the dominant ideology. It is in the will to secure this stability – to repose, as Johnson hoped, on 'the permanence of truth' – that criticism runs into all those strange divagations of sense which mark the history of Shakespeare studies. Textual scholarship and interpretation are likewise afflicted by this chronic uncertainty of aim. As Johnson labours against multiplied errors and delusions, so Leavis rebuts the 'potent and mischievous' influence of Bradleian criticism, only to write another chapter in the casebook of endlessly dissenting views. Shakespeare's meaning can no more be reduced to the currency of liberal-humanist faith than his text to the wished-for condition of pristine, uncorrupt authority. All we have are the readings which inevitably tell such partial and complicated stories of their own devising.

4

DECONSTRUCTING SHAKESPEARE'S COMEDIES

Malcolm Evans

I AFFECTING THE LETTER

In one of the earliest of Shakespeare's comedies a mirror is held up to deconstruction by one who has a nose for the whole business *avant la lettre*:

> HOLOFERNES Ovidius Naso was the man: and why, indeed, *Naso*, but for smelling out the odoriferous flowers of fancy, the jerks of invention? *Imitari* is nothing; so doth the hound his master, the ape his keeper, the tired horse his rider.
>
> (*Love's Labour's Lost*, IV. ii. 118–22)

Imitation, the pedant Holofernes suggests, is beneath human dignity. At best *mimesis* is for animals. But elsewhere in Shakespeare's comedies even the hound is in two minds about it. In *The Two Gentlemen of Verona*, roughly contemporary with *Love's Labour's Lost*, Launce's dog shows a dogged Brechtian reluctance to abandon the actor's canine quiddity, remaining 'as one should say, one that takes upon him to be a dog indeed, to be, as it were, a dog at all things' (IV. iv. 11–13). When called upon to act like a human being the dog proves unable to sustain his mimicry for longer than 'a pissing while': 'When didst thou see me heave up my leg and make water against a gentlewoman's farthingale?' asks the indignant Launce, 'Didst ever see me do such a trick?' (IV. iv. 37–9). But in such times of distress the dog 'sheds not a tear, nor speaks a word' (II. iii. 30–1).

Already, in these early plays, the status of mimesis is problematic. Defined as fit only for animals then spurned even by them, this mimicry in crisis is a gift to deconstruction, and these divided, contradictory formulations of the problem are further compounded by the return of a naive concept of imitation – a deceptive affirmation of mimesis as that which was, after all, the mark of the distinctively human. Just as Proteus can transform himself into a spaniel for the love of Silvia (IV. ii. 14), so Launce can become a dog out of love for his dog: '"You do him the more wrong", quoth I, "'twas I did the thing you wot of"', and the dog-whipper to the Duke, offended by the smell of urine, 'makes me no more ado, but whips me out of the chamber'. (IV. iv. 28–9). Holofernes, who wishes to play no less than three of the Nine Worthies, is as accomplished an imitator as Launce or even Bottom. And in all this concern with acting, representation and identity, so characteristic of the Comedies, the mirror that reflects deconstruction is always itself divided and already in more than one place – at the site of a mimetic sign or action, but also broken in the signifier released in the enactment of acting, the representation on the stage of the process of mimesis itself which may, as Holofernes maintains, be no more or less than 'nothing'.

In the Comedies the process of representation is never finally effaced from its product, leaving these categories themselves indistinct. This denigration of a 'represented' to which representation must always subordinate itself, or a 'meaning' which can be located beyond the play of signifiers, radically undermines from within those metaphorical constructions through which meaning is constituted. What Derridean deconstruction removes is this 'reassuring certitude, which is itself beyond the reach of play' (Derrida 1978, p. 279), a certitude designated in metaphysical thought as simultaneously part of a total structure but not of it – a paradox which calls into question the metaphysical concept of coherence itself. If the structure proposed by mimesis and metaphysics is a structure only because it has a centre, and if that centre must also always be outside – in the object or the signified on which the structure is grounded – then in Derrida's terms 'the center is not the center' and coherence is constituted in contradiction. Thus, as Holofernes asserts, 'Imitari is nothing', a principle which invades each stage of the practice of signification. But this 'nothing' is also in Renaissance literary theory the site of the poetic imagination, functioning as a kind of absence upon which a variety of actions can be inscribed. In this context Holofernes's 'nothing' is liberated from any intrinsic meaning to become an index of the plurality of devices deployed in the Comedies.

Action in the Comedies culminates in the 'jerks of invention' described by Holofernes, which indicate serious business already deferred for too long. Malefactors are converted and a god appears from the trees; a messenger arrives with the worst news imaginable, or the twins at last pop up in the same place together; the heroine is slandered and seems to die, or is captured by outlaws before the protean protagonist abandons thoughts of rape, accepts the stamp of form and is 'charactered'. And yet, in the interim, imitation 'is nothing': the process about which there is much ado, the material from which the poet creates in Puttenham's Arte of English Poesie and in A Midsummer Night's Dream. It is what the poet 'affirms' in Sidney's Defence of Poetry and that which, in King Lear, 'can be made out of nothing' and which will eventually 'come of nothing'. It is also, with its manifestly theatrical connotation, the 'nothing' signified by the poor player and the idiot's language in Macbeth, and the 'nothing' which Ophelia 'thinks' as an epitome of the feminine – and which is 'a fair thought to lie between a maid's legs', a genital delirium of presence and absence as she/he waits for the entrance of a fellow boy-actor who performs the part of a boy-actor representing the Player Queen.[1] These intervals, which install themselves in the action through its word-games, maskings and conundrums, may, in one way or another, account for the body of the play, functioning as signifiers always surplus to 'meaning', or as signifieds no longer present to or identical with themselves. These 'nothings' are the traces of production itself, or visible erasures in the 'finish' of the product – the forces which constitute, and are thus more immediately and palpably 'something' than, the illusory subjects, objects and predicates of the poet's 'created world' as it unfolds itself on stage. Indeed, the text of *Love's Labour's Lost* gives them their own theoretical exergue when Holofernes 'affects the letter' (IV. ii. 53), deconstructing distinctions of age and gender which may be thought to inhere in the signifiers 'deer', 'pricket', 'sore' 'sorel' into the grammatological spacing of Derridean *différance*,[2] the process in which semantic *differentiation* is caught up in a signified which is endlessly *deferred*:

> The preyful princess pierc'd and prick'd a pretty pleasing pricket;
> Some say a sore; but not a sore, till now made sore with shooting.
> The dogs did yell; put 'ell to sore, then sorel jumps from thicket;
> Or pricket sore, or else sore'll the people fall a-hooting.
> If sore be sore, then 'ell to sore makes fifty sores-O-sorel!
> Of one sore I an hundred make, by adding but one more I.
>
> (IV. ii. 54–60)

While plots and themes idle at such moments, *mimesis* conspicuously refused to put its house in order to make up its mind. Launce passes the time with something which approximates to an early draft of the mock-trial in *King Lear* where madman, Fool and actor ('Edgar I *nothing* am') confront a joint-stool in the part of Goneril. On this occasion the objects to be 'translated' are shoes, hat, staff, the dog, possibly Launce himself. The wooden shoes are almost as resistant as the dog to this project of imitation:

> This shoe is my father. No, this left shoe is my father; no, no, this left shoe is my mother; nay, that cannot be so neither. Yes, it is so, it is so: it hath the worser sole. This shoe with the hole in it is my mother; and this my father.
>
> (*The Two Gentlemen of Verona*, II. iii. 14–18)

By exploiting the limitations of the 'wooden O', here the literal 'nothing' in the sole/soul of the wooden shoe, Launce sketches some of the rudimentary divisions that constitute the cultural law of gender, while displaying the residual *substance* of the signifier, which can never be fully transformed, absorbed or made transparent in a represented 'nature'. The unyielding materiality of the shoe suggests other transformations, which lie beyond its power of acting. It would be appropriate if it 'could speak now like a wood [mad] woman' (lines 26–7) to represent the grief of the mother at the departure of her son, but this is not to be. In the event it has to be passed over in the business of assigning other parts before the action can begin:

> this staff is my sister; for, look you, she is as white as a lily, and as small as a wand. This hat is Nan our maid. I am the dog. No, the dog is himself and I am the dog. O, the dog is me, and I am myself. Ay; so, so.
>
> (II. iii. 19–23)

It is only his lack of logical and rhetorical finesse that fixes Launce, tautologously, as the subject who evades the shifting of identity from object to object, and who can say 'I am myself'. This assertion stands in defiance of that other play, *The Two Gentlemen of Verona*, in which 'Launce' is in the process of being made from other, no less recalcitrant materials – the staff, the hat, the shoes, the dog and his master's voice. Only the closure through which Launce asserts his own 'character' keeps him erroneously, monstrously Launce, 'the Prodigious Son' (II. iii. 3), but the identity of the dog is an altogether more protean affair. It is at once one with its master ('the dog is me'), but it is also already on its way to becoming something else. When called upon to imitate Launce's grief at the parting from his family, the 'real' scene which is constituted as the horizon of these receding actions, the dog, the Shakespearean actor *par excellence*, is transformed into 'a stone, a very pebble stone and has no more pity than a dog' (II. iii. 10–11).

In the popular dramatic tradition dogs add the human touch. We need look no further than the best-loved of imaginary beasts – Lassie, Old Shep and Blue Peter. But Holofernes, in his insistence that imitation is only for apes, horses and dogs, contravenes Aristotle, for whom *mimesis* is proper and natural only to humanity, and a far cry from the mimicry practised by other animals.[3] This, however, is only a minor oversight in Aristotle, whose *Poetics* can move on magisterially from 'Plot' and 'Character' to 'Thought' and 'Diction' while the Shakespearean text goes on fumbling with pre-fundamentals. Before *The Two Gentlemen of Verona* even broaches the problem of achieving a workable distinction between man, dog, and the mimetic offices appropriate to each, Speed and Proteus throw a comparable opposition into crisis from the angle of the sheep, rendering the elements of logic first to rhetoric and then to the inarticulate:

> SPEED The shepherd seeks the sheep, and not the sheep the shepherd; but I seek my master, and my master seeks not me: therefore, I am no sheep.
>
> PRO The sheep for fodder follow the shepherd; the shepherd for food follows not the sheep; thou for wages followest thy master; thy master for wages follows not thee: therefore, thou art a sheep.
>
> SPEED Such another proof will make me cry 'baa'.
>
> (I. i. 86–93)

In *Love's Labour's Lost* the same tired joke resolves the 'indivisible sound' of the beast which, in Aristotle, resembles the letter but falls short of its potential for combination in intelligible sounds, into the randomness and play of what Derrida, in 'White Mythology', describes as a 'non-sense' which exceeds signification and in which 'language is not yet born' (Derrida 1974, p. 41). By reversing the 'a, b,' of his hornbook 'with a horn added', Holofernes becomes 'Ba, most silly sheep with a horn', confirmed by Moth in the last two of the five vowels 'o, U' (V. i. 43–52). The jest is the making of Moth as an element of drama, a literal 'character' – 'thou consonant' (line 49) – ranked alongside the women of France, who find themselves 'Beauteous as ink' in the 'O's', 'text B' and 'red dominical' of their wooers' letters (V. ii. 41–5), and the 'cipher' Armado (I. ii. 52). This last figure appears again in *As You Like It*, in the guise of 'good Master What-ye-call't' (III. iii. 66) or 'Monsieur Melancholy' (III. ii. 289–90), the Jaques/'jakes' of a language which contains both the waste 'matter' of proverbial wisdom and the momentary awakening of 'all the men and women merely players' (II. vii. 140), in which discourse is once again alerted to its conditions of production. This too is a unified rounded character only in the sense of a 'cipher' (III. ii. 285), a word which connotes, behind the *excreta* of the sign, at once 'nothing' and, from the sixteenth century on, 'a secret or disguised manner of writing' (OED).

So the figures who speak and gesticulate on stage in the Comedies are much more than imaginary people. They are literally and ostentatiously 'characters' – hieroglyphs, letters, elements in a signifying system which flaunts its own abstractions against the claims of a mimesis which strives for the unmediated presence of its represented world. This combination of the image of writing and a foregrounding of the process of theatrical production once again brings the preoccupations of deconstruction and their particular bearing on these plays sharply into focus. For Aristotle 'written words are the signs of words spoken' just as speech is a symbolization of 'the affections or impressions of the soul' (On Interpretation, 16a) (Aristotle 1938, p. 115). So writing is the sign of a sign, doubly fallen from the immediate presence of thought and the subject to itself, an essence twice mediated. Here the letter exists only as something secondary and excrescent – in Derrida's terms a 'supplement'. In the metaphysical construction of language it holds a position similar to that occupied in drama by the materials mimesis banishes to the bustle and babble of a mise en scène which must be occulted in the interest of Aristotle's 'Plot', 'Character', 'Diction' and 'Thought' – in other words the represented world and its predications or the apparently seamless quality of a production whose process is transparent, decorously absent.

Thus mimesis and the view of writing as no more than a supplement, an inadequate representation of speech, share the same metaphysical stage. In contrast Holofernes, who rejects imitation, also shares with Derrida the conviction that writing, far from being merely supplementary, in fact precedes speech, even 'thought',[4] and believes that those who refuse to speak words as they are written are prisoners of a phonocentric madness – 'It insinuateth me of insanie: ne intelligis, domine? to make frantic, lunatic' (V. i. 24–5). The constitutive 'letter', relegated by mimesis and metaphysics to the status of a mediation, doubles back and dispels the monomania of the voice, presence and the signified in the characteristic gesture of Shakespeare's comedies declaring themselves as they are not. An erased 'nothing', a materiality which bears traces of the 'letter', reappears in the puns, rhymes and burlesques of comic language, the tautology, acyrologia and cacozelia of social and aesthetic inferiors (clowns, fools, caricatured 'low-comic' figures, women[5]), and the productivity recovered from the ciphers of mimesis in theatrical allusions, plays within plays, and the animated props of Launce and his co-actors.

The identity of this 'letter' is itself always divided, conditional, that of a supplement which has usurped the ideological and metaphysical dominant. The comedies say 'I am not what I am', 'Nothing that is so, is so', 'if your four negatives make your two affirmatives', 'If I were a woman', 'the truest poetry is the most feigning', 'all mirth and no matter', 'If this were played upon a stage now, I could condemn it as an improbable fiction', and 'If truth holds true contents'.[6] This provisional reversal of polarities – in which the supplement takes priority and hierarchical or centred structures are undermined – is its own undoing. The 'letter' in the comedies declines to vouch for the priority of an originary scripting and rehearsing represented in the text, an irreducible signified which can, in turn, compel the mimetic 'action' to be no more than its disposable, supplementary signifier. Launce presenting a play with shoes, hat, staff and dog no more vouches for a 'Shakespeare' who presents Launce than the theatrically produced dog who enacts the 'pebble stone' by showing no more pity than a dog. Contrary to the opinion fashionable in the 1960s and early 1970s, there is no 'meta-language' or 'meta-drama' in the comedies, no level of representation which can fix 'what is *really* going on', only more production, more text. In the language of deconstruction:

> The supplement, which is neither simply the signifier nor simply the representer, does not take the place of a signified or a represented, as is prescribed by the concepts of signification and representation or by the syntax of the words 'signifier' or 'representer'. The supplement comes in the place of a lapse, a nonsignified or a nonrepresented, a nonpresence. There is no present before it, it is not preceding [*sic*] by anything but itself, that is to say by another supplement. The supplement is always the supplement of a supplement. One wishes to go back *from the supplement to the source*: one must recognize that there is a *supplement at the source*.
>
> (Derrida 1976, pp. 303–4).

This unending supplementation is the force of 'affecting the letter' as practised by Holofernes, a process more concretely discernible in the detours of a specifically *theatrical* signifier around Launce, his costume, props and dog. This same process is in evidence in the movement of 'writing', in Derrida's sense, as *metaphor*, the figure in which a signifier's signified is always another signifier, one in a shuttle of 'vehicles', each lacking the 'tenor' of a literal or 'proper' name, each standing in as the driver of the one in front. In metaphor language, as an 'arche-writing' behind speech, embarks on 'a voyage into a long and hidden sentence, a secret recitative', with no guarantee of returning to an unmetaphorical name, a signifier which perfectly captures a present signified (Derrida 1974, p. 44). Outside the 'white mythology' of western philosophical discourse ('white', 'characterless', 'imperialist', the mythology of no mythology), even 'metaphor' itself is a metaphor, a translation of a translation with no source, incapable of stepping outside writing to 'represent' its own essence (Derrida 1974, pp. 29–30).

In *A Midsummer Night's Dream*, a series of transformations in a world of shadows and darkness is designated 'translation', a synonym for 'metaphor' in Elizabethan English.[7] Bottom, who joins Holofernes in being 'translated' into an ass, expounds the 'bottomless overdeterminability' of what Derrida calls the 'metaphorization of metaphor' (Derrida 1974, p. 44). The ballad of 'Bottom's Dream', a silent text within the text recording, within the *Dream*, a dream of a ('real') translation, is so called 'because it hath no bottom' (IV. i. 215), containing as it does both infinity and a great deal of nothing. 'The eye of man hath not heard, the ear of man hath not seen, man's hand is not able to taste, his tongue to conceive, nor his heart to report, what my dream was' (lines 209–12): while echoing the mystical illuminations of St Paul and Erasmus's Dame Folly, the dream is also the world turned upside-down, a radical unhinging of empirical and metaphysical givens. It is as if 'natural' language had taken an afternoon nap and woken to find that the bottom has fallen out of its world and the world out of its bottom. Holofernes, who thinks of the afternoon as 'the posterior of the day' (V. i. 81) would find this a 'congruent epitheton', evoking both the proverbial *logorrhoea* of the trainee-Bard and the gargantuan physical release of carnival. But the text's dream of itself also succeeds in arriving back at the most bland and mundane of realisms, a world of intact subjects and property ('Methought I was, and methought I had') in which each sense and faculty is capable only of the functions proper to it. This glimpse of solid ground is, however, suspended – in a double sense – in the multiple negations of a writing. Here, as in the comedies generally, the bottom line is always a spacing, a perforation.

II FUNDAMENTAL ISSUES

Deconstruction arrives at the scene at an inopportune moment. In 1938 H. B. Charlton, looking back over a critical tradition which assumed that the comic was generically 'unserious', complained of an 'enormous lee-way' in theoretical rigour between the criticism of Shakespeare's comedies and the work on his tragedies. But by 1976 Michael Long could claim, with some plausibility, that the criticism of the Comedies had begun 'to understand a basic feature of Shakespeare's thinking and to get close to some fundamental elements in his vision', while interpretations of the tragedies remained at a more primitive stage of development.[8] This reversal of fortunes, attributable less to the interventions of the Shakespearean heavy-weights – Charlton, Tillyard, Dover Wilson – than to the work of C. L. Barber (1959) and Northrop Frye (1965), gave rise to a growing conviction of something soon to be grasped and an uncharacteristic generosity and certainty among the commentators themselves: 'the best that has ever been written on the subject' (Lerner 1967, p. 12, on Barber), 'the only critic who surpasses Barber' (Salgado 1973, p. 78, on Frye). With the final whistle only seconds away there should be little to add.

The arrival is unfortunate for a critical tradition already beginning to display a comic hubris of its own. Deconstruction has a way with 'basic features of thinking' and the 'fundamental elements' of a 'vision'. But the moment is also inopportune for deconstruction itself. C. L. Barber's work on the relationship between the Comedies and popular festivity, echoed in Frye's emphasis on licence and the Saturnalia, has identified an 'inversion', 'play' and a 'release' already at work in the text. Filtered through Bakhtin's account of the medieval carnival and its legacy, which can compensate in this case for the endemic lack of a coherent theory of ideology in Anglo-American Shakespeare criticism, this material points to the text's particular production of a historical 'deconstruction', which may be read out, at least in part, by more conventional forms of analysis. And Robert Weimann's *Shakespeare and the Popular Tradition in the Theater* (1978), which really is, by a long stretch, the best book not only on the Comedies but on a more general erosion of mimetic earnestness in Shakespeare which puts the usefulness of a separate 'comedy' category in some doubt, fills the historical gap between the Bakhtinian carnival and the Elizabethan and Jacobean stage.

In Shakespeare's plays, as Weimann shows, language and action are already turned against themselves, divided between the relatively 'naturalistic' mode of the *locus* (upstage), which circulates humanist learning and other productions of the dominant ideology within the bounds of a sealed illusion, and the popular tradition of ritual nonsense, burlesque and topsy-turvydom which occupies the *platea* (downstage) and makes the time of the mimetic action contemporary with its performance by extending a traditional utopian levelling across the line that divides stage from audience.

This dual movement and play of what Weimann calls 'enchantment' and 'disenchantment' (1978, pp. 216, 247) readily translates into '*mimesis*' and 'deconstruction', pre-empting within the text as a historical production the space of the eager post-Derridean poised at its margins. Faced with an already heterogeneous text, the options for a contemporary deconstruction are either to co-operate with its precursor, deconstruct the prior 'deconstruction', or to be itself deconstructed. The last eventuality is by no means out of the question. 'The movements of deconstruction', writes Derrida, are accomplished not by a destruction of structures which is effected from outside, but by 'inhabiting them in a *certain way*', operating 'from the inside' and 'borrowing all the strategic and economic resources of subversion from the old structure' (Derrida 1976, p. 24). Holding to its article of faith that there is no 'outside', deconstruction relocates itself 'inside' by postulating an inner 'old structure' which may be recognized, exploited and undermined. But the main difficulty in Shakespeare's comedy, where there is a supplement at the source, is precisely the determination of *which* structure, or unstructuring, is the more or less '*old*'. Through this *aporia*, which admits age, chronology, history, leaks the dimension of the text occulted by deconstruction itself particularly in its North American phase as a souped-up, mildly hallucinogenic formalism, a New Criticism now in three dimensions but still playing down the crucial historical axis, the only site for distinguishing recurrences of a formally homologous process (call it 'deconstruction') in the medieval carnival, the English theatre of the late sixteenth and early seventeenth centuries, and the arcane 'humanizing' rituals of contemporary education systems.

After a prolonged period of theoretical preening, deconstruction, fully domesticated Eng. Lit. style, claims its moment as another 'approach' to the close reading of the 'great works' on a syllabus which must not exclude Shakespeare. In the Comedies, the 'old structure' to be infiltrated from within is determined either on the toss of a coin or by liberally allowing the deconstructionist soothsayer his/her narcissistic and impossible gesture of drawing lines with a wand on the sky. But by a remarkable coincidence, unless we subscribe to an historical and dialectical view of criticism as ideological production and reproduction, the Comedies, as they have been understood in recent decades, make this task easier by proffering just such a structure, charged with the major figures of Derrida's 'phonocentrism', 'logocentrism' and 'metaphysics'. Love's Labour's Lost, for example, were it not so impenetrable, would already be a classic of western phonocentrism, ranked alongside Plato's Phaedrus and Rousseau's Essay on the Origin of Languages (see Derrida 1976, pp. 37, 165 ff). Navarre and his friends fight 'the huge army of the world's desires' (I. i. 10) to gain immortality from a book-learning which reveals the 'light of truth' inaccessible to the senses. Berowne warns his fellows about 'continual plodders' who know nothing but 'base authority' (lines 86–7) and 'fame' (line 92), a superficial knowledge comparable to the 'semblance of wisdom' that Socrates has Thamus ascribe to the breed of pedants born of literacy (Phaedrus, 275–5b). In Love's Labour's Lost, as in the Phaedrus, writing is set against the presence and fecundity of speech. The women of France are talkers, reciprocators who fill the time with formal 'sets of wit' (V. ii. 29) while waiting for the Academe's edict for writing and against speech[9] finally to collapse. As the men move from learning to love, the tyranny of writing remains in place, in their view of women's eyes as 'the books, the arts, the academes' (IV. iii. 348) and in the letters, masks, rhetorical contrivance and 'penn'd speech' that insulate an essentially self-regarding love, which celebrates the transcendent Petrarchan lady as a bestower of superhuman powers while cowering in the shadow of the physical, mortal woman perceived as 'pitch that defiles' (IV. iii. 3). With Marcade's entrance, death finally begins to break the spell of the speciously immortal, in reality *deadly*, letter and to restore it to its proper place as a supplement. The 'present breath' of life (I. i. 5) becomes one with the *living* language's 'converse of breath' (V. ii. 727), as the play that began with a juvenile initiation into writing ends with a more taxing initiation into speech and adult responsibility which, in the penances imposed on the scholar-lovers, imply 'nature', reciprocation, community and self-knowledge.[10]

This construction of the relationship between speech and writing, central to one possible reading of the 'old structure' of the play, is, for Derridean deconstruction, the inaugural gesture of metaphysics, which privileges the signified ('self', 'nature', 'represented') at the expense of the signifier. In this hierarchy identity is recovered from *différance* and a transcendent *logos* is conjured up from the inscription and spacing which, from the perspective of grammatology, 'exceeds and comprehends' the work of language itself (Derrida 1976, pp. 8–9). The priority of speech over writing ultimately signifies the priority of that 'presence' to which speech is closer and more responsive – a source *beyond* the supplement, a place of unmediated self-presence and self-identity, in which 'meaning' is not yet subject to the unending chain of metaphoricity. In a reading of the Comedies informed by these metaphysical assumptions the letter is no longer the inescapable supplement *at* the source but the mark of the secondary, the external, the repressive. As such it becomes the lynchpin of what Frye calls the 'anti-comic society', often centred on 'a harsh and irrational law', which tends to predominate during the first phase of a typical Shakespearean comedy (Frye 1965, pp. 73–4).

This obstruction, which is often presented as being both incomprehensible and impersonal, must be overcome for the fulfilment of what Frye calls the 'comic drive'. The essential, unproblematic nature of this drive is to seek out 'atonement' and an 'identity' which integrates the individual with her/himself, reality with desire, youth with age, and the 'spirit' of community with its outer social forms. Moreover, all of this is to be accomplished in the larger synthesis of Art, which represents 'the recovery by man of the energy of nature' (Frye 1965, pp. 78–87, 115–18, 159). If the central thrust of comedy is towards unity, identity and synthesis, then the 'letter' is a force to be overcome or expelled, whether it manifests itself as a harsh law or as some other form of the supplement seen merely as a decline from the integration and presence of the metaphysical source. The Comedies provide numerous instances of this 'letter' which, in Frye's interpretation, becomes the scapegoat of the comic drive. It appears in the edict that enforces book-learning and later in the obtrusive contrivance of rhetorical 'penn'd speech' in *Love's Labour's Lost*; it is there also in the triple hold of the bond, the law and Shylock's Judaic legalism in *The Merchant of Venice*, and in the written 'will' of the dead father which must override the living, breathing 'will' of Portia (I. ii. 24–5). In *A Midsummer Night's Dream* the construction appears again in the form of an inscribed 'law' which diffuses itself through the social institution of the play; the 'sharp Athenian law' which, as Theseus maintains, 'by no means we may extenuate' (I. i. 120) secures Egeus's hold on Hermia who must in turn consider herself 'but as a form in wax, / By him imprinted, and within his power / To leave the figure, or disfigure it.' (I. i. 49–51). Moreover, Hermia's predicament is underlined by a further 'law', that of everything written in 'tale or history', which confirms that 'the course of true love never did run smooth' (I. i. 134–5).

There are many other instances of this obtrusive 'letter', which can be seen not as the Derridean 'supplement at the source' but as the supplement *tout court* posited by metaphysics – the secondary, denigrated term which underwrites the apparent unity, priority and self-sufficiency of its opposite. Malvolio as an embodiment of Puritan literalism and denial is caught out by a detour of the 'comic drive' through the 'great P's', 'C U T's' and 'M.O.A.I.' of writing (*Twelfth Night*, II. v. 80–109), mistaken by him as the presence and accessibility of a physical Olivia. Further examples of the survival of the letter in Frye's second comic phase of confusion, licence and 'temporarily lost identity' (1965, p. 76) occur when the young lovers from *The Two Gentlemen of Verona* to *As You Like It* are trapped in the impersonal literary stereotypes of pastoralism and Petrarchan love, a writing which reduces all to 'whole volumes in folio' (*Love's Labour's Lost*, I. ii. 174–5) and will 'tire the hearer with a book of words' (*Much Ado About Nothing*, I. i. 287). The tyranny of this dead letter marks the fall or division from which the youthful lovers will eventually return to the various 'integrations' and 'identities' centred on mature adult love. According to this construction of the Comedies, which achieves its fullest and clearest expression in Frye, the 'letter' fades at the point of marriage, the moment of social renewal which is accompanied by the dance as a symbol of cosmic harmony.

If this pattern of fall and atonement, a division associated with some aspect of the 'letter' followed by a reintegration and recovery of real identity, holds true for the Comedies in general, then deconstruction, to repeat Derrida's formulation of its project, has a suitable 'old structure' to inhabit and subvert from within. This structure, in effect, recapitulates some of the central strategies of metaphysics in giving priority to speech over writing, identity over difference, and in privileging the signified at the expense of the signifier. If this is indeed the dominant structure of the Comedies, its logocentrism threatens to eclipse the other, more contorted and self-reflexive mode, associated with such figures as Holofernes, Launce and Bottom, and to despatch it to the supplementary space of 'sub-plots', 'anti-masques' and 'low-comic' action. Here, with their subversive potential doomed to failure by convention and the aesthetics of unity, 'affecting the letter' and cognate practices can serve only to elaborate more central themes and devices. Meanwhile, in the order which comes to dominate in their place, confusion and release are merely strategic means to a higher harmony and recuperation whose structure is essentially that of the Christian *commedia*, the movement from Innocence through Fall to Redemption.

Frye, the prime theoretician of this order, compounds the Christian patterns with elements of the Greek *komos*, Roman religious festivity, Judaism and the Hindu *Sakuntala* (Frye 1965, pp. 64, 73), making the structure of the Comedies mirror that of a collective *psyche*. His concept of the student of literature is the apotheosis of Matthew Arnold's 'disinterested' reader who explores the 'religion of culture'. While deconstruction may occupy and undermine this version of the text's 'old structure', Frye's discourse cheers it on its way and inflates it to its full capacity, knowing nothing else, inscribing moral and aesthetic certainties as a meta-mythology which occupies a historical void. There is no trace here of the slave or plebeian solidarity of the Saturnalia and carnival, no historical sense of divided interests and a topsy-turvydom which may momentarily *relativize* the pompous constructions of metaphysics and the ruling ideologies, and place them within imaginary explorations of social equality. Even C. L. Barber (1959) turns the festive familiarity and disorder back towards an affirmation of metaphysical absolutes ('love', 'nature') and a critical formalism which can detach the Shakespearean text from its network of historical relations to deliver it as a commodity for consumption in the modern theatre and classroom.[11]

This pattern of release and reintegration, from its valorization of speech and writing through to its emphasis on atonement and the 'identity' which, for Frye, constitutes the goal of the comic drive, is precisely the sort of thing that mobilizes the full Derridean vocabulary. It is time to repeat the arguments of 'Affecting the Letter', with the added insistence that the mode of Holofernes and Launce cannot in the end be marginalized or rendered innocuous. This is not froth to be blown off the top of the text but froth that sits at the bottom, problematizing any comic 'spirit' or essential meaning that a theological mode of criticism in quest of the Shakespearean *logos* might wish to recover from the impenetrability of the 'letter'. The Comedies confront interpretation with surfaces that are concerned not so much with yielding textual depths as with reflecting other surfaces or deconstructing the surface-depth opposition. Thus *Love's Labour's Lost*, for example, in its persistent play with light and darkness, doodles with 'dark' ('ambiguous', 'secret') ciphers that yield 'light' meanings which are at once 'illuminating', 'insubstantial' and 'unchaste'. If the play does allude to a traditional phonocentric preference for the spoken over the written word, it nevertheless enacts a contradictory primacy of writing – or the priority of the opaque 'letter' (signifier) over the 'spirit' (signified) – in its foregrounding of the 'great feast of languages' (V. i. 35), both verbal and theatrical, that constitutes the text. Here the densely patterned movement of words and of bodies on the stage affirms the materiality of language itself and the residues of signification that exegesis can never finally dissolve in its quest for a source or a pure signified. In his *exemplum* of the heathen philosopher who, when hungry, would put grapes in his mouth 'meaning thereby that grapes are made to eat and lips to open' (*As You Like It*, V. i. 31–2), Touchstone suggests that the operation of recovering the spirit from the letter usually produces only another letter, or at best a linguistic impasse in which two signifiers are pinned together and claimed to be identical in the hope that this will yield a transcendent truth beyond language. Hymen's precondition in the same play for the marriages that will signal 'atonement' – 'If truth holds true contents' (V. iv. 124) – makes similar gestures towards the truth contained at the heart of truth, identical with itself, only to break down in a delirium of wordplays on 'truth', 'holds', 'true' and 'contents' which leaves no centre but tautology, endless supplementation, and a textual process whose closure can only be as you like it.[12] The truth about such texts is inevitably conditional, inscribed in contradiction and absence, the work of the poet who affirms 'nothing'. 'The truest poetry', as Touchstone tells Audrey, 'is the most feigning' (III. iii. 16–17), a definition which puns on *feigning* and *faining* ('affectionate', 'wistful') to deny the metaphysics of identity and self-presence even the comfort of a simple paradox.

Hymen's tautologous demand that the truth should be true speaks from a masque-within-the-play to the audience of *As You Like It* on the subject of a divided 'truth' which is at once present and impossible in this most outrageous and threadbare of romantic fictions. This climactic utterance of the Comedies comes, appropriately, from a *deus ex machina* with no serious function to perform but who mirrors the work of one of Derrida's favourite rhetorical devices – also named the 'hymen'. In Derrida, as in Shakespeare, this figure marks the point beyond which interpretation has no jurisdiction: 'the limit to the relevance of the hermeneutic or systematic question' (Derrida 1979b, p. 99), 'the violence of a truth stronger than truth' (Derrida 1979a, p. 155). This final coincidence completes the conspiratorial work of deconstruction in the Comedies.

But here deconstruction, 'which always in certain way falls prey to its own work' (Derrida 1976, p. 24), begins again. Its next move can only be to move the inner 'old structure' to be inhabited and subverted from within to another place – from the authorized version of the Comedies which reaches its highest fulfilment in the work of Barber and Frye to the newly authorized deconstructed version now, in turn, waiting to be undermined. On the grounds that the popular precedes the learned just as ritual comes before mimesis, it can be argued that the mode of Holofernes, Launce and Bottom rather than that of Frye and his critical predecessors is the true 'old structure' of the plays. What then? Possibly to show, in the manner of Derrida on Saussure and Lévi-Strauss (1976, pp. 27 ff. and 101 ff.) that the apparent displacing of idealism and the transcendental signified in the Comedies is not all it appears to be: that somewhere a gap opens, a contradiction of a contradiction which allows the text, like its Jaques, to arrive through a double-negative of scepticism back at a positive commonplace. Perhaps, the plays are finally guilty of the platitudes and pieties that fall out of their bottomlessness to be represented in humanist criticism as fundamental issues. Let us, after all, attribute to Shakespeare an affirmation of 'Love's Wealth', 'Love's Truth', 'Love's Order' and the rest of it,[13] a weakness for claptrap about 'exquisite heroines', and a mimesis of delightful confusion before the advent of 'atonement', 'self-knowledge', 'balance' and 'legitimacy' that just happens to universalize the individualism, political quietism and sensibility of the 'disinterested' critic. Perhaps the comedies themselves, viewed as self-conscious discourses on a textual 'materialism', lack a certain theoretical rigour. If so, applying deconstruction's off-side law, blow the whistle and shout 'Metaphysics!'

III COOKING THE BOOKS

'It is the critic's task, and there is hardly a more comical one, to coagulate an island of meaning upon a sea of negativity' (Kristeva 1980, p. 109). Julia Kristeva's assessment gives theoretical confirmation to the truism that the funniest thing about Shakespeare's comedies is the criticism. This critical tradition's unpropitious beginnings during the academic apprenticeship of English Literature are hardly surprising given the 'triviality' of the Comedies and the ponderously paternalistic and moralizing discourse employed to situate Shakespeare in a national education system. The Newbolt Report (1921) put Shakespeare at the heart of a heritage which was at once a universal 'means of grace' and the focus on a specifically English unity and pride (Newbolt 1921, pp. 202, 252). The set 'Discourse' for Shakespeare Day, an annual rite compulsory for pupils at elementary schools in all parts of the country, spoke of his solid commitment to England and his conviction that 'English ideals make for righteousness, for freedom, for the recognition of human rights and liberties', the core of Shakespeare's broader appeal in an Anglo-centric universe – 'his sovereignty . . . well-nigh universal', his genius 'the power to pleasure and entrapture, and to instil in men's hearts his manifold observations on the myriad problems of life and eternity' (Gollancz 1916, pp. 10, 12, 21). After this build-up the Comedies were a potential source of embarrassment. *A Midsummer Night's Dream*, for example, would not be the first text that leapt to mind for a defence of literary study against the charge of being one of the 'unintelligible and futile trivialities of "middle-class" culture', recorded in the *Newbolt Report* as a response from organized labour (Newbolt 1921, pp. 202, 252). It was not until later that moral fibre could be proved to have anything to do with fairies.

Within this ideological and institutional framework the 'serious' study of Shakespeare's comedies was, understandably, slow to develop. And when it did its emphasis was on the affirmation of metaphysical values (love, self-knowledge, 'nature', atonement) or on the purely formal or generic concerns of a more technocratic mode of criticism which was sustained by the 'humanizing' ideologies of institutional literary study but not called upon to reaffirm their values beyond fine-tuning the already 'unified' textual commodity. These two modes of criticism, which still flourish, were both challenged and reinforced by Northrop Frye's *A Natural Perspective* (1965). Such strenuous theorizing, coupled with a heretical willingness to generalize the structure of a 'typical' comedy, drew empiricism's reflex response of reaching for the 'reductionist' label, the scapegoat/supplement of its own 'white dogma' – the dogma of *no theory* which is based on the three unities of modern humanist criticism: the 'organic' text, the sign, and the discreet bourgeois subject as representative 'man'. But Frye's reductivism was ultimately acceptable, as it constituted in its way a *langue* of the previous criticism, a structure based on the identity of identity, which could generate any number of formalist and interpretative inanities, based on the innate drive in individuals, objects and societies to be as they really are. Frye's text is situated at the limit of a criticism which systematically misrecognizes its own ideological work as a recovery of the essential nature of its literary object – at the point where this discourse soars into the cosmos and swoops into the collective unconscious. Had deconstruction not at this moment existed, someone would have had to invent it.

'– They order, said I, this matter better in France –' So begins *A Sentimental Journey*, and in the space of a hundred words Sterne has packed, caught the Dover stage to the steam-packet and, already anticipating death by indigestion, is dining 'upon a chicken fricassee . . . incontestably in France'. While the *Larousse Gastronomique* calls for a painstaking preparation and seasoning of numerous ingredients, the *Penguin English Dictionary* sketches Anglo-Saxon priorities and the limits of *entente cordiale* by defining 'fricassee' as 'a white stew'. Sterne's own fate at the hands of criticism repeats this central culinary dichotomy. While Victor Shklovsky's description of *Tristram Shandy* as 'the most typical novel of world literature' pointed European priorities in the direction of 1970s French deconstruction, the domestic tradition has felt less at home with Sterne's typographical experiment, the black/blank page and the impossibility of narrative than with Defoe's double entry book-keeping. The 'sensible' English response to Sterne's concoction, from Dr Johnson to the notorious footnote in *The Great Tradition*,[14] has been to boil it in a cloth bag and feed it to the animals. The cries of 'foreign muck' which resounded during the Cambridge 'structuralist' controversies of 1980/1 brought the same fear of indigestion and exotic intestinal disorders to bear directly on literary theory, a fear which will inevitably be magnified as deconstruction approaches Shakespeare, so monumental a signifier of 'Englishness', with its traditional tolerance of everything but foreigners, theory and fuss. But there always was something odd about Shakespeare's comedies, particularly the early ones, which has made their canonization conditional, part of an apprenticeship always to be redeemed by something else. Their linguistic doodles, unhealthy self-proddings, and obsession with finding as many ways as possible of referring to the genitals and cuckoldry have always suggested that there might be more room in the bag beside Sterne, and promoted in audiences at the subsidized theatre a type of mis-timed rhetorical braying otherwise heard only in parliamentary broadcasts, a cheer-leading prompt set off less by the performance than by a familiarity with the *Arden* notes. This 'oddness' is one of the best ports of entry for deconstruction, not only into the Comedies but into Shakespeare's work as a whole, a place to begin affecting the letter and to speed the disintegration of a hegemonic, monumentalizing critical tradition.

'Shakespeare one gets acquainted with without knowing how', says Henry Crawford in Mansfield Park. 'It is part of an Englishman's constitution.' In the Arnold/Newbolt tradition, reading, complicit with the national myth of the Bard, is scarcely more arduous than this. For those who seek grace, Shakespeare is 'open to all the world', while 'the literature of England belongs to all England, not to the Universities or to any coterie of the literary or the learned: and all may enjoy it who will' (Newbolt 1921, p. 204). To read is a matter only of opening oneself to refinement, responding uniquely and imaginatively, hearing[15] and thereby absorbing 'the best that is known and thought in the world' through the empirical and ideal presence of the text, 'the object as in itself it really is' (Arnold 1962, pp. 258, 282). Deconstruction at least manifests the problem of reading and dismantles its mythical 'object': 'The so-called "thing in itself"', writes Derrida, 'is always already a representamen shielded from the simplicity of intuitive evidence. . . . The self-identity of the signified conceals itself unceasingly and is always. on the move' (1976, p. 49). And the fetishized 'unity', which retains its hold not only on Frye and Barber but, to some extent, even on Weimann's work,[16] is undone in Derrida's practice of reading, summed up by Culler as a 'double mode' which shows the text to be 'woven from different strands which can never result in a synthesis but continually displace one another' (1979, p. 155). But as a means of attacking traditional assumptions about culture, reading and the text, deconstruction, already moved from the institutional site of philosophy to that of the 'literary', is being put to specific ideological uses, targeted in ways that ultimately imply a politics of criticism. In relation to Shakespeare's work and its place in culture and ideology, Derrida's now proverbial proclamation 'There is nothing outside the text' (il n'y a pas de hors-texte) (1976, p. 158) needs perhaps to be amplified by Macherey's description of the text as always irrevocably encrusted by the criticism, which is assimilated to it as part of the material history that must determine, at any moment, perceptions of the object 'as in itself it really is'.[17] Thus deconstruction, while placing itself 'inside' will always work on an *occupied* text, a *used* text, deconstructing prior constructions of its meaning or form rather than an immanent and absolutely determinable 'old structure'. In this sense deconstruction as in itself it really is can only remain a supplement, its politics, imposed from outside, capable of a variety of shadings and cryptic colorations.

So far, in the criticism of Shakespeare's comedies, there is very little evidence to cite. In an essay in *Textual Strategies* (1980), René Girard points to a 'delirium and frenzy' in *A Midsummer Night's Dream* to show that *'all their minds transfigured so together'* and *'something of great constancy'* (V. i. 24–6) imply the final arrival at 'a common structure of mythical meaning' – in other words that Hippolyta is right during the exchange at the beginning of Act V and 'Theseus must be as deaf and blind to his bride's arguments as Shakespeare's audiences and critics seem to have been ever since' (Girard 1980, pp. 192, 211–12). This is not only a brand new reading of an old text, but a brand new old reading. In 1965 J. L. Calderwood showed how commentaries on the play tend to divide evenly into 'Theseus' and 'Hippolyta' camps (Calderwood 1965, p. 506). Behind this perhaps pedantic quibble lies a deeper disappointment at the way in which Derrida's intervention, with its initial *ideological* force, can peter out into another 'approach' to literature in which the objects and institutional frameworks of study are not only left intact but refurbished while the historical specificity of the text's *polysemia* is overlooked.

The same can be said of A. B. Dawson's reading of *Much Ado About Nothing* as 'itself a play of signification', a text in which 'the *"jeu de signification"* (Derrida's term) exceeds what is signified' (Dawson 1982, p. 221). This formulation is a blueprint for any number of readings not only of the Comedies and Shakespeare's other plays, but of every work in the 'canon' of English Literature, which will suffer very little damage from being read in this way. The recipe for Shakespeare would be to take the instances of what Weimann (1978) calls 'disenchantment', based on festivity and the popular tradition in drama, use them to undercut or problematize *mimesis*, and season with some Derridean terminology (optional). The outcome, at best, could only be an updating of a New Criticism still innocent of the social connotations of its 'complexity' and 'taste' (Hawkes 1977, pp. 152–5), a *technique* of reading which can treat its institutional site, along with the simplicity of its basic 'humanizing' claims, as something already consolidated and bearing the quiet assurance of a fact of nature. This type of reading is always uncomfortably close to confirming again the 'genius' of the Bard, a 'universal wisdom' with the emphasis moved from a transcendental signified to the ceaseless productivity of a transcendental signifier. When D. J. McDonald argues that the alternation of 'presence' and 'absence' in Hamlet 'enables us to describe the fluid and intangible qualities of the play' and locate 'the source of its vitality' (1978, pp. 52–3), the work of recuperation is almost complete. We are back not only with Arnold but with Carlyle, who predicted that in Shakespeare 'the latest generations of men will find new meanings . . . new elucidations of their own human being' (Carlyle 1841, p. 174).

In the wake of theoretical invasions always from outside England (Paris, Cardiff, Yale), the 'excesses' of this mode of reading may still be too much for surviving members of Newbolt Man, now an endangered species whose full-throated cry is heard mainly in the nooks and backwaters.[18] But in some ways deconstruction arrives like Touchstone, rotten before it is ripe, its celebration of a textual 'materiality' long since challenged by more thorough-going materialisms.[19] Given the open-door policy of the Comedies (as you like it, what you will), we can confidently anticipate, all else being equal, a decade of Shakespearean Derrideana and Derridoidia, transnational fricassee-burgers à la mode. In one way these may be a harmless celebration of play, but in the context of what they displace or institutionally impede they also constitute a political reaction. At Yale, as Michael Ryan points out, 'textuality' has greatly revived the 'literary' and its fetishes 'in the face both of the politicization of the canon by women's and black studies and the inevitable coming to the fore of media and popular culture studies' (Ryan 1982, p. 103). At risk here is not just a political criticism, which is only what all criticism has been, by design or default, all along, but the 'pluralism' and 'balance' on which the liberal academy has always prided itself, a doctrine now being called to account institutionally for the first time. Deconstruction permits a delirium of dissent which is also a babble of compliance, an equalizing of all voices in the irreducibility of écriture. If the liberal subject 'man' knew no divisions of gender, race or class and the politics of criticism these divisions imply, the textual panoply of crazed signifiers, supplements at the source, and subjects-in-process does little better. And if the 'literary' text is the space of a near-total iconoclasm, 'critical awareness' may be developed there without reference to the other languages and other texts which, since Newbolt, have become the most pervasive means of control in the west. There might be some point in deconstructing and thus laying bare the mimetic contrivance of television news and documentary, for example, or the 'textuality' of advertising, but as long as Shakespeare can keep up with progressive thinking such texts can be held safely outside the balanced, nominally a-political parameters of academic 'English'.

Shakespeare's comedies, because of the associations that make them so amenable to its methods, can assist in locating deconstruction historically. In this process the medieval carnival is a useful third point of reference. Comparing carnival with deconstruction, Terry Eagleton has argued that the former implies much more than a dislocation of familiar structures:

> in rendering existing power structures alien and arbitrary, it releases the potential for a golden age, a friendly world of 'carnival truth' in which 'man returns to himself'. . . . [Carnival's] estrangement effects are reconstitutive as well as deconstructive, dialectical images in which the parodic dissolution presumes and produces its 'normal' representation, reassembling it in the figures of what it denies. The laughter of carnival is both plebeian derision and plebeian solidarity, an empty semiotic flow which in decomposing significance nonetheless courses with the impulse of comradeship.
>
> (Eagleton 1981, pp. 145–6)

In itself, the process of 'decomposing significance' can only be radical or subversive in an extremely limited, a-political sense. Hence the plebeian carnival can become the measure of other loosely 'deconstructive' discourses or practices, and a pretext for the question 'deconstruction for and *accompanied by* what?' In this historical light the deconstructive mode of literary criticism, particularly in its North American forms, appears to be a conservative rather than a progressive force. But carnival can also serve as a foil for an historical description of some of the 'deconstructive' effects of the Shakespearean text. The reproduction of certain festive materials and discourses in Shake-speare's comedies pictures, across the differences of mimesis and topsy-turvydom, humanism and the popular tradition, not so much a separation and solidarity of social classes as the collaboration of stage and audience in a self-reflexive exchange in the theatre which suspends divisions of class in the relentless pursuit of its own 'secondariness' or supplementarity. In their foregrounding of the signifier, the theatrical, madness, holiday and dream, the Comedies suggest a spiralling of the supplement into itself, a process which proposes an order more 'real' than the unknowing 'stage' of the world. But the divided, indefinitely deferred 'truth' of this order is, in the last instance, only that of a semiotic asylum – an institutional place of containment outside the ideological norm, and one in which the gesture of crossing a dividing line (stage/audience, theatre/world) produces the line itself as undeniably there (cf. Foucault 1967, pp. 18–19).

The echoes of a festive or carnivalesque 'deconstruction' in the Comedies may, then, be regarded as part of the historical decline and eclipse of the carnival tradition, as described by Bakhtin (1968, pp. 33–4). The aspects of these plays that seem to invite a Derridean appropriation are also located in the late sixteenth- and early seventeenth-century crisis in representation, or rather from the dis-continuities in language and concepts of language, out of which an unproblematic modern notion of 'representation' finally emerges. Foucault writes of this as 'the privileged age of trompe l'oeil painting, of the comic illusion, of the play that duplicates itself by presenting another play, of the quid pro quo, of dreams and visions'. Between the sixteenth century's construction of language as an opaque 'thing in nature', a cipher folded back into the grammar of existence, and the 'mathematical plainness' which appears in the seventeenth, with its subjection of words to empirical 'things', and its representation of 'representation' as something which has value 'only as discourse' (Foucault 1970, pp. 17 ff., 29–35, 42–3; my italics), opens the space of a historical 'textuality'. This is the moment of Don Quixote, in which 'words wander off on their own, without content, without resemblance, to fill their emptiness', and the chivalric protagonist is a literal character, 'a long, thin graphism, a letter that has just escaped from the open pages of a book'. It is also the moment of the other first 'great works' of modern literature, texts in which language, according to Foucault, 'breaks off its old kinship with things and enters into that lonely sovereignty from which it will reappear, in its separated state, *only as literature*' (Foucault 1970, p. 49; my italics).

Malvolio's promise of retribution at the end of *Twelfth Night* (V. i. 377) is partly fulfilled when this 'textuality' resurfaces within an institutional production of the 'literary'. What made the relatively indeterminate text, for the emergent Puritan middle class, something akin to what Foucault calls '*only literature*' ('pastime', 'idleness', 'play') became a material condition of the bourgeoisie's deployment in education, at the height of its power, of 'literature' with a vengeance. For Foucault the 'Classical age' of European discourse, which follows the semiotic crises of the late sixteenth and early seventeenth centuries, ends by precipitating again, in the nineteenth century, a 'knowledge closed in upon itself', a 'pure language' considered 'in nature and function, enigmatic – something that has been called, since that time, *Literature*' (Foucault 1970, p. 89). The naming of this discourse, its ideological reproduction, and the formal categorizing of its periods, genres and 'great traditions' fell to the liberal and humane disciplines of the popular education systems instituted throughout Europe from this time on. In academic curricula literary studies, at first considered in England to be most suitable for women and inferior male students, or for worker-education (Eagleton 1983, pp. 27–8), gradually replaced the Classical languages as the primary 'humanizing' force. Through the rites of exegesis, literary criticism administered appropriate versions of the dominant ideology to each mass ejected from the education system between its 'elementary' level and its intellectual summit in higher education, focusing on what the *Newbolt Report* calls the 'nobler, more eternal and universal element' of the text at the expense of its status as a historical production (Newbolt 1921, p. 205). But beyond the process of explanation and reduction lies an affirmation of the transcendent inexhaustibility of 'Art', exemplified nowhere more fully than in Shakespeare. The urbane, pluralist 'debate' of humanist criticism, as Macherey and Balibar point out, produces 'literature' itself *within* education as 'something outside (and above) the process of education, which is merely able to disseminate literature, and to comment on it exhaustively, though with no possibility of finally capturing it'

(Macherey and Balibar 1978, p. 7). And beyond the competing interpretations, circumscribed by the unities of text, sign and subject, stands the less tangible ideological work of reproducing, within the imaginary unity of a national language and culture, distinctions between the classes more fully in command of their riches and those who remain tongue-tied to a 'basic' fraction, doomed at the lower echelons of the system to have the plenitude administered as the tantalizing inaccessibility of a law of culture, power and creativity (ibid., pp. 6–7).

So deconstruction arrives at a text which is also institutionally 'deconstructed', elected to the 'literary' by virtue of its stylistic tremors, its work, as defined by Macherey and Balibar, of 'displacing the ensemble of ideological contradictions on to a single one, or a single aspect, the linguistic conflict itself' (ibid., p. 9). To parody the object of traditional criticism as the universal felicities and eternal verities, what the Shakespeare Day programme for 1916 called 'the power to please and enrapture' and 'the myriad problems of life and eternity', is to account for only a fragment of the discourse whose signified is inexhaustible, always, even at the moment of being pinned down, already somewhere else saying 'Yes, but . . .' As a mode of literary close-reading, formalism's jeux sans frontières, deconstruction may catch the earlier critical discourse in the act of metaphysical and ideological closure and move the occasional text to a more 'central' position in the canon. Such texts might well include Tristram Shandy for example, Sterne's attempt, a century and a half later, to rewrite Don Quixote in England, or the early Comedies as a privileged instance of a 'writing', theatrical supplement and metaphoricity which suspend mimesis in the Shakespearean text at large. But confronted with 'literature', deconstruction, like the critical discourses it succeeds, can only endlessly rediscover its own first principles, now in the form of a meta-tautology or solipsism twice removed. Its 'practical' uses in processing the great works, undertaken in defiance of deconstruction's theoretical challenge to the very basis of conventional literary study, tends towards self-parody, 'affecting the letter', nominally subverting ideologies while continually reproducing those that underwrite the discipline, in a persistent confusion of 'writing' itself with the 'arche-writing' which Derrida calls 'écriture' on the misleading (and undeconstructed) grounds that 'it *essentially communicates* with the vulgar concept of writing' (Derrida 1976, p. 56).

Such a processing of Shakespeare's comedies, which could undoubtedly permit its own urbane pluralism and prolonged 'debate', would slow down the broader politicization of English Studies – and be accomplished through an institutional recognition of other (non-'literary') texts, other literatures, and a legitimate conflict among theories of literature and ideology. It could also muffle the impact of other post-1968 developments in critical theory on the study of Shakespeare's text. The work of Lacan, Althusser, Macherey, Foucault, Kristeva and Cixous opens up other possibilities, other modes of *historical* reading. Behind 'textuality' and 'play' there are questions of conflict and discontinuity in the discourse on the subject, gender, the family, legitimacy, speech, writing and 'representation' itself.[20] There is also the history of transformations in a specific 'deconstructive' trope which affects not only medieval festivity and Shakespeare's comedies but also the political practice and the writing, never subsequently dignified with the name 'literature', of the late sixteenth- and seventeenth-century radical Puritan groups who aimed to 'turn the world upside-down' on a more permanent basis, culminating in the theatricality of a royal beheading and the delirious Ranter 'carnival' of the late 1640s.[21] Last there is the matter of how expandable texts prepared for oral performance in the popular theatre came to be produced as the centre-piece of a national and universal 'literature' – an ideological history which brings us, eventually, to the question of deconstructing Shakespeare's comedies. The scene is occupied, perhaps, not by 'deconstruction' but deconstructions, with one version currently threatening to upstage the others. Assuming that nine out of ten pieces of Shakespeare criticism will as ever remain unreadable and unread, some sign or declaration of intent would, in future, seem appropriate. This could be located somewhere near deconstruction's impossible source: at the point where literature claims to foster the distinctively 'human', or at the elided supplementary question of power expressed somewhere in Shakespeare's text, possibly by Launce, as 'a dog's obeyed in office'.

5

SEXUALITY IN THE READING OF SHAKESPEARE

Hamlet and *Measure for Measure*

Jacqueline Rose

I

What fantasy of the woman has figured in readings – psychoanalytic and other – of *Hamlet* and *Measure for Measure*, plays which have repeatedly been defined as a 'problem', as requiring an interpretation which goes beyond their explicit, or manifest, content? How far has the woman been at the centre, not only of the internal drama, but also of the critical drama – the controversy about meaning and language – which each of these plays has provoked? In this essay, rather than apply psychoanalysis to literature, as if psychoanalysis were a method to be mapped onto the literary text, I will try to show how psychoanalytic and literary criticism share with the literature they address a terrain of language, fantasy and sexuality – a terrain in which the woman occupies a crucial, but difficult, place. In both of these plays, the central woman character finds herself accused – Gertrude in *Hamlet* of too much sexuality, Isabella in *Measure for Measure* of not enough. In both cases, the same notion of excess or deficiency has appeared in the critical commentaries on the plays. *Hamlet* and *Measure for Measure* have each been described as aesthetic failures which ask too much of – or offer too little to – the act of interpretation itself. By focusing on the overlap of these two accusations, of the woman and of the play, we might be able to see how the question of aesthetic form and the question of sexuality are implicated in each other.

T. S. Eliot linked the two plays when he described their material as 'intractable', resistant to interpretation and infringing the proper boundaries of dramatic form. In his famous essay (1919) on *Hamlet* (Eliot 1975), which was later picked up by Ernest Jones in his psychoanalytic reading of the play (Jones 1949), Eliot first put forward his central concept of the 'objective correlative' in the form of a critique: of *Hamlet* for its aesthetic failure and of Gertrude for being its cause. For Eliot, the aesthetic matching of emotion to object, which is the precondition of proper aesthetic form, fails in *Hamlet* because Gertrude is not sufficient as a character to carry the weight of the affect which she generates in the chief character of the play. Without this correlation, emotion in literature, or drama, becomes too insistent. Unless it can be seen as the inevitable response to the character presented on stage, it draws attention to itself, uneasily suggestive of something in the artist which he has failed to get under control. The deficiency of the character is therefore not only the cause, but also the result of an emotional excess. In *Hamlet*, the failing is Gertrude's, who thus deprives not only her son, but also the play, of the proper emotional support.

In his essay, Eliot lays down the terms for a way of assessing literature and its values whose influence has by no means been restricted to Shakespeare, but it is important that he first does so with reference to Shakespeare, and that the formulation centres so crucially on a woman. The importance of the woman in Eliot's theory appears as more than arbitrary when we notice that he uses another image of a woman to embody what he sees as the consequent failure of the play. *Hamlet*, Eliot writes, is 'the *Mona Lisa* of literature' (Eliot 1975, p. 47), offering up in its enigmatic and undecipherable nature something of that maimed or imperfect quality of appeal which characterizes Leonardo's famous painting. Like the *Mona Lisa*, *Hamlet* is a flawed masterpiece whose very failing acts as a pull on spectator and critic alike. Its very imperfection brings with it the power to seduce. Thus the idea of emotional excess shifts across the different levels of analysis – from drama to author to spectator. The appearance of the *Mona Lisa* in Eliot's essay suggests that the problem with *Hamlet* is that the 'inexpressibly horrible' content which he identifies beneath the surface of the text fascinates as much as it repels. The danger which *Hamlet* poses to Eliot's definition of proper aesthetic form resides – as much as in the play's origins – in its effect.[1]

To this extent, Eliot's analysis – like other readings which will take their authority from his conception of literature – repeats the drama which is acted out inside the plays he describes. In both *Hamlet* and *Measure for Measure*, sexuality entails danger and violates propriety, or form. Gertrude's impropriety (her 'o'erhasty' marriage) and Isabella's excessive propriety (her refusal to comply with Angelo's sexual demand) produce an image of sexuality as something unmanageable which cannot be held in its place. In both plays, it is the woman who provokes a crisis which overturns the sexual identity of the central male character of the drama. Hamlet, in response to his mother's 'fla-grancy', projects that same flagrancy onto the image of the innocent Ophelia whom he then spurns along with life itself. Angelo places sexual licence under penalty of death and then, provoked into desire by the total virtue of Isabella, he shifts from his role of legislator into that of 'vice'. In both plays, sexuality appears as infringement, and in each case it is the woman who is the cause. For Hamlet, Gertrude's blatant sexuality makes her less than human, less even than a beast lacking 'discourse of reason' (I. ii. 150) (Isabella also hurls the epithet 'beast' at her brother Claudio when he asks her to submit to Angelo's sexual demand (III. i. 135)). But it is Angelo who states most clearly the *more* and *less* that the woman becomes when she fails to contain for the man the sexuality which she provokes:

> Be that you are,
> That is, a woman; if you be more, you're none.
>
> (II. iv. 133–4)

In relation to *Hamlet*, the charge of failure, as well as the horror, can be lifted straight out of the play: Hamlet and his dead father united in their reproach of Gertrude for her sexual failing ('O Hamlet what a falling off was there' (I. v. 47)), and horror as the old Hamlet's exact response to the crime which precedes the play and precipitates its drama ('O horrible! O horrible! most horrible!' (I. v. 80)).

Eliot's essay suggests that the question of the woman and the question of meaning go together. The problem with Hamlet is not just that the emotion it triggers is unmanageable and cannot be contained by the woman who is its cause, but that this excess of affect produces a problem of interpretation: how to read, or control by reading, a play whose inscrutability (like that of the Mona Lisa) has baffled – and seduced – so many critics. Eliot's criticism is normative in two senses which he himself makes explicit. It demands a particular aesthetic of formal constraint (this demand is part of his critique of Romanticism) and it entails preferences – a particular selection of texts as the model of what literature should be (Eliot later had to qualify his essay on Hamlet by stating that his critique did not detract from the value and unity of Shakespeare's work as a whole (Eliot 1933, p. 44)). The objective of Eliot's critical writing is therefore to validate literature at the same time as holding it to account. The task of the writer, and the critic, is ethical. Emotion must be controlled by meaning, and an always potentially chaotic and fragmentary reality must be ordered by art. In Eliot's writing, the objective correlative carries the burden of social order itself. Gertrude's weakness as a character provokes a crisis in which the chaos latent in social cohesion refuses to submit itself to form.

Paradoxically, the importance of psychoanalysis for a questioning of this critical tradition lies not in its distance from it, but in the proximity of its terms, in the striking similarities and echoes which connect the psychoanalytic account of subjectivity to the drama of representation and its dangers which Eliot so graphically describes. That there is risk in the human utterance, and uncertainty behind its apparent security of form, could be seen as the most fundamental discovery of Freud. For psychoanalysis, speech is always a drama which contains something in excess. It always bears the traces of a conflict of positions and identities which can only ever momentarily be arrested or resolved. The unconscious upsets the proper order of representation most clearly in dreams, in slips of the tongue and in jokes, but it can also threaten the most normal or seemingly ordered protocols of representation and speech. Eliot identifies in Hamlet something 'excessive', 'inexpressibly horrible' and 'unknowable' which, because it cannot be managed, brings 'buffoonery' in its train. But by linking his demand for artistic coherence so closely to a recognition of its demise, Eliot suggests in this essay on Shakespeare not an incompatibility, but a relation, between these two extremes. The supremacy of the artist (the most supreme of artists) and the ideal conception of form come together at the precise point of their collapse. Instead of looking down on chaos from the heights of artistic mastery and control, Shakespeare in Hamlet slips off the edge of representation itself.

Order for psychoanalysis is also sexual order: the division of human subjects into male and female and the directing of desire onto its appropriate objects, but again this is effected only partially and at a cost. This process is also described by psychoanalysis as a drama – the Oedipal drama which allocates subjects to their sexual place while also showing that the norm can be violated by the one who most firmly believes that he is submitting to its law. As with language, so with sexuality, an insistence on order always speaks the other and more troubled scenario which it is designed to exclude. Again the link can be made with Eliot. In 'Tradition and the individual talent', published in the same year (1919) as the Hamlet essay (Eliot 1975), Eliot provides the complement to his concept of aesthetic form in what can fairly be described as an 'Oedipal' reading of literary tradition itself. In order to control his disordered subjectivity and transmute it into form, the artist must give himself up to something outside himself. and surrender to the tradition which precedes and surrounds him. Only by capitulating to his literary ancestors can the artist escape his oppressive individual-ity and enter into historical time: 'Set [the artist] for contrast and comparison among the dead' for 'the most individual parts of his work may be those in which the dead poets, his ancestors, assert their immortality most vigorously' (p. 38). Thus, just as in the psycho-analytic account the son pays his debt to the dead father, symbol of the law, in order fully to assume his own history, so for Eliot, the artist pays his debt to the dead poets and can only become a poet by that fact.

Eliot's conception of literary tradition could therefore be described as a plea for appropriate mourning and for the respecting of literary rites. Once again the echo of *Hamlet* is striking. But, as has been pointed out by Jacques Lacan (Lacan 1959), it is the shameful *inadequacy* of mourning which is the trigger and then the constant refrain of the play: the old Hamlet cut off in the 'blossom' of his sin, Polonius interred 'hugger mugger', Ophelia buried – wrongly because of her suicide – in sacred ground.

In this context, where order is constantly both asserted and fails, the fact that it is a woman who is seen as the cause of the excess and deficiency in the play, and again, a woman who symbolizes its aesthetic failure, takes on a further resonance, seeming to echo another funda-mental drama of psychic experience as described by Freud. This is the drama of sexual difference where the woman appears as the cause of just such a failure in representation, as something deficient, lacking or threatening to the systems and identities which are the precondition not only of integrated artistic form but also of so-called normal adult psychic and sexual life. Located by Freud at the point where the woman is first seen to be different (Freud 1924, 1925), this moment can then have its effects in that familiar mystification (or fetishization) of the woman which makes of her something both perfect and dangerous or obscene (obscene if *not* perfect). And perhaps no image has embodied this process more clearly than that of the *Mona Lisa* itself, which at exactly this historical moment (the time of Eliot and Freud alike) started to be taken as the emblem of an inscrutable femininity, cause and destination of the whole of human mystery and its desires:

> The lady smiled in regal calm: her instincts of conquest, of ferocity, all the heredity of the species, the will to seduce and to ensnare, the charm of deceit, the kindness that conceals a cruel purpose, – all this appeared and disappeared by turns behind the laughing veil and bur-ied itself in the poem of her smile. Good and wicked, cruel and compassionate, graceful and feline, she laughed.
>
> (Angelo Conti, *cit.* Freud 1910, p. 109)[2]

The enigma of the woman and the enigma, or undecipherability, of the image are inseparable: 'No one has solved the riddle of her smile, no one has read the meaning of her thoughts' (Muther, *cit.* Freud 1910, p. 108). It is their combination which produces the excess: 'a presence . . . expressive of what in the ways of a thousand years men had come to desire' (Walter Pater, cit. Freud 1910, p. 110), as well as the danger: 'the kindness that conceals a cruel purpose' (p. 109). Freud also picks up the tone, in one of his most problematic observations on femininity, when he allows that writers have recognized in this painting:

> the most perfect representation of the contrasts which dominate the erotic life of women; the contrast between reserve and seduction, and between the most devoted tenderness and a sensuality that is ruthlessly demanding – consuming men as if they were alien beings.
>
> (Freud 1910, p. 108)

What other representation, one might ask, has more clearly produced a set of emotions without 'objective correlative', that is, in excess of the facts as they appear? The place of the Mona Lisa in Eliot's reading of Hamlet suggests that what is felt as inscrutable, unmanageable or even horrible for an aesthetic theory which will only allow into its definition what can be controlled or managed by art, is nothing other than femininity itself.

What requires explanation, therefore, is not that Gertrude is an inadequate object for the emotions generated in the play, but the fact that she is expected to support them. Hamlet's horror at Gertrude (like the horror Eliot sees behind the play) makes her a focus for a set of ills which the drama shows as exceeding the woman at the same time as it makes of her their cause. It has often been pointed out that Hamlet's despondency seems to centre more on his mother's remarriage than it does on his father's death even after the revelation of his uncle's crime. Eliot does suggest that it is in the nature of the sentiments dealt with in Hamlet - a son's feelings towards a guilty mother – that they are unmanageable by art. But he does not ask why it is, in the play as in his own commentary, that the woman bears the chief burden of the guilt.

At the end of Eliot's essay, he refers to Montaigne's 'An Apologie of Raymond Sebond' as a possible source for the malaise of Shakespeare's play (its discourse on the ephemeral, contradictory and unstable nature of man has often been taken as the origin of Hamlet's suicide soliloquy) (Florio 1885, pp. 219–310). In relation to the woman, however, another smaller essay by Montaigne – 'Of three good women' – is equally striking, not necessarily as a source, but for the exact reversal which it represents vis-à-vis Gertrude herself, each of these women choosing self-imposed death at the point where her husband is to die (pp. 378–82). The image is close to the protestations of the Player Queen in the Mousetrap scene of Hamlet who vows her undying love to her husband, whereupon Gertrude, recognizing perhaps in the Player Queen's claims a rebuke or foil to her own sexual laxness, comments 'The Lady doth protest too much' (III. ii. 225) (a familiar cliché now for the sexual 'inconstancy' of females). So what happens indeed to the sexuality of the woman when the husband dies, who is there to hold its potentially dangerous excess within the bounds of a fully social constraint? This could be seen as one of the questions asked by Hamlet the play, and generative of its terrible effect. Behind Eliot's reading we uncover a whole history of the fantasies that the woman embodies and the order that she is required to uphold.

The presence of sexuality to this concept of aesthetic form has important implications for recent literary debate whose terms echo, from the opposite side, those of Eliot's critique. Taking their cue from psychoanalysis, writers like Roland Barthes (1970 and 1971) and Julia Kristeva (1974 and 1980) have seen the very stability of the sign as index and precondition for that myth of linguistic cohesion and sexual identity which we must live by, but under whose regimen we suffer, with literature as one of the chief arenas in which that struggle is played out. Writing which proclaims its integrity, and literary theory which demands such integrity (objectivity/correlation) of writing, merely repeat that moment of repression when language and sexuality were first ordered into place, putting down the unconscious processes which threaten the resolution of the Oedipal drama and of narrative form alike. In this context, Eliot's critical writing with its stress on the ethical task of writer and critic becomes nothing less than the most accomplished (and influential) case for the interdependency and centrality of language and sexuality to the proper ordering of literary form. Much recent literary theory can be seen as an attempt to undo the ferocious effects of this particularly harsh type of literary super-ego – one whose political repressiveness in the case of Eliot became more and more explicit in his later allegiance to Empire, Church and State.

Hamlet fails, therefore, at the two precise points where Eliot calls literature to account – the coherence of the aesthetic object and the proper ordering of historical time. What in his terms is the play's failure could be taken now as the sign of the oppressiveness – for criticism and for literature – of these very demands, of their aesthetic and moral constraint. It is as if the woman becomes both scapegoat and cause of the dearth or breakdown of (Oedipal) resolution which the play enacts, not only at the level of its theme, but also in the disjunctions and difficulties of its aesthetic form. Much has been made of the aesthetic problem of *Hamlet* by critics other than Eliot, who have pondered on its lack of integration or single-purposiveness, its apparent inability to resolve itself or come to term (it is the longest of Shakespeare's plays), just as they have pondered on all these factors in the character of Hamlet himself.

Hamlet therefore poses a problem for Eliot at the level of both matter and form. Femininity is the image of that problem; it seems in fact to be the only image through which the problem can be conceptualized or thought. Femininity thus becomes the focus for a partly theorized recognition of the psychic and literary disintegration which can erupt at any moment into literary form.

II

The overlap of aesthetic and sexual failing appears again in commentaries on *Measure for Measure* in which Isabella has become the focus of a generally acknowledged sense of deficiency in the play's dramatic form. F. R. Leavis saw the play as one of the most 'consummate and convincing of Shakespeare's achievements' (Leavis 1942, p. 234), but in doing so, he set himself explicitly against a list of critics which include 'Hazlitt, Coleridge, Swinburne, the Arden editor, Sir Edmund Chambers, Mr Desmond McCarthy, the editors of the New Cambridge Shakespeare and innumerable others' (p. 234). Isabella is not the only 'problem' in this play (the term 'problem' was introduced at the turn of the century by analogy with the naturalist dramas of Ibsen and Shaw); but criticism has alternatively revered and accused her in such a way that her sexual identity has become the site on which dissatisfaction with the play, and disagreement about the play, have turned. No character in the play has produced a 'wider divergence of opinion' (R. M. Smith 1950, p. 212), opinions which, despite the differences between them, once again have in common their *excess*. Isabella has been the object of 'excessive admiration' and 'excessive repugnance' (Smith, p. 212) uniting in her person those extremes of attraction and recoil which were latent in T. S. Eliot's comparison of the *Mona Lisa* with *Hamlet*.

Strangely, the accusations against Isabella have, if anything, been stronger than those against Gertrude, suggesting that it is the desire provoked by the woman which is above all the offence, and that the woman who refuses to meet that desire is as unsettling as the one who does so with excessive haste. Isabella has been described as a 'hussy' (Charlton, cit. R. M. Smith 1950, p. 213), 'hysterical' (Lever, Introduction to Arden edition, Shakespeare 1965, p. lxxx), as suffering 'inhibition' (Knight 1930, p. 102) or 'obsession' (Jardine 1983, p. 192) about sex. She has also been revered as divine. The two positions are, however, related and the second can easily tip over into the first. Angelo himself makes the link:

> Shall we desire to raze the sanctuary
> And pitch our evils there?
>
> What is't I dream on?
> O cunning enemy, that, to catch a saint,
> With saints dost bait thy hook!
>
> (II. ii. 171–2, 180–1)

Wilson Knight's essay on *Measure for Measure*, which Leavis refers to as the only adequate account which he knows of the play (Knight 1930), gives the strongest illustration of the proximity between Isabella's evil and her sainthood. 'More saintly than Angelo' with a 'saintliness that goes deeper, is more potent than his', Isabella gradually turns in the course of the analysis into a 'fiend'. Her rejection of Angelo's sexual demand and her refusal to sacrifice herself for the life of her brother makes that same sanctity 'self-centred', 'ice-cold', lacking 'humanity', 'feeling' or 'warmth'. In the face of this refusal criticism blows hot and cold, becoming in itself a participation in the act. Isabella's 'sex inhibitions' show her 'horribly as they are, naked'. Shakespeare 'strikes mercilessly against her once and deep' and she is 'stung', 'lanced on a sore spot of her soul'. Her final intercession for Angelo's life shows the response beneath the denial: 'his strong passions have moved her . . . thawed her ice-cold pride' (Knight 1930, pp. 100–3).

In the case of Isabella, it is lack of sexuality which is the failing, but as with Gertrude it is the woman who bears the burden of the reproach. The basic accusation, which is shared by Lever in the Arden edition of the play, does not greatly differ from the more measured interpretations of Isabella's slow growth into humanity which have been offered against it (Traversi, cit. Maxwell 1947; R. M. Smith 1950; French 1982).

The critical premisses on which this interpretation rests are, however, as important as its content, and these can be related back to Eliot. One implication of the objective correlative is that drama relies on the credibility of the character to give coherence to its form. If the character fails, then meaning cannot be pinned down or drawn into its proper bounds. It starts to circulate and goes out of control. For Eliot, such lack of control is ultimately that of the author himself who, like the character on stage, has failed to hold together. The aesthetic consistency of the character and the psychological cohesion of the author are interdependent. If meaning is not properly ordered through the dramatic personae, it is therefore the very limits of human subjectivity which are put at risk.

The critical investment in Isabella, of which Wilson Knight's essay is only one of the most extreme instances, can be seen as deriving from this way of conceptualizing literature, which is of course not restricted to Eliot alone. Eliot's assessment of Gertrude was predominantly an aesthetic one (he distanced himself from criticism of Hamlet as a character by insisting that the problem was the play), but it does contain within it the idea of a norm. To judge Isabella – whether positively or negatively – is already to pre-judge the issue of meaning and subjectivity by transposing it into moral terms. If the problem is how a character behaves, then the limits of characterization are not called into question. Given that Measure for Measure is one of Shakespeare's plays where it is generally recognized that his method of characterization cannot fully be grasped psychologically (the weakness of Claudio as a character, the allegorical role of the Duke), then the extent to which Isabella has been discussed in terms of consistency, credibility and ethics is striking. In the critical debates about Isabella, it is as if we can see anxiety about aesthetic or representational cohesion turning into a sexual reproach.[3]

The fact that there is a question of language and meaning at stake in relation to Measure for Measure is made explicit by Leavis himself whose article 'The greatness of Measure for Measure' was written as a reply to an article by L. C. Knights called 'The ambiguity of Measure for Measure', both of which were published in Scrutiny in 1942.[4] For Leavis, the charge of ambiguity must be answered if Shakespeare is not to be seen as the 'victim of unresolved contradiction, of mental conflict or uncertainty' (Leavis 1942, p. 240). His critical task is therefore to establish the integrity of the text, which entails aesthetic and moral certainty, that is, the power to identify and judge. The easiest identification is with Angelo ('it is surely easier for us to put ourselves in Angelo's place and imagine ourselves exposed to his temptations', p. 247), while the supreme judgement falls on Isabella herself ('a supreme test on Isabella' at the end of the play). Lack of ambiguity therefore involves unequivocal sexual identity and a corresponding (and uneven) distribution of moral roles.[5]

If we overturn this certainty – as L. C. Knights does in his article – we can therefore expect to find an ambiguity or dislocation at the heart of sexuality itself – one which upsets the very form of judgement which this type of character-based analysis enshrines. What is sexuality in Measure for Measure? Who bears the responsibility for the problem posed to ethics by desire? What is it that criticism is forced to leave aside when it asks the woman to transform sexuality from outrage into something moral and human and safe? It would seem to be the excess of sexuality itself, an excess which disrupts linguistic, fully as much as ethical, form. Apologetically – given his own commitment to the idea of Shakespeare's mastery – L. C. Knights identifies such a dislocation in these lines:

> Our natures do pursue,
> Like rats that ravin down their proper bane,
> A thirsty evil; and when we drink, we die.

(I. ii. 120–2)

The problem with these lines (like those of Sonnet 129 to which Knights also refers) is that sexuality is given as an evil which belongs to the act, to the desire, to the object and to nature itself, but it can be limited to none of them. Instead Shakespeare's language shifts awkwardly across them all:

> The illustrative comparison has, we notice, three stages: (i) rats 'ravin down' poison, (ii) which makes them thirsty, (iii) so they drink and – the poison taking effect – die. But the human parallel has, it seems, only two stages: prompted by desire, men quench their 'thirsty evil' in the sexual act and – by the terms of the new proclamation – pay the penalty of death. The act of ravening down the bane or poison is thus left on our hands, and the only way we can dispose of it is by assuming that 'our natures' have no need to 'pursue' their 'thirsty evils' for it is implanted in them by the mere fact of being human. This is of course pedantry and – you may say – irrelevant pedantry, for Shakespeare's similes do not usually demand a detailed, point by point, examination, and the confusion between desire (thirst) and that from which desire springs does not lessen the general effect. The fact remains, however, that there is some slight dislocation or confusion of feeling, comparable, it seems to me, to the wider confusion of Sonnet 129, 'An expense of spirit in a waste of shame . . .' (for not even the excellent analysis by Robert Graves and Laura Riding in their *Survey of Modernist Poetry*, pp. 63–81, can make me feel that the sonnet forms a coherent whole). And even if you accept the simile as completely satisfactory, nothing can prevent 'our natures' from receiving some share of the animus conveyed by 'ravin', a word in any case more appropriate to lust than to love.
>
> (Knights 1942, pp. 226–7)[6]

L. C. Knights' analysis of these lines moves as far from Leavis's (and Eliot's) conception of artistic cohesion as the more recent analyses of Shakespeare's *Sonnets* and of the language of the first scene of *Hamlet* given by Stephen Booth (Booth 1977 and 1969b), where what is always at stake is the insecurity of meaning which Shakespeare imposes on the reader of the *Sonnets* and on the spectator of his play (*Hamlet* as 'the tragedy of an audience which cannot make up its mind', Booth

1969b, p. 152). The two critical positions – the one which would contain and the one which would explode the text – confront each other around Hamlet in that it is precisely the first twenty-two lines of the play that Eliot describes as masterly for being transparent to the dramatic meaning of the play (Eliot 1951, p. 135). Language as something transparent or as something which calls attention to itself has been another issue of recent critical debate. What is interesting in relation to Hamlet and Measure for Measure is that the concentration on the woman seems to siphon off or distract attention from the difficulty of language itself. Slippage of meaning and sexuality as excess seem therefore to be the sub-text of the critical focus on Isabella and Gertrude. If they fail as characters and/or as women, then what is required of criticism, and of dramatic form, is their moral aesthetic completion.

III

One remark of Isabella has been especially condemned. When Claudio asks her to submit to Angelo in order to save his life, she reacts:

> Is't not a kind of incest, to take life
> From thine own sister's shame? What should I think?
> Heaven shield my mother play'd my father fair:
> For such a warped slip of wilderness
> Ne'er issued from his blood.
>
> (III. i. 138–42)

Lever calls this a 'hysterical conceit . . . in keeping with the speech as a whole' (Shakespeare, 1965, p. 75 n.); Charlotte Lennox in 1753 criticized it for 'its coarse and unwomanly reflections on the virtue of her mother' (Lennox, cit. R. M. Smith 1950, p. 213). In relation to these lines, Isabella is 'hysterical' and 'unwomanly', not through lack of humanity (her refusal to relent), but because of the aspersion which she casts on the proper sexual ordering of humanity itself. Accusing her brother of incest (if he takes his life from her sexual act), she then immediately releases him from the charge by claiming that he cannot – because of this very demand – be her legitimate brother. The sexual scandal shifts generations and becomes a mother's sexual crime (like

Gertrude's). This way of thinking makes Isabella 'hysterical' and 'unwomanly' because it overturns the most fundamental of sexual laws.

The charge of neurosis is brought to bear, therefore, on behaviour and language which is an affront to – or does not make – sense. Leavis ended his article on Measure for Measure by objecting to a recent Cambridge production which had presented Angelo as a 'twitching study in neurosis'. If the meaning of the play is coherent and unambiguous there must be no neurosis, just as the charge of neurosis (or hysteria) is brought to classify and organize meaning which goes out of control. Refusal of difficulty and diagnosis of disorder become complementary ways of managing the literary text, each one subjecting the text to the control of an ego which denies, or surveys at a distance, any trouble of meaning which it might present.

Ernest Jones's famous psychoanalytic reading of Hamlet (Jones 1949) seems to put interpretation firmly on this path of diagnosis, which then works in the service of critical and artistic control. Jones makes it explicit that his intention is also to establish the integrity of the literary text, that is to uncover factors, hidden motives and desires, which will give back to rationality what would otherwise pass the limits of literary understanding and appreciation itself: 'The perfect work of art is one where the traits and reactions of a character prove to be harmonious, consistent and intelligible when examined in the different layers of the mind' (p. 49). Jones's reading therefore belongs with that psychoanalytic project which restores to rationality or brings to light, placing what was formerly unconscious or unmanageable under the ego's mastery and control. It is a project which has been read directly out of Freud's much contested statement 'Wo es war, soll Ich werden', translated by Strachey 'Where id was, there ego shall be' (Freud 1933 (1932), p. 80; 2, p. 112). Lacan, for whom the notion of such conscious mastery is only ever a fantasy (the fantasy of the ego itself) retranslates or reverses the statement 'There where it was, so I must come to be' (Lacan 1957, p. 524; my translation).

For Jones, as for Eliot therefore, there must be no aesthetic excess, nothing which goes beyond the reaches of what can ultimately be deciphered and known. In this context, psychoanalysis acts as a key which can solve the enigma of the text. The chapter of Jones's book which gives the Oedipal reading of the text, the one which tends to be included in the anthologies (for example, Lerner 1963), is accordingly entitled 'The psychoanalytic solution'. Taking his reference from Freud's comments in *The Interpretation of Dreams* (Freud 1900, pp. 264–6; 4, *pp.* 366–8), Jones sees Hamlet as a little Oedipus who cannot bring himself to kill Claudius because he stands in the place of his own desire, having murdered Hamlet's father and married his mother. The difference between Oedipus and Hamlet is that Oedipus unknowingly acts out this fantasy, whereas for Hamlet it is repressed into the unconscious, revealing itself in the form of that inhibition or inability to act which has baffled so many critics of the play. It is this repression of the Oedipal drama beneath the surface of the text which leads Freud to say of *Hamlet*, comparing it with Sophocles' drama, that it demonstrates 'the secular advance of repression in the emotional life of mankind' (Freud 1900, p. 264; 4, p. 366).

If Hamlet cannot act, therefore, it is because he is locked into an unconscious drama which has not been elucidated, or resolved. The psychoanalytic solution therefore answers not only Hamlet's but also the critic's dilemma. The diagnosis of the character's *disorder* produces for the reader the *order*, or intelligibility, of the text.

Jones's reading involves a psychological interpretation of character, but it cannot, by its own definition, stop there. If Hamlet's dilemma is to be understood in terms of a failing, then that failing must have a cause. Jones's interpretation has often been discredited for its psychological speculations about Hamlet's early childhood as well as for its conjectures about Shakespeare's personal life, both of which lead him necessarily off the edge of the text. But these are in a sense only the logical consequence of a critical method which takes the reality or consistency of the character as its norm. Just as Eliot read into *Hamlet* a momentary loss by Shakespeare of the self-possession which is the precondition of art, so Jones reads Shakespeare's private psychic drama out of that of the character on the stage (Jones 1949, pp. 115 ff.). (Psycho-)analysis of the author is latent to the concept of the aesthetic inadequacy or breakdown of the text. Inside the play, Eliot located this inadequacy in Gertrude. Jones sees this same failing as psychological – Gertrude's too great possessiveness and her too little constraint produce those overwhelming feelings in Hamlet which then threaten to engulf the character and the play. In Jones's reading, Hamlet also bears the guilt of his own desire (the mind of the infant is, Jones writes in a less known chapter, 'tragic' under the weight of this desire – chapter IV, pp. 81–103), but Gertrude none the less becomes the vanishing point of the problem represented in the play.

Yet the drift of this analysis also starts to give an opposite impression, which is that responsibility for the psychological drama cannot in fact be pinned down. At the very moment when psychoanalysis produces its Oedipal reading, with the implied account of what could – or should – have been the successful resolution or norm, then, as was the case with Eliot, the origin or source of the failure starts to move across the different levels of text. From Hamlet to Shakespeare and back to Gertrude, the question arises as to what would be needed, precisely, to get matters straight? Or is it that what is felt as the *deviation of Hamlet* exposes the futility of asking this question at all? Another look at the psychoanalytic engagement with *Hamlet* suggests that the second of these questions might be closer to the point.

The relationship of psychoanalysis to *Hamlet* has in fact always been a strange and repetitive one, in which Hamlet the character is constantly given the status of a truth. When Hamlet is described as Oedipus, psychoanalysis has been brought in to solve a problem of reading or aesthetic form. But when he is described as melancholic or hysteric, the relationship works in reverse. Then literature becomes the place where psychoanalysis can seek illustration for those aspects of subjectivity which bring us up against the limits of interpretation and sexual identity alike. The interpretative distinction between rationality and excess, between normality and abnormality, starts to crumble for instance when the melancholic is defined as a madman who also speaks the truth. Freud uses *Hamlet* with this meaning in 'Mourning and melancholia' written in 1915:

> We can only wonder why a man has to be ill before he can be accessible to a truth of this kind. For there can be no doubt that if anyone holds an opinion of himself such as this (an opinion which Hamlet holds of himself and everyone else) he is ill, whether he is being more or less unfair to himself.
>
> (Freud 1917, pp. 246–7; 2, p. 255)

Taken in this direction, Hamlet illustrates not so much a failure of identity as the precarious distinction on which this notion of identity rests. In 'Psychopathic characters on the stage' (Freud 1942 (1905 or 1906)), Freud includes Hamlet in that group of plays which rely for their effect on the neurotic in the spectator, inducing in her or him the neurosis watched on the stage, crossing over the boundaries between onstage and offstage, and breaking down the habitual barriers of the mind.[7] A particular type of drama, this form is none the less effective only through its capacity to implicate us all: 'A person who does not lose his reason under certain conditions can have no reason to lose' (Lessing, cit. Freud 1942 (1905 or 1906), p. 30 n.). Jones makes a similar point, and underscores its fullest social import, when he attributes the power of Hamlet to the very edge of sanity on which it moves, and the way that it confuses the division which 'until our generation (and even now in the juristic sphere) separated the sane and responsible from the irresponsible insane' (Jones 1949, p. 76). T. S. Eliot also gave his version of this, but from the other side, when he described poetry in 'Tradition and the individual talent' as an escape from emotion and personality, and then added 'but, of course, only those who have personality and emotion can know what it means to want to escape from these things' (Eliot 1975, p. 43). So instead of safely diagnosing Hamlet – his Oedipal drama, his disturbance – and subjecting them to its mastery and control, the psychoanalytic interpretation turns back onto the spectator and critic, and implicates the observer in those forms of irrationality or excess which Jones and Eliot, in their different ways, seem to be ordering into place.

Calling Hamlet a hysteric, which both Freud and Jones also do (Freud 1887–1902, p. 224; Jones 1949, p. 59), has the same effect in relation to the question of sexual difference, since it immediately raises the issue of femininity and upsets the too tidy Oedipal reading of the play. Freud had originally seen the boy's Oedipal drama as a straightforward desire for the mother and rivalry with the father, just as he had first considered the little girl's Oedipal trajectory to be its simple reverse. The discovery of the girl's pre-Oedipal attachment to the mother led him to modify this too easy picture in which unconscious sexual desires in infancy are simply the precursors in miniature of the boy's and the girl's later fitting sexual and social place (Freud 1924,

1925, 1931). This upset of the original schema led Freud to re-think the whole issue of feminine sexuality, but it also has crucial effects on how we consider the psychic life of the boy. In a section called 'Matri-cide' (Jones 1949, chapter V, pp. 105–14), which tends to be omitted from the anthologies, Jones talks of Hamlet's desire to kill not the father, but the mother. He takes this from Hamlet's soliloquy before he goes to his mother's bedchamber in Act III, scene ii of the play:

> Let not ever
> The Soul of Nero enter this firm bosom;
> Let me be cruel, not unnatural.
> I will speak daggers to her, but use none.
>
> (III. ii. 384–7)

and also from Gertrude's own lines: 'What wilt thou do? Thou wilt not murder me. Help, Ho!' (III. iv. 20–1) (the murder of Polonius is the immediate consequence of this). Thus desire tips over into its opposite and the woman becomes guilty for the affect which she provokes.

This is still an Oedipal reading of the play, since the violence towards the mother is the effect of the desire for her. But desire then starts to trouble the norms of identification, involving Jones in a discussion of the femininity in man (not just desire for the woman but identification with her), a femininity which has been recognized in Hamlet by more than one commentator on the play (Jones 1949, pp. 88, 106)[8] Thus Hamlet, 'as patient as the female dove' (V. i. 281), becomes Renaissance man only to the extent that he reveals a femininity which undermines that fiction (the image of the female dove was objected to by Knight in 1841 as a typographical error (Shakespeare 1877, I, p. 410 n.)). Femi-ninity turns out to be lying behind the Oedipal drama, indicating its impasse or impossibility of resolution, even though Freud did talk of its 'dissolution', as if it suddenly went out of existence altogether. But this observation contradicts the basic analytic premiss of the persistence of unconscious desire.

Thus on either side of the psychoanalytic solution we find some-thing which makes of it no 'solution' at all. The ascription of melan-cholia and hysteria to Hamlet appear at first as traditional diagnoses of the character and the text. In fact they entail a different interpretative scenario altogether, one which exposes not the failure of the play, but of the fantasy which lies behind the aesthetic critique – that there could be a straightforward resolution to the drama of our own psychic and sexual life. For Jones, as for Eliot, this problem of *Hamlet*, the challenge which it poses to interpretation, is then best embodied by femininity itself: 'The central mystery [of *Hamlet*] has well been called the Sphinx of modern literature' (Jones 1949, pp. 25–6). What seems most important is not, therefore, whether Hamlet suffers from an excess of femininity (what form of diagnosis would that be?), but the way that femininity itself functions *as* excess, the excess of this particular inter-pretative schema (hence presumably its omission from the extracts and summaries of Jones), and the very image once again for the troubled and troubling aesthetic boundaries of the play.

IV

It should therefore come as no surprise that the opposite of this dis-turbance – an achieved aesthetic or even creativity itself – then finds its most appropriate image again in femininity, but this time the reverse: the good enough mother herself. As if completing the circuit, André Green turns to D. W. Winnicott's concept of the maternal function as the basis for his recent book on *Hamlet* (Green 1982).[9] In this psycho-analytic reading, femininity appears as the very principle of the aesthetic process. Shakespeare's Hamlet forecloses the femininity in himself, but by projecting onto the stage the degraded and violent image of a femininity repudiated by his character, Shakespeare manages to preserve in himself that other femininity which is the source of his creative art:

> Writing *Hamlet* had been an act of exorcism which enabled its author to give his hero's femininity – cause of his anxieties, self-reproaches and accusations – an acceptable form through the process of aes-thetic creation. . . . By creating *Hamlet*, by giving it representation, Shakespeare, unlike his hero, managed to lift the dissociation between his masculine and feminine elements and to reconcile himself with the femininity in himself.
>
> (Green 1982, p. 256)

The reading comes from Winnicott's paper 'Creativity and its origins' (Winnicott 1971, pp. 65–85) which ends with a discussion of Shakespeare's play. It is a fully psychological reading of the author, but its interest, once again, lies in the way that femininity appears as the enigma and source of the analysis, as of the play. More clearly and explicitly for Winnicott than for the other writers discussed here, aesthetic space itself is now conceptualized in terms of sexual difference and the place of femininity within it. Creativity *per se* (the creativity in all of us, so this is not just the creativity of the artist) arises out of a femininity which is that primordial space of being which is created by the mother alone. It is a state of being which is not yet a relationship to the object because there is as yet no self, and it is, as Green defines it, '*au delà de la représentation*', that is, the other side of representation, before the coming of the sign (this comes very close to French feminists such as Luce Irigaray on femininity and language).[10] But it is worth noting how the woman finds herself thus situated either at the point where language and aesthetic form start to crumble or else where they have not yet come to be.

'Masculinity does, femininity is'[11] – Winnicott's definition, like Green's, and that of Eliot before them, starts once again to look like a repetition, which reproduces the fundamental drama of Hamlet, cleaving the image of femininity in two, splitting it between a degradation and an idealization which, far from keeping each other under control (as Green suggests), set each other off, being the reverse sides of one and the same mystification. And like Eliot, Green also gets caught in the other face of the idealization, the inevitable accusation of Gertrude: 'Is the marriage of Gertrude consequence or cause of the murder of Hamlet's father? I incline towards the cause'. ('*Je pencherai pour la cause*', Green 1982, p. 61); and at the end of the book, he takes off on a truly wild speculation which makes Gertrude the stake in the battle between the old Fortinbras and the old Hamlet before the start of the play.

But the fact that Hamlet constantly unleashes an anxiety which returns to the question of femininity tells us above all something about the relationship of aesthetic form and sexual difference, about the fantasies they share – fantasies of coherence and identity in which the woman appears repeatedly as both wager and threat.

Lacan, in his essay on Hamlet (1959) (see pp. 101–2 above), puts himself resolutely on the side of the symbolic – reading the play in terms of its dearth of proper mourning, and the impossibility for Hamlet of responding to the too literal summons of the dead father, who would otherwise represent for the hero the point of entry into his appropriate symbolic place (the proximity between this article and Eliot's 'Tradition and the individual talent' is truly striking). Lacan therefore places the problem of the play in the symbolic, on the side of the father; Green in the 'before' of representation where the mother simply is. The difference between them is another repetition, for it is the difference between the law of the father and the body of the mother, between symbol and affect (one of Green's best-known books in France was an exposition of the concept of 'affect' in Freud and a critique of Lacan's central premiss that psychic life is regulated by the exigencies of the linguistic sign (Green 1973)). But it is a difference with more far reaching implications, which link back to the question – of the fantasy of the woman and her guilt – with which this investigation started. For the concentration on the mother – on her adequacies and inadequacies – was the development in psychoanalytic theory itself which Lacan wanted to redress, precisely because, like Hamlet, it makes the mother cause of all good and evil, and her failings responsible for a malaise in all human subjects, that is, in men and in women, which stems from their position in the symbolic order of culture itself (Lacan 1957–8 and 1958). The problem of the regulation of subjectivity, of the Oedipal drama and the ordering of language and literary form – the necessity of that regulation and its constant difficulty or failing – is not, to put it at its most simple, the woman's fault.

Finally the reference to the Mona Lisa and to the Sphinx have another relevance to psychoanalysis, one which refers to the act of interpretation itself. The Sphinx presents meaning as a riddle, the Mona Lisa seems to hold a meaning which it refuses to divulge. The psychoanalytic concept of resistance also assumes that meaning is never simply present to the subject, but is something which disguises itself, is overwhelming or escapes. Freud came to recognize that its very intractability was not a simple fault to be corrected or a history to be filled. It did not conceal a simple truth which psychoanalysis should aim to restore. Instead this deviation or vicissitude of meaning was the 'truth' of a subject caught in the division between conscious and unconscious which will always function at one level as a split. Paradoxically, interpretation can only advance when resistance is seen not as obstacle but as process. This simultaneously deprives interpretation of its own control and mastery over its object since, as an act of language, it will necessarily be implicated in the same dynamic.

In both Hamlet and Measure for Measure, the play itself presents this deviant and overpowering quality of meaning which appears in turn as something which escapes or overwhelms the spectator. In Act III of Hamlet the two effects are staged, the one fast upon the other, in the Mousetrap scene: the Dumbshow discloses its meaning only partially or postpones its effects, while the spoken and too explicit words of the play which follows send their chief spectator into crisis. The Dumbshow gives the shadow of a meaning, the play speaks its meaning too loud. Together they divide the play in two, forcing us to ask for whom is meaning intended and does it always unfailingly reach its goal (does the King see the Dumbshow or is it intended for the audience and not for his eyes?). The disparity between these two moments also reflects the Renaissance division between non-representational and illusionistic stage space (Weimann 1978), but the problem of interpretation they have provoked (Jenkins, in Shakespeare 1982a, pp. 501–5) equally points to repetition, discontinuity and excess, all of which run right through the fabric of the play. In Hamlet, the murder of the old King is represented three times over – in the Ghost's speech, in the Dumbshow and in the play, although the chief horror is directed at the sexual act (the one act that cannot be staged). Hamlet himself hovers between the word and a deed whose sole meaning, when it comes, is to bring death. The dilemma of Hamlet (character and play) could also be seen in terms of an analytic scenario in which focus brought to bear on the problem and difficulty of meaning leaves the relationship between word and action held in unbearable suspense.

In Measure for Measure, speech is also offered as a drama which can be too present – in this case the drama of a woman who dares to speak and show her face. When Isabella is called upon to plead for her brother, she is poised on the edge of a vow which will forbid her to speak with her face uncovered to a man (I. iv. 10–13). The play therefore opens with a sexual danger which it places within the utterance itself. This danger – to which Angelo's desire comes as the immediate and anticipated response – resides in something given as the too physical voice of the woman, the overwhelming presence of her speech.

In *Measure for Measure*, sex unlegitimated by marriage is therefore forbidden, but speech itself in relation to the woman is placed under the weight of a law. The penalty which falls on the too blatant sexuality of Juliet and Claudio is matched by this injunction against the act of expression which can also be felt as too glaring or exposed. As if, by analogy, the sexuality of the utterance will by definition be overpowering unless it disguises itself or is covered from view.

In *Hamlet* and *Measure for Measure* words either fail to complete themselves in action or else they reach their destination too fast. This may be at least part of the discomfort which is aroused for interpretation by these plays. More than the theme of an illicit or adulterate sexuality, this tension may be what is felt as intractable to a form of analysis which wants meaning to be balanced or to be held in its proper bounds. The same tension could perhaps explain why Gertrude and Isabella have, in their different ways, served so much as the critical focus of these plays. Failing in a woman, whether aesthetic or moral, is always easier to point to than a failure of integration within language and subjectivity itself. If we try to read Shakespeare in terms of the second, however, it might be possible to lift the onus off the woman, who has for so long now been expected to take the responsibility, and to bear the excessive weight.

6

READING THE SIGNS

Towards a semiotics of Shakespearean drama

Alessandro Serpieri
translated by *Keir Elam*

The works of Shakespeare have represented over the past fifteen to twenty years one of the major fields of critical enquiry for structuralist and semiotic readings of literature and drama.[1] Literary semiotics, and more specifically the semiotics of drama, offer a very wide and complex network of interrelated theories and methods; here I can present only some of the basic principles relevant to the main purpose of this essay, namely the sketching out of a particular mode of analysis of Shakespearean drama. After reviewing these theoretical parameters, I will endeavour to exemplify my own version of semiotic criticism, in a necessarily brief hermeneutic reading of two plays, *Julius Caesar* and *Othello*.

The literary *sign* is powerfully overdetermined, that is to say, it gathers sense through a wide network of syntactic and semantic relations manifest in the text itself by its very textual situation – a situation that endows it at once with syntagmatic (horizontal) and paradigmatic (vertical) meanings – over and above those values that it assumes through its macrotextual and intertextual allegiances.[2] But it likewise, and no less crucially, takes on meaning from the historical, cultural and pragmatic contexts within which it is produced. The literary sign, in other words, brings together a complex of meanings at the crossroads between different routes of signification: textual and extratextual, linguistic and semiotic. One might take, as a more or less casual example, a categorematic sign like the word 'ceremony' in Shakespeare, a word often textually and macrotextually overdetermined by ritualistic-symbolic values. This sign serves as a paradigmatic vehicle for the very sense of the symbolic world-order, and of the idea of regality which represents that world-order: such overdetermination is evident, for instance, in *Henry V* (see in particular IV. 1. 101 ff.) and is implicit but no less significant in *Julius Caesar* (especially in the Republican and anti-symbolic position of the tribunes – 'Disrobe the images / If you find them decked with ceremonies' (I. i. 64–5) – and in the symbolic stand of Caesar: 'Set on, and leave no ceremony out' (I. ii. 11)). As the figure of an entire model of the world (at least in its political aspects), the term 'ceremony' thus acquires its full sense only within the lexical connotations and within the epistemic and ideological contrasts of the Elizabethan period.

The literary text, in a far more complex fashion than the literary sign, proves to be overdetermined by a functional multiplicity of semantic levels of an (a) discursive and (b) contextual-cultural kind. Semiotic criticism, while drawing on the hermeneutic insights provided by structuralism with regard to the linguistic-discursive make-up of the text, moves towards a more complete investigation of textual structures within the historical-cultural systems underlying them. From a semiotic perspective, in fact, the literary text is seen as a *dynamic* object that unfolds in a complex formal-semantic-pragmatic elaboration of models of reality (epistemic frames), of axiologies (systems of value), ideologies (production of values, often implicit or hidden), codes (correlations between given signifiers and given signifieds in the production and communication of meaning), subcodes, genres, conventions (discursive, presentational and rhetorical orientations): in a word, virtually all the semiotic systems at work in a given culture.[3] And this culture itself may in turn be interpreted, more or less metaphorically, as a global Text within which texts proper, with their different cognitive, communicative and expressive functions, are generated (Foucault 1970; Lotman 1973).

The range of interpretative tasks open to literary semiotics is too vast, then, to permit an exhaustive critical enquiry, not so much into the multiple cultural sectors activated by textual structures (one can always list them, but the result will be simply an inert catalogue) as into the *modes* of manifestation whereby cultural elements are filtered and organized in the text according to peculiar and original semantic hierarchies. If the literary work communicates its own *extra*-text, and thereby interprets its own historical period, it does so within a form of communication that reflects back upon the communicative system itself. Thus the critic, while exercising as wide-ranging a semiotic awareness as possible, will orient his reading towards what he takes to be the *dominant* communicative factors in the text, so as to identify its most functional cultural and pragmatic axes from the point of view of its *construction*.

At this constructive level, the text – obeying norms or violating them so as to create others – fits into that particular supra-individual system of textuality called *genre*. A single story may be told not only in various ways but also, and above all, according to the various semiotic and discursive *modes* predicted by different genres: for example, according to epic, narrative or dramatic modes, articulated in the peculiar forms of these genres expressed by a given age. In bringing into relationship *modes* and *contents*, the genre offers specific types of presentation, structure and convention for the actualization of the material in discourse. The genre offers 'norms of cohesion' (Segre 1979) of a more than linguistic nature, in that they are not limited to the sentence but are valid for the entire transphrastic dynamic of the text. Such norms give form to the themes and materials of the *fabula* according to predicted or predictable schemes: the text in itself, especially in its allegiance to a genre, gives indications, as it were, *for its own use*, directions indispensable to the appropriate reception of its specific mode of textuality. A semiotic reading tends to bring to the fore these parameters also, at once internal and external, for the construction and 'inbuilt' reception of the text.

These parameters take on particular weight when one is dealing with the *dramatic* text: a text which has a quite special status, in the field of literary production, on account of the powerful marks of genre which stamp onto it very particular indications for use. These indications call for a new or supplementary form of semiotic attention. Because if it still remains necessary to correlate the linguistic structures and semantic values of the dramatic text with its cultural context (a pragmatics of the construction of textual meaning), it is no less pressingly important to orient such structures towards a semiotic co-operation with non-verbal systems, those specific to the theatrical performance *for which* the drama is written: mimic, gestural, proxemic and kinesic systems or codes, etc. The dramatic text assumes such systems, potentially or manifestly, in its own particular verbal semiosis (thus calling for a pragmatics of the theatrical destiny of textual meaning, in potential or mental form in a reading, and in actualized form within its various stage realizations).

A semiotic reading of the dramatic text must be aware not only of the cultural pragmatics of its historical context, but also of the potential pragmatics of the *stage* relationships that are inscribed in the strictly verbal make-up of the text itself in accordance with the codes and conventions (both general and historical) of the genre. In a word, critical enquiry into the contextual values of the drama should be carried out with a view to its specific semiotic complexity, a complexity quite distinct from that of literary genres, which are not conditioned by directions for a more-than-verbal use.

But even with respect to its strictly linguistic aspects, the drama *tells its stories* in a quite different fashion from narrative and poetic genres. The drama 'narrates' through the direct interplay of utterances: i.e. it is not the narration of facts from a particular perspective but the unfolding, rather, of a dynamic development of speech acts, the succession of which traces a story. In speaking within situations (or scenes) defined according to specific conventions,[4] the *dramatis personae* influence each other, come into conflict (thereby representing opposing models of the world, ideologies or existential attitudes), overpower one another or join each other, in accordance with tragic or comic or grotesque canons. Their action also develops through non-verbal means (in part registered at another linguistic level of the dramatic text, namely in the stage directions), such as facial expressions, gestures, movements, proxemic relations. The dominant mode of action, however, remains far and away the linguistic kind, which is, strictly speaking, action performed through words. Not having as its final end a reading, unlike the literary text *tout court*, the drama is structured verbally as language that *acts* (illocutionary and perlocutionary levels) and that *refers* to the situation and to the space in which it is pronounced (deictic level).

Setting out from such premises, I proposed some years ago a method for the segmentation of the dramatic text, designed to identify units of performative-deictic orientation in the speech-act continuum of the drama (Serpieri 1977; Serpieri *et al.* 1978). The speeches of the *dramatis personae*, in this perspective, should be segmented on the basis of units of deictic orientation, which change every time the axis of reference (of the speaker towards himself, towards another character, or towards an absent or abstract addressee) changes within discourse, conceived as discourse *in situation*. Some brief examples will be given below.

What should be stressed here is the *peculiarity* of dramatic language.[5] If in its 'predisposition towards the stage' the drama may be conveniently analysed at deictic and performative levels, no less important is the study of other linguistic levels typical of the dramatic enunciation: beginning with the rhetorical level that governs the articulation, often implicit or secret, of the illocutionary and perlocutionary acts by which dramatic action lives (Ohmann 1971, 1973; Serpieri 1977). The drama is a *mise en scène* of language (mimesis in Aristotelian terms), which is predisposed towards the theatrical *mise en scène* proper through a functional and dynamic relationship with the codes of non-verbal communication.

Dramatic rhetoric must likewise be considered *in situation*: so-called figures of word or thought possess only a relative, not an absolute, linguistic autonomy in the drama, since they are produced so as to function, within the speech exchange, in at least potential combination with other codes. As such, the privileged figure is, virtually in the drama and actually in performance, *referential* in character. Not by chance, even at first glance, Shakespearean tragedy is marked by the prevalence, in the construction of the drama, of institutionally referential tropes such as irony, hyperbole, paradox, etc., and the comedies give no less weight to the stage functions of figures, privileging puns, hyperbole, paradox, irony, etc.

One might take, as a single representative example, the rhetorical repertory of Hamlet. This repertory is always circumstantial and referential, and constitutes a formidable form of linguistic action (replacing direct pragmatic action) upon Hamlet's interlocutors, upon the context, upon the ideology and axiology of the world view towards which Hamlet is opposed. He offers riddles and replies with enigmas; he does not allow his interlocutors to finish their speeches, upsets their system of expectations, inserts semantic-figural 'noise' or interference, derails isotopies, literalizes others' metaphors and metaphorizes the literal, and so on. The fulcrum of his linguistic-stage action lies in *equivocation*, that is in the collision of levels of meaning or isotopies, with suppression or substitution of the automatized senses which converge to form the false and scleroticized model of the world expressed by his antagonists. The effect of his linguistic-stage operations is to expose the topological structure of the 'global semantic field' of the age,[6] and thus to ridicule the mystifying semiotic processes of traditional power and language: power asserts itself here mainly through language, assertive language is power.

If dramatic language is always potentially circumstantial, the rhetoric on which it often draws appears, by necessity, referential and metalogistic[7] because it brings about a prospective alteration of the referent (Serpieri 1980, p. 41), namely, person or prop or stage-space or language itself. Certainly, in the drama there exists also a largely 'literary' rhetoric, made up of tropes which weave paradigmatically the semantics of this or that character's discourse, and of the drama as a whole, but what appears more powerfully marked is the rhetorical level inextricably bound to the situation of utterance, to the illocutionary-perlocutionary dynamic and to the pragmatic context. Dramatic criticism, in general, and Shakespearean criticism in particular, have tended to privilege, instead, the less marked 'poetic' levels of the rhetoric of drama, dedicating themselves above all to paradigmatic readings of tropical systems, of fields of imagery, of figural patterns on the page rather than for the stage. It appears more productive now, without neglecting the results achieved by paradigmatic studies, to shift attention to the mechanisms of discursive-rhetorical interaction, and thus to the *syntagmatics* of figures within speech exchanges.

It follows, clearly, that more attention should also be paid to the *syntactic* level of dramatic discourse, which is probably what best characterizes the 'predisposition towards the stage' of the expressive modes, and thus of the tactical and epistemic functions, of the *dramatis personae*. It is through syntax that the semantic competence and dramatic functions of characters unfold, that illocutionary-perlocutionary tactics are manifested, and thus that the representation of elements in conflict achieves its dynamism. The drama, constitutionally the *mise en scène* of a conflict, of an *antithesis*, draws above all on linguistic, deictic and rhetorical syntagmatics in the task of presenting, in what Pirandello has called 'spoken action', the clash of epistemic, ideological and psychological models.

All these traces of a predisposition towards the stage are actualized to an extraordinary degree in Shakespearean dramaturgy, as in varying degrees certain commentators have already observed.[8] Here I will endeavour to illustrate, in a necessarily summary fashion, the marked levels of dramatic language, together with their cultural correlates, with specific reference to *Julius Caesar*, a *political* and *public* drama that represents an exemplary clash of axiological and ideological models, and to *Othello*, a *psychological* and *private* drama, which secretly transcribes an anthropological opposition rooted within the tensions of the bourgeois-puritan episteme.

The complex relations between semiotic and more specifically rhetorical structures on the one hand, and ideological structures on the other, have a powerful constructive weight in Shakespearean drama. This is particularly true in the plays dealing with historical subjects, where one perceives more clearly the terms of the great structural and epistemological crisis that occurred between the sixteenth and seventeenth centuries, a crisis that can be summarized as the conflict between a *symbolic model* of the world (a classical-medieval-Renaissance heritage) and a *syntagmatic model* of the world, inaugurating the relativism of the modern age. In the former, according to the Soviet semiotician Yuri Lotman, 'The importance of the sign lay in its substitution function: the substituted element was considered as content and the substituting element as expression. For this reason the substituting element could never have an autonomous value: it acquired value according to the hierarchic position of its content in the general model of the world'; in the latter, 'The meaning of a man or of a phenomenon was determined not by its relationship with their essences at another level but by its insertion into a given level' (Lotman 1973, pp. 44, 52).

The two models have a quite different historical, socio-cultural and epistemological status, since they organize reality, at a material as well as a cognitive level, along the vertical axis and horizontal axis respectively. Every social formation, every system of signification and of communication, is structured, in consequence, according to radically different topological-semantic orientations. The two models reflect, moreover, two distinct visions of language itself as the primary modelling system of a culture: *motivated* language versus *arbitrary* language. As a consequence, the word will be, in the first model, a linguistic interpretation, reserved mainly for the leader, of the general Sense of the world; whereas in the second model, arising out of a conflict with the first, the word will present itself as a deconstruction of this symbolic hermeneutics, in the name of a social project involving, if not 'the people' itself as the subject of history (democracy), at least the many who are able and willing to lead human affairs.

Shakespearean drama encodes the crumbling of the symbolic model, with its centripetal ideology and its stabilizing rhetoric, but rarely permits a positive perception of the syntagmatic model that erodes it through its centrifugal ideology and its destabilizing rhetoric. The symbolic world-order still offers semantic co-ordinates of reference, while the new relativistic episteme appears above all as a laceration of sense, a loss or dispersal of values. But with all his undoubted nostalgia for this lost sense, Shakespeare represents the great conflict in its profoundest movements, *without* committing himself directly to either ideological option. In dramatizing history as a clash of models, he is careful not to declare allegiance to one side or the other, thereby transmitting a message. He limits himself, rather, to an attentive comparison of the ideologies in question, anchoring them to discourse and to the speaking subjects, and always revealing in them components of partiality and blindness.

All of this is particularly clear in *Julius Caesar*. One might distinguish the axiological-ideological spaces involved in this play by means of a series of oppositions:

Space of Caesar and Antony	*Space of Brutus and Cassius*
symbolic world-order	syntagmatic world-order
power of the one	power of the many
motivated name	arbitrary name
superstition	scepticism
passion	reason

The political dimension of this play is so powerful that the characters, while shown also in certain personal and private aspects, can have only a public space and a public destiny. The crowd, the 'supposed' subject of history, is very often on stage in order to register, through its own orientations, the ideological and political clash. The privileged scene is the street, the square or the forum. The play begins and culminates with a persuasion of the crowd as force, as material, on which to try out the transformation of ideology into power (in the first scene the republican ideology of the tribunes; in the third Act, the republican ideology with Brutus as its spokesman, and the Caesarian-monarchical ideology espoused by Antony).

During his political seduction of Brutus, Cassius attacks, among other things, the very heart of the symbolic world-order, i.e. the motivated Name:

> Brutus and Caesar: what should be in that 'Caesar'?
> Why should that name be sounded more than yours?
> Write them together, yours is as fair a name;
> Sound them, it doth become the mouth as well;
> Weigh them, it is as heavy; conjure with 'em,
> 'Brutus' will start a spirit as soon as 'Caesar'.

> (I. ii. 140–5)

He questions, that is, the signifier 'Caesar', just as he had earlier questioned the man Caesar, limited, weak, not able to live up to his monarchical ambitions; and thus he reduces the motivated to the arbitrary, demythologizing the proper name. Caesar has no right to interpret, for all, the Sense of the world.

By contrast, Caesar identifies himself completely with his name. His ideological self-deception lies in his living and dying for that name, which he hammers out continually by speaking of himself in the third person. See, for example, the moment of the great decision – in Act II, scene ii – to go to the Capitol despite the prodigious signs and evil omens: 'Caesar shall forth' (line 10); 'Yet Caesar shall go forth' (28); 'And Caesar shall go forth' (48), where the verb of motion, in conjunction with the symbolic name, assumes in turn symbolic value as a sacred public manifestation, indispensable to the leader as the sun of the world (for this symbolism, compare, for example, *Richard II*, III. iii. 7–9, where York says 'It would beseem the Lord Northumberland / To say "King Richard"; alack the heavy day, / When such a sacred king should hide his head').

The symbolic world-order is entirely sewn with secret interpretations and is constantly intent on deciphering the sense of that parallel plane of which it is but the ephemeral substitute. Its ideology thrives on the tumult of the passions (superstitions, guilt, fear) which can be exorcized only through the guidance of the Leader, who has mysterious access to Sense.

To the paradigm of superstition, Cassius and Brutus endeavour to oppose a secular scepticism on the level of human events, even if at the end of the play they will die *in the name of Caesar*, recaptivated by the suggestiveness of the symbolic world-order, and this is the greatest tragic irony of this ideological play. Brutus, in particular, intends to refute every irrational value in his defence of the purity of the Idea. See, for instance, his refusal to swear fidelity to the undertaking, as Cassius had proposed:

> No, not an oath. If not the face of men,
> The sufferance of our souls, the time's abuse –
> If these be motives weak, break off betimes,
> And every man hence to his idle bed.

> (II. i. 114–17)

Since swearing involves the summoning up of a 'third' (a god, etc.) as guarantor of the human transaction, the oath is not acceptable to him, angers him; note the recurrent invective in this speech, significantly his longest in the entire play. Only the Idea, pure reason, an exclusively human relationship, is valid. For that Idea, against the advice of Cassius, he commits various political errors – rejecting the elimination of Antony and conceding to Antony himself the right to speak at Caesar's funeral – together with a number of military misjudgements. Repressing his passions in the name of the Idea, he is in turn subject to the partiality, and to the mystification, of ideology. And thus he loses the confrontation with Antony, whose ideology is able to draw upon a far more convincing rhetoric than his own.

Antony's is a rhetoric that can be geared with extreme subtlety to the dramatic situation, in particular through a wide network of deictic orientations (that is to say, the semiotic units which emerge through the shifting from one object of reference or from one addressee to another) which allow him the mastery of every stage space. Here I will limit the discussion to a single example of the direct stage impact of his language, namely his first entrance onto the scene of Caesar's murder:

BRUTUS   But *here* comes Antony. Welcome Mark Antony.
ANTONY   O mighty Caesar dost *thou* lie *so* low?
          Are all *thy* conquests, glories, triumphs, spoils,
          Shrunk to *this* little measure? Fare *thee* well.
          I know not, gentlemen, what *you* intend,
          Who else must be let blood, who else is rank:
          If *I myself*, there is no hour *so* fit
          As Caesar's death hour; nor no instrument
          Of half that worth as *those your* swords, made rich
          With the most noble blood of all this world.
          I do beseech *ye*, if *you* bear *me* hard,
          Now, whilst *your* purpled hands do reek and smoke,
          Fulfil *your* pleasure. Live a thousand years,
          I shall not find myself *so* apt to die;
          No place will please me *so*, no mean of death,
          As *here* by Caesar, and by *you* cut off,
          The choice and master spirits of this age.

                                                (III. i. 147–63;)

The circumstantial deictics, of which Antony makes frequent use, are italicized here. Despite the formal greeting of the new leader, Brutus, Antony ignores the conspirators, turning immediately to the dead Caesar. His emotion is authentic, even though, as usual, it is also played out within a political strategy. Antony must remain attached to Caesar, must rail upon his killers in some way, pushing himself at times to the utmost limit of danger (see lines 204–10 below). The more he risks, the more he convinces the conspirators of his honesty, and thus of a possible political pact. As such, the dramatic movement of his discourse has to be ably balanced *between* Caesar and the conspirators, with varied deictic orientations. If his accusations, bound to direct references to Caesar's body, often assume violent and explicit terms, even if under metaphorical guise, *within* these accusations a high esteem for his opponents must infiltrate. Antony is careful above all to close his speech, here as later, with a homage to the conspirators, so that the semantic emphasis of the conclusion counterbalances his attachment to Caesar and the consequent challenge, both manifest and implicit. Note in particular the linguistic and dramatic pregnancy, and the calculated ideological ambiguity, of the syncategorematic term *by* in line 162: '*by* Caesar', the tie with Caesar underlined; '*by* you', the dignity of a possible death at the hands of the artificers of that death itself, men of another ideology but none the less respectable for that, indeed hyperbolized in their status in line 163. The signifier, even of a syncategorematic kind, (i.e. fulfilling a 'linking' function) is employed with formidable ability by Antony. Playing on *by*, he shifts the discourse from the level of lament for the dead leader to the level of the (fictitious) agreement with the new leaders.

Let us examine briefly, now, the ideological clash, at the level of the respective rhetorical forms, of the two orations in the Forum (Act III, scene ii). Brutus's succinct oration is delivered in prose, despite his 'high' social status, because prose is the vehicle of logical argumentation. While employing rhetorical figures, his oration is in fact a theorem, logical but tautological, brief but redundant. Brutus does not need to convince, knowing he is right; he has only to demonstrate the purity of the Idea, ignoring the passions. He sets out by requesting attention, without interruptions: 'Be patient till the last' (line 12). He will offer his demonstration, then the crowd will judge. It is the opposite attitude to the one embraced by Antony, who will let himself be interrupted often and artfully, thus allowing the crowd to believe itself protagonist of the oratorical (emotional, ideological, political) event. Brutus offers a series of circular figures with an apparently conative function which is nevertheless completely subordinated to his demonstrative logic – see lines 13–18:

(a) hear me for my cause
(b) and be silent
(a) that you may hear

(a) Believe me
(b) for mine honour
(b) and have respect to mine honour
(a) that you may believe

(a) Censure me
(b) in your wisdom
(b) and awake your senses
(a) that you may the better judge

The circular figures prove constrictive, caught in the inexorable semantic (and logical) progression of verbal functions: *hear, believe, judge,* where the perlocutionary effect is predetermined, taken for granted, at a rational level: to *hear* Brutus means to *believe* in his honour and thus *judge* him honest. The demonstration of the theorem is then developed not through the artifices of tropical persuasion but by means of hypotheses, rhetorical questions, parallelisms, in an abstract lexis. Given certain premisses, the syllogism must work. The cardinal phrase is 'but, as he was ambitious, I slew him'. At the end, Brutus invites the people to respond ('I pause for a reply'), but no one will speak ('None, Brutus, none'), because in fact he has *taken the word* from the people, in whose name he had struggled ideologically against Caesar, who had *taken their power*. Only when he adds, almost incidentally, that each one of them will bear some weight in the Republic, do the people, their passions finally aroused, grant him a provisional *triumph* ('Bring him with triumph home unto his house', line 50), an *iconic celebration* ('Give him a statue with his ancestors', line 51), a *symbolic nomination* ('Let him be Caesar', line 52), and even a *coronation* ('Caesar's better parts / Shall be crown'd in Brutus', lines 52–3), in a superb crescendo of dramatic irony.

If Brutus moves only along the referential (logical-demonstrative) axis of the communicational model, Antony, when he takes over from him on the stage, plays on all the functions of language in situation, unleashing multiple deictic orientations and illocutionary-perlocutionary modalities. The emotional function alternates with the conative function, the referential with the phatic and with the metalinguistic. He has to overturn the assertion 'ambitious Caesar' = 'honourable Brutus' into the opposite assertion 'non-ambitious Caesar' = 'ungrateful and murderous Brutus', but he can do so only within the limits imposed on him by Brutus himself ('You shall not in your funeral speech blame us, / But speak all good you can devise of Caesar, / And say you do't by our permission', III. i. 245–7). It is precisely these limitations that induce Antony to construct his masterpiece of 'indirection', of occult rhetorical persuasion, based not on the *énoncés* (at the level of propositional content he respects Brutus's prescription) but on the enunciational perspective or context from which they are presented and subsequently upturned. It is Brutus himself who provides Antony with the *modes* of his triumph.

Overall, Antony brings into play *ductus subtilis*, whereby the orator

> simulates at a first level (*thema*) an opinion [Brutus is an honourable man], with the secondary purpose (*consilium*) of achieving through provocation an effect on the audience which is the exact opposite of this opinion [Brutus is not an honourable man]. The whole speech is thus an irony of simulation.
>
> (Lausberg 1949, p. 66)

An irony of simulation, but also of dissimulation (*dissimulatio*) which, according to classical rhetoric, makes use of the modes of grammatical *immutatio* (change of type of sentence: *interrogatio, exclamatio, syntaxis obliqua*), in addition – apart from irony – to the tropes of emphasis and litotes, of periphrasis and of paralepsis, which serve to hide one's opinion, together with the *detractio* of thought, whereby one dissimulates one's very oratorical capacity. Antony makes abundant and theatrically functional use of all these modes.

The basic axes of his speech are indirect, founded on a continuous game of assertion and negation: he affirms through irony and emphasis in order to negate, while he negates through litotes, through paralepsis and through *detractio*, in order to affirm. His technique of hidden persuasion appears, in this, strictly related to that of Iago. Not by chance the third Act of *Julius Caesar* and the third Act of *Othello* provide perhaps the greatest scenes of 'seduction' in Shakespeare: in one case, public and ideological seduction, in the other private and psychological seduction. In both plays the artificers of persuasion make great use of litotes, a figure which insinuates an affirmation by emphasizing it under the guise of a negation, an unreal affirmation which therefore cannot be expressed directly: that Brutus has betrayed the people, and that Desdemona has betrayed Othello.

In addition to the use of irony, the primary rhetorical mode of Antony's utterance is that which employs litotes. The litotic mode is understood as a figure of thought, of word, and of dramatic (and potentially stage) illocution. Litotes of thought pervades the entire oration in its various articulations: he has come to rouse the people in the name of Caesar against the name of Brutus who had acted on behalf of the people; he cannot say so directly, and indeed has to maintain the contrary, but working through upsets in sense he manages to overturn the explicit propositions and reach his ideological and political end. Litotes of word is frequent and very effective: 'I come to bury Caesar, not to praise him' (line 76); 'I speak not to disprove what Brutus spoke' (102); 'I will not do them wrong' (line 127), etc. When he exhibits Caesar's will, his trump card which will demonstrate beyond any doubt the generosity of the murdered leader, Antony immediately 'hides' it ('Which, pardon me, I do not mean to read', line 133), and in fact he only reads it some 100 lines later, when the crowd is already wild without having received this decisive proof. Then he reinforces litotes through prohibition (i.e. Brutus's): 'I must not read it' (line 142), followed immediately by paralepsis that affirms negatively: 'It is not meet you know how Caesar lov'd you' (143) and ''Tis good you know not that you are his heirs' (147). And between the two paralepses he inserts another kind of negation that suggests rebuke and praise at once: 'You are not wood, you are not stones, but men' (line 144). Negation is always used by way of enticement, and so is always, basically, a litotes, a figure which transmits the very sense that it claims to hide.

It is a figure which has, moreover, an immediate dramatic and theatrical import. At a certain point, Antony arranges the crowd in a circle around Caesar's body and calls attention to Caesar's corpse covered by the toga (lines 171–99). But for almost all his speech, he stresses not the massacred body of Caesar, which in fact he does not uncover, but the leader's torn and bloody toga, an emblem at once of rank and of suffering. The toga is a double sign on which Antony can work, appealing to all the emotional registers: the pathetic (the first evening he saw him wear it), the epic (that evening was the eve of the great victory against the Nervii), the blasphemous (the hole caused by the wretched blade of Brutus, 'Caesar's angel'), the stoical (Caesar, destroyed by Brutus's ingratitude, covered his face with the same toga). At once sign and simulacrum, the toga unleashes all the emotions, and the crowd weeps. But at the end, in an extraordinary *coup de théâtre*, Antony benevolently rebukes the people for having let themselves be moved only by Caesar's 'vesture', by a mere simulacrum, and then uncovers the massacred referent itself:

> Kind souls, what weep you when you but behold
> Our Caesar's vesture wounded? Look you here!
> Here is himself, marr'd, as you see, with traitors.
>
> (III. ii. 197–9)

Even this move, exquisitely dramatic as it is, falls under the rubric of litotes: negating or suspending in order to affirm; working on the emotions through a minor point in order to unleash them through the major point; allowing only a part of the sense or evidence to filter through, precisely so that the meaning may burst out because of the blocking of a direct flow, or, as here, of a direct reference to the 'object'. Everything has to be rendered indirect, oblique.

Thus triumphs the Word that *makes* History. But Shakespeare then undercuts this word, exposing the mystification on which it is founded, in a brief remark of Antony's when he is finally left alone:

'Now let it work. Mischief, thou art afoot, / Take thou what course thou wilt' (lines 262–3). It is a stepping back from the Caesarian ideology, although one should not forget the analogous move attributed to Cassius, alone after he has convinced Brutus in favour of the Republican conspiracy: 'Well, Brutus, thou art noble; yet I see / Thy honourable mettle may be wrought / From that it is dispos'd . . .' (I. ii. 305–9). Shakespeare remains equidistant from the rationale and the mystifications of the symbolic model and from those of the syntagmatic model.

If in *Julius Caesar* it is the ideological sense of the world that is at stake, in *Othello*, no less than in *Hamlet*, it is the existential and relational sense of the subject. Who is Iago and who is Othello? Why does Iago fabricate a *fabula* in order to destroy the others? By what techniques does he succeed in provoking mental confusion and tragedy? How and why is it that every sign of Iago's is not, and cannot be, more than a *simulacrum*, the function of an imaginary semiosis? What is the system, the historical context, in which such imaginary turbulence can be produced? I have attempted to answer these and other questions in a book-length study of this play (Serpieri 1978). Here I will restrict myself to a few summary comments.

Iago is the artificer of a *destructive projection*, in the sense that he deflects onto others, in particular onto Othello and Desdemona, profound obsessions of which he is not fully aware himself. The textual journey that the critic undertakes in exploring these obsessions amounts to a search for a motive for Iago's actions. A search that, in the play, is conducted by Iago himself: see the 'motive-hunting' of which Coleridge wrote. In the first scene he reveals to Roderigo a comprehensible motive, the desire for revenge against Othello, who has not nominated him Lieutenant, preferring Cassio. But under this expressible motive there already shows through an unstated and unstatable disquiet. At the level of syntactic articulations, in fact, recurrent binary patterns emerge: 'I know my price, I am worth no worse a place; / But he . . .' (lines 11–12); 'but he, sir, had the election; / And I . . .' (27–8); 'He, in good time, must his lieutenant be, / And I . . .' (32–3). These are patterns of *disjunction* (phrasal figures for the discrimination he has suffered) which place in opposition first and third person pronouns: *I, me* versus *he, him, his.* The latter refer alternately to Othello (unnamed at first) and to Cassio. A basic opposition of the play thus emerges: I versus *him, them, the others.*

It is a social opposition, of rank or of status, which also turns out, immediately, to be an anthropological (and racist) opposition between the white Iago and black Othello, and which moreover takes on, in a more secret but for that none the less functional way, the status of a metaphysical antithesis between the elect and the doomed, in accordance with the theory of predestination so deeply rooted in protobourgeois puritan society (there are traces of such a theory in various parts of the drama; see the explicit signalling of it in II. iii. 95–104). The problem of discrimination and of the clash between 'I' and the others is framed within the anthropological and historical category of *extrane-ity*, in which the individual finds himself in continual struggle with the others for his own existence and for his own survival (See Hill 1967; Horkheimer 1969).

The strategy of Iago is not that of open confrontation but of indirect attack. He dissimulates from the outset, even if for the purpose, at first, of social rather than imaginary scheming:

> . . . for sir,
> It is as sure as you are Roderigo,
> Were I the Moor, I would not be Iago:
> In following him I follow but myself . . .
> . . . I am not what I am.
>
> (I. i. 55–65)

The latter statement appears, however, more than a Machiavellian tactic, expressing as it does, under the aegis of a negation of being, not only the game between appearance and reality but also the possible loss of identity. Iago, in fact, is a prisoner of his own *imaginaire*, and is thus condemned to *not being* in reality: his manifest desires and motives are only the slidings of an *unspeakable* desire. If criticism considers him at the level of *being* (and of identity: jealous, Machiavellian, diabolic, etc.), it is in danger of missing his actual dramatic depth.

Iago's unspeakable desire appears as a constellation of perturbations and of frustrated sexual impulses. The obscenity of his language is constantly designed to deny the positiveness of Eros, to represent

Othello as the repulsive black champion of a degraded hyperbolical sexuality, and to expose Desdemona as an insatiable whore. Let us consider a few examples, drawing attention to the rhetorical techniques involved. Iago warns Brabantio of his daughter's flight in these terms:

> Zounds, sir, you are robb'd, for shame put on your gown,
> Your heart is burst, you have lost half your soul;
> Even now, very now, an old black ram
> Is tupping your white ewe . . .

(I. i. 86–9)

The emphasis put on the action that takes place elsewhere simultaneously with its very naming (note the redundancy of the temporal reference – 'Even now, very now' – and the progressive form) forces open the eyes of the interlocutor onto an unbearable vision of bestially degraded sex (see the later 'Your daughter, and the Moor, are now making the beast with two backs'). The rhetorical figure of *hypotyposis* is used here: a figure of circumstantial utterance typical of Iago, as is *litotes*, his chief mode of imaginary temptation. Sex is an emergency, an out-and-out disaster, which he censures but which he vicariously and perversely enjoys. This can be seen with Roderigo in I. iii. 319 ff., or in an aside in II. i. 167 ff., where Iago comments on the gallantry of Cassio, who, in welcoming Desdemona to Cyprus, kisses her hand and converses with her. This is a significant example of an utterance as it were in top gear, which not only comments on but invades a purely formal action, replacing it with fantastic meanings. It is a process typical of Iago's contortion of the real, a process which goes beyond the tactics of temptation, thus confirming the more than instrumental nature of his imaginary creations. The passage is given here in prose, segmented into deictic orientations of a gestural and intonational character:

> [1]He takes her by the palm; [2]ay, well said, whisper: [3]as little a web as this will ensnare as great a fly as Cassio. [4]Ay, smile upon her, do: [5]I will catch you in your own courtesies: [6]you say true, 'tis so indeed. [7]If such tricks as these strip you out of your lieutenantry, it had been better you had not kiss'd your three fingers so oft, [8]which now again you are most

> apt to play the sir in: ⁹good, well kiss'd, an excellent courtesy; ¹⁰'tis so
> indeed: ¹¹yet again, your fingers at your lips? ¹²would they were clyster-
> pipes for your sake.
>
> (II. i. 167–77)

Iago always invades the *énonciations*, or the *énoncés*, or the actions of others distorting their meaning, so that every external sign becomes a simulacrum of his vision. We have here an imaginary interpretation of the action, with a series of deictic orientations which keep the rhythm of its moves, its gestures and its pauses, and which are equivalent to ostensions, fantastic direct addresses which vary the pronominal schemes: I/he-they, with an axis that directly involves the audience (1, 3); I/thou-you (2, 4, 5, 6, etc.). The first segment is an ostension or a demonstration of the action that is taking place and that he pre-tastes in keeping with the meaning he attributes to it; the second represents a formidable approach towards the scene, as if he were whispering in Cassio's ear to urge him on in performing the act; the third changes the axis again, distancing Cassio so as to indicate, presumably to the audience, how he will trap him in the semiotic system to which the action in progress leads; in the fourth segment, he approaches the 'you' again with exhortatory emphasis, ironical and morbid at once, so as to implicate him and participate vicariously in the seduction; in the fifth, the orientation is still towards 'you', but on a different level of direct address, because what is foregrounded is the predatory function of the 'I'; the sixth segment is an ironical comment; the seventh takes up in the form of direct address what has already been threatened in the third person in segment three; in the eighth, Iago brings himself close to the action again, anticipating it; in the ninth he comments on the act which in the meantime has taken place, with voyeuristic pleasure and at the same time with ironical detachment; in the tenth segment he underlines another phase immediately following it; in the eleventh he feigns surprise; in the twelfth and last he attacks the 'you' in an anal fantasy that transforms the courteous scene – already changed into an erotic scene – into a perverse exchange within which Cassio becomes the victim, punished by his own erotic signal-symbol.

It should by now be evident that the levels of Iago's utterances shift continuously, even when the referential axis appears to be the same, because he opens onto the real action an imaginary backcloth within the theatre of his mind, no less than in the shifts of interpretation into which he forces his interlocutors (in particular Othello). Thus he cannot be clear even in his own monologues: he sets up one level and then immediately jumps from it or modifies it; he cites one motive for his hatred, but then immediately produces others. He is jealous of Othello, who is supposed to have betrayed him with his wife Emilia; he is jealous of Cassio for the same reason; he is in love with Desdemona . . . Let us examine this latter revelation:

> now I do love her too,
> Not out of absolute lust, (though peradventure
> I stand accountant for as great a sin)
> But partly led to diet my revenge,
> For that I do suspect the lustful Moor
> Hath leap'd into my seat, the thought whereof
> Doth like a poisonous mineral gnaw my inwards,
> And nothing can, nor shall content my soul,
> Till I am even with him, wife, for wife:
> Or failing so, yet that I put the Moor,
> At least, into a jealousy so strong . . .
>
> (II. i. 286–96)

Iago spins his web not through the stability of the subject and the predication of a purpose, but through the very sliding, curiously decentred, of the enunciation, in a tangled syntax in which meaning never reaches firm ground but is continuously consumed, mixed and overturned, without finding an énoncé in which to rest. He uses the emphatic do (lines 281 and 286) to convince himself, but his ideas and feelings are always partial, the skiddings of a complex and evasive impulse. He claims to love Desdemona, but the claim is immediately followed by a negation which none the less only partially silences his lust (censured/unbridled), precisely because of the qualification he attaches to it: absolute. The negation almost seems to vanish in lines 287–8, but is in fact still operative in his defensive sliding, signalled at a syntactic level by the very status of the interpolated clause ('though peradventure . . .'), and at a semantic level by the concessive conjunction 'though', followed immediately by a dubitative adverb: 'though peradventure'.

This rendering opaque of sense is also due to an apparently incongruous metaphor: 'stand accountant'. Iago is accused 'for as great a sin' in the courtroom of his puritanical and schizophrenic (obscene/censuring) mind. After having affirmed, even if through negation, he derails the offered meaning by bringing out another motive, purely instrumental to his love for Desdemona: 'But partly led'. Note how his logic unfolds in keeping with his typical disjunctive syntax ('I love Desdemona, not from unbridled lust but for revenge'), which nevertheless drags along with it signals of the rejected hypothesis ('partly' places in question the disjunctive 'But' introducing the supposed 'real' motivation). Only at this point does the motive expounded in the first monologue (I. iii.) re-emerge, while the social motivation indicated to Roderigo at the outset is completely forgotten. The now-remembered motive is his jealousy regarding Emilia. But in the act of betrayal, again only 'suspected', it is not so much his wife that is present as his own usurped function: 'Hath leaped into my seat'. He feels continually robbed of his role, and thus justified in his aggressiveness. The substitution of a function in fact arouses envy of being, since the function is part of being, predicated of a subject who is and who does, and who is in *as much as* he does: thus at a more abstract and formal level of analysis, it is envy of the *énoncé*. Iago cannot identify with any situation or sign or *énoncé*, and is thus condemned to deconstruct through his own *énonciations* the *énoncés* of others, transforming them into simulacra.

Othello is precisely the lord of the *énoncé*. A cultured barbarian, used and subtly discriminated against by Venetian society, he represents himself as a humanistic and epic hero. What dominates in him is self-representation (but not in the negative and moralistic sense in which it was interpreted by Eliot and Leavis), versus the representation (for others, of others, of himself) to which Iago is bound. Othello, from his first entry on stage, trusts only in the *énoncé*:

> 'tis yet to know –
> Which, when I know that boasting is an honour,
> I shall provulgate – I fetch my life and being
> From men of royal siege, and my demerits

May speak unbonneted to as proud a fortune
As this that I have reach'd

(I. ii. 19–24)

His position is frontal, assertive, well balanced. He endeavours to transform the present into the documentary past, the precariousness of relationships into the stability of the role, of the story, of memory. This can be seen in the tale through which he won Desdemona, or at his arrival in Cyprus:

It gives me wonder great as my content
To see you here before me: O my soul's joy,
If after every tempest comes such calmness,
May the winds blow, till they have waken'd death,
And let the labouring bark climb hills of seas,
Olympus-high, and duck again as low
As hell's from heaven. If it were now to die,
'Twere now to be most happy, for I fear
My soul hath her content so absolute
That not another comfort, like to this
Succeeds in unknown fate.

(II. i. 183–93)

Even in this happy moment in which he is reunited with Desdemona after the separation at sea, Othello is not able to represent himself in the flow of the present, but he has to distance himself in some way in the security of the *énoncé*, in the transcription of the image. While Iago is condemned to a continuous mental present – of thinking, of projecting, of seducing – Othello tends to elude the present in symbolic certainties. Beneath his frontal security broods the weakness of the precariously cultured alien, of the 'stranger'. The temptation of Iago wrecks his every defence.

We can only examine the beginning of the great seduction here, when Iago and Othello enter on stage and Cassio, who is talking to Desdemona, begging her to intercede on his behalf with the Moor so that he may be reinstated to his position of lieutenant, sneaks away furtively in his embarrassment at the situation. It is one of many unpredicted acts, and signs, that Iago exploits with extreme ability:

IAGO   Ha, I like not that.
OTHELLO   What dost thou say?
IAGO   Nothing my lord, or if – I know not what.
OTHELLO   Was not that Cassio parted from my wife?
IAGO   Cassio, my lord? . . . no, sure, I cannot think it,
            That he would sneak away so guilty-like,
            Seeing you coming.
OTHELLO   I do believe 'twas he.

(III. iii. 35–41).

There is already present here the germ of the basic rhetorical strategy of the seduction. Iago begins with an exclamation designed to capture Othello's attention emotionally, and then affirms that he does not like the fact indicated by the deictic *that*. The deictic term leaves the precise sense suspended, and Othello reacts, as he will continue to do throughout, with a demand for explication of the meaning, that is for a semantic disambiguation of the deixis. Iago responds with the annulling of the deictic term ('Nothing'), only to reopen the spiral of sense with a suspended hypothesis ('or if . . .') and then to reclose this sense with a further negation ('I know *not*'). It is such reticence, entrusted, as always with Iago, to litotes and suspension, which plants the first seed of suspicion in Othello, who asks whether Cassio was not the person who crept away at their arrival – something that he already *knows*, but which has been *transformed* from a fortuitous event into *a sign of something else*, to which Iago appears to be elliptically referring. The ensign is astonished and denies, first absolutely ('no, sure') and then by tracing the negative of the image that he wishes to fix in Othello's mind: 'I cannot think it . . .'. At this point, Othello affirms emphatically ('*do* believe') what he already knew, but which has now become loaded with sinister sense.

Iago's rhetorical operations always involve referential falsifications, and as such cannot be considered only on the literary plane, but have to be appreciated within the dramatic situation. A further example, among many, of such semiotic complexity, which transforms signs into simulacra, occurs in IV. i., when Iago makes Othello decodify a dialogue of his with Cassio regarding the whore Bianca *as if* it were a dialogue on Desdemona.

The most widely used figure, litotes, may be seen here as a manifestation of the puritan code: a figure of persuasion which, by denying, affirms in the 'other' all that – the diabolical, the lustful, the alien – which it refutes or censures in the 'self'. A figure of projection, litotes is thus the emblem of the *imaginaire*. Its force is so much the greater in that it is designed to destroy its opposite, the hyperbole of Othello, for whom the codes of the adoptive civilization – especially the classical-epic-humanistic and the Christian codes – have to be magnified so as to demonstrate his definitive appropriation thereof. A figure of acculturation (introjection), hyperbole is thus the emblem of the *symbolic*.

If Iago is therefore the perverse rhetorician of the profound, Othello is the fragile bard of an idealized reality in his epic cadences that presume to exhaust reality within the bounds of the all-comprehensive *énoncé*. It might be said that for Othello even syntax is a metaphor, while for Iago even the image is a segment, a link, of a metonymic thought. *Beneath* this opposition, however, the extremes touch. There is, between these two rhetorical modes, a hidden resemblance that constitutes an important key to the understanding of the complementary relationship between the two characters. Iago is imprisoned in negation, the negation of eros, and in the void and envy of being, which he translates into litotic form in order to attack and punish the 'other'. But Othello is likewise imprisoned, in hyperbolic affirmation. They live according to opposed modes of unreality: Iago through closure to others, bourgeois-puritan *extraneity* or isolation; Othello through the weight of a manifest or hidden *discrimination*. Thus the psychological level of the play comes to coincide with the anthropological-cultural level. And the two characters look at each other as in a mirror, as the negative or positive image of the same tragic cultural mask. If Othello is the victim in dramatic terms, Iago, artificer of a destructive projection, is in turn victim at an epistemic level, namely of the very category of extraneity and of the very historical fantasies that go along with it and that he is doomed to take with him.

The two exemplary readings offered here have indicated only *some* of the possible terms of a semiotic reading of Shakespearean drama. The theoretical framework for such a reading is extremely wide and is still in an interesting phase of definition regarding (i) the very *techniques* of discursive, argumentative and rhetorical analysis and (ii) the procedures for verifying the *functional connections* between the linguistic-semantic dynamic of the text and, on the one hand, cultural models and, on the other, the theatrical realization of the drama. What is certain, however, is that Shakespearean dramaturgy remains one of the most stimulating tests for semioticians of drama, both for the theoretical returns it offers regarding dramatic operations, at the highest possible level of complexity and of semiotic polyvalency, and for the critical-interpretative paths it opens to a coherent, but at the same time problematic, textual exploration.

7

SHAKESPEARE IN IDEOLOGY[1]

James H. Kavanagh

I

... literary criticism is not an expensive luxury. To the contrary, as what has proved to be the most potent vehicle for the peddling of all sorts of ideological wares and mythologies, it is money well spent. The uses to which literary texts are put within the social process constitute the most privileged mode of reproduction and social relay of the bourgeois myths which disperse men and women into a frozen world of idealist and essentialist categories. Myths of creation, of genius, of man's essential nature, of the eternity and universality of the forms in which we express ourselves are all strongly supported in this way.

(Bennett 1979, pp. 169–70)

To discuss Shakespeare is to discuss the study of English itself. The word 'Shakespeare' is less the name of a specific historical figure, than a sign that has come to designate a vaguely defined, but fiercely defended, set of characteristics that function as the touchstone of value for what we commonly call the 'English literary tradition'. Shakespearean criticism is often less interested in analysing an historically specific practice (whether we call it a writing, a dramatic, or an ideological practice) than in presenting the products of that practice, and the proper name associated with it, as instantiating the formal strategies and substantive concerns that form the consensually defined core of all 'great literature'.

For contemporary marxism,[2] to discuss Shakespeare is to discuss the conditions and effects of a complex, changing set of ideological practices, including the historically specific practice which produced Shakespeare's plays for an Elizabethan audience, and the various specific practices which have helped produce Shakespeare as the emblem of the literary for modern readers. An ideological analysis of 'Shakespeare' is less a matter of searching out and extracting some circumscribed dimension of 'ideology in Shakespeare', than a matter of understanding how the work of an historical and discursive subject is implicated – indeed, constituted – in the history of an ideological practice. Shakespeare is in ideology(ies) at least as much as ideology is in Shakespeare, and an ideological analysis of the work inevitably becomes as well an analysis of how and why the name has become a key signifier in the ideology of the literary, whose social function Tony Bennett describes so succinctly above.

This essay uses the term ideology, as developed in Althusserian Marxism,[3] to designate a system of representations that offer the subject an imaginary, compelling, sense of reality in which crucial contradictions of self and social order appear resolved. Ideology in this sense is less a set of explicit political ideas[4] than what Althusser calls a ' "lived" . . . relation to the real' (Althusser 1970, pp. 231 ff.) – a set of pre-conscious image-concepts in which men and women see and experience, before they think about, their place within a given social formation, with its specific structure of class and gender relations. Ideology is imaginary not because it is in any sense unreal, but because it gives the subject an image that satisfies an unconscious need for coherence, an image that is in fact the specular means for constructing the subject (Althusser 1971, pp. 162 ff.; Belsey 1980, pp. 55–6). Contemporary marxism understands that the subtlest and strongest forms of ideological address are those pitched not in narrowly political or abstractly conceptual terms, but those – including what we call literature and art – pitched in concrete, overdetermined images appealing to the primary unconscious fears and desires that underpin the subject's sense of reality and identity. It is this 'reality-effect' (Macherey and Balibar 1980, p. 53) – the capacity of certain discursive and dramatic practices to disturb or displace prevailing forms of social and sexual subject-ion through an address to the unconscious – that has prompted recurring demands for the exclusion, and schemes for the management, of such practices.[5]

Of course, ideology is always politically significant, because the lived relation to the real in which it situates the subject provides the condition of political thought and practical activity, and solicits the subject's free (even if grudging) participation in a social world experienced as natural and inevitable. Ideologies address, fascinate, worry, and fix social subjects in ways appropriate to the reproduction of a given social order; they present as obvious, simple, and universal – as reality itself – what is peculiar, complex, and historically and socially specific. Thus, the ideology of the literary renders an endless stream of texts, written in diverse – even incommensurable – conditions, for divergent – even opposed – purposes, into a coherent realm of obviously meaningful and valuable works embodying shared universal truths recognizable by any thinking subject. Ideological work is always directly or indirectly affiliated with political work, constructing a realm of experience that seems to universalize and stabilize a social project serving particular class interests.

Ideology, then, is not a thing, but *a type of relation*, a relation that is 'indispensable in any society' (Althusser 1970, p. 235), and that is the product and support of a specific form of indispensable social practice. For contemporary marxism, ideological practice – along with economic, political, and theoretical practices – is one of the four major practices whose work constitutes a social formation. Each of these interrelated practices is a process of production, using raw materials (including products of the other practices), instruments of labour, and labour processes to produce specific effects necessary for the functioning and reproduction of the social whole. Each of these practices finds its condition of possibility in the others; and in complex social formations, each of the practices becomes further differentiated into a set of sub-practices or activities – like aesthetic and literary activities – whose specific effects have become important for a given social structure. In a class-divided society, ideological practices seek to offer a 'lived relation to the real' in which a conflicted social order, appropriate to particular class interests, has the force of a necessary, unified, natural structure in which subjects find their rightful place, and conflicts resolve, disappear, or are 'produced' as ratifying a given set of social relations.

A discussion of Shakespeare, then, must certainly render an account of the socio-ideological conditions of Elizabethan dramatic practice. And if there is one thing we can say about Shakespearean theatre, it is that it was not intentionally implicated in what we now call 'the literary'. Raymond Williams reminds us that 'In its modern form, the concept of "literature" did not emerge earlier than the eighteenth century and was not fully developed until the nineteenth century.' The word 'literary', he points out, 'did not acquire its specialized modern meaning until the eighteenth century', even if 'the conditions for its emergence had been developing since the Renaissance' (Williams 1977, pp. 46–7). So Shakespeare's work is more accurately 'pre-literary', at the threshold of a new practice which lacks the word that will give it a discursive ideological presence – a word (and concept) that will be produced and elaborated only in the context of modern industrial society and modern forms of class struggle.

Indeed, all drama – extending as it does beyond the bounds of language, writing and individual expression into the realms of 'properties', bodies and collective performance – fits somewhat askew within the general notion of the literary. Shakespearean theatre, which escapes both the frame of the page and the frame of the proscenium arch, seems particularly ill-suited to a modern notion of the literary associated with the careful boundaries of a formalist aesthetics. One favourite literary strategy for dealing with this problem has been to ignore it, to treat Shakespeare's work as poetry, his medium as language, and to forget all the rest. Its strong anaclitic relation to language has helped make this critical strategy so prevalent that one cannot easily get back behind it; its assumptions saturate even the ostensibly alternative 'stagecraft' commentary, which tends to produce a kind of para-literary ideological discourse. The point is not to denounce or dismiss the construction of Shakespeare as literary, but to emphasize that this work configures Shakespeare for its own ends as actively as any other, and that Shakespeare's 'literariness' as we know it is clearly produced by modern criticism, a designation of his language and practice that would be incomprehensible to a subject in Elizabethan ideology.

Thus, this essay does not share what Catherine Belsey calls the common-sense 'expressive realist' assumption, shared until recently by most marxist as well as bourgeois critics, that 'literature reflects the *reality* of experience as it is perceived by one (especially gifted) individual, who *expresses* it in a discourse which enables other individuals to recognize it as true' (Belsey 1980, p. 7). We do not seek in Shakespeare the perfect expression of a coherent literary 'truth', even one now invested with a radical or proto-socialist content, but rather the traces of a complex semio-ideological *work*, designed to resolve conflicting determinations.

Like the other figures whom we call 'authors', Shakespeare is both less in control and more active than this expressive realist ideology would have it. He is a principal – but not the only – agent of a productive ideological practice, most of whose conditions remain out of his control: the patronage system, the market/audience, the technical possibilities of the theatre, the political constraints and social ideologies in place, even the exigencies of his own personal formation. Like any other 'author', Shakespeare does not 'create' something perfect out of an evanescent mental or spiritual plasma, but is implicated in an objective material and social process, beyond the control of any individual 'consciousness' (especially in the case of theatrical production!), whose conditions he must take for granted, and whose significance or effect he cannot anticipate.

Yet Shakespeare's authorial work within this process has a definite effect, and constitutes a *productive* ideological practice that transforms the raw materials it takes up, producing a new ideological ensemble that was not there before. A text, whether conceived as 'dramatic' or 'poetic', that issues from this practice is not a transparent window on a prior universal truth that the author has seen and now allows the reader/spectator to recognize in exactly the same form; it is the material means for evoking a specific imaginary experience, associated with specific ideas in unprecedented ways – ways that even the author 'himself' cannot anticipate. An illusion of transparency may be part of the textual effect, but it is just that. Terry Eagleton's forceful presentation of ideology's relation to the literary text as analogous to the dramatic text's relation to the dramatic production is particularly apt in this context:

> The literary text is not the 'expression' of ideology, nor is ideology the 'expression' of social class. The text, rather, is a certain *production* of ideology, for which the analogy of a dramatic production is in some ways appropriate. A dramatic production does not 'express', 'reflect', or 'reproduce' the dramatic text on which it is based; it 'produces' the text, transforming it into a unique and irreducible entity. . . . Text and production are incommensurate because they inhabit distinct real and theoretical spaces.
>
> (Eagleton 1976, p. 64)

Rather than searching for the true (or false) ideas expressed by Shakespeare, then, we are interested in specifying Shakespeare's place within what Williams calls 'the conditions of emergence' of the literary, analysing in terms of class and ideology – terms that Shakespeare did not understand any more than he understood the terms of the literary – the strategy and effectivity of Shakespearean language. In Eagleton's terms, we want to understand how 'the literary text's relation to ideology so constitutes that ideology as to reveal something of its relations to history' (Eagleton 1976, p. 69). Shakespearean language is not only a significant ideological gesture within a peculiar class-conflicted conjuncture that anticipates the 'conditions of emergence' of a new, 'literary', discursive practice. It also becomes one of the primary ideological conditions of a more systematic literary ideological practice that only develops its full social potential in distinct but related socio-historical circumstances.

Concerning the situation of Elizabethan dramatic practice, one critic has aptly noted that,

> although the facts are well known, it seems still not to be well understood that the English Renaissance dramatists, Shakespeare included, were the first writers to work in the marketplace situation which has since become the characteristic social and economic condition of the literary artist.
>
> (Kernan 1982, p. 138)

Shakespeare occupied a unique proto-professional position of economic semi-independence between patronage and the market, while
still under severe ideological compulsion – dependent on the whims of
court and council, caught in an ideological space between modified
absolutism and insurgent Puritanism. This position of relative economic independence combined with relative ideological constraint
was itself the effect of a transitional alignment of classes, implying a
temporary and precarious stabilization of conflicting social projects.
The 'new aristocracy' created by Henry VIII's re-assignment of
expropriated Church property provided a fulcrum on which the Elizabethan monarchy stabilized itself, balanced between the interests of the
traditional nobility of landed estates and the rising bourgeoisie of the
towns. This situation made room for a pragmatic – i.e. politically
opportunistic and conciliationist – ideology. The traditional feudal
barons had lost significant ideological legitimacy as a result of the
prolonged and costly War of the Roses, and were losing economic
power relative to the commercial and mercantile bourgeoisie. The
image of the warrior-Lord, disdaining any education except in valor-
ous combat, whose wealth was absolutely secured by his immense
fixed landholdings and the accompanying rents, was weakening
severely under the impact of a town- (and especially seaport-) oriented
bourgeoisie, whose productive use of flexible wealth in the form of
money capital, and proto-scientific reasoning in the form of technical
innovation, gave them growing economic, and therefore political,
influence – especially since this class was increasingly taking on the
role of creditor for the aristocracy and the monarchy.

The imaginary version of the Elizabethan monarchy – a sovereign
whose absolute divine right is tempered and justified by her/his education in Christian virtue and responsibility – held dominance in this
transitional conjuncture against the centrifugal pressures of the more
'Italianate', Machiavellian absolutism of the English feudal 'princes',
often tinged with Catholic discontent, and the nascent, potentially
egalitarian, individualism of the merchants and artisans of the towns,
which took the form of Puritan and Calvinist dissidence.[6] Even
the most dramatic displays of Elizabethan power – the execution of
Mary Queen of Scots, the defeat of the Spanish Armada and the
suppression of Essex's rebellion – marked the regime as one which

held precariously in check, at the cost of undermining the monarchy's own future legitimacy, the opposed social forces that would later clash in open civil war.[7] Marxism would thus see the ideal Elizabethan 'golden age' as a conjuncture in which an expansion of capital (based largely on piracy), exogenous military victories and conciliationist ideological ensembles, worked to defer the sharpening of incipient internal contradictions.

As a playwright in this field of ideological practice, Shakespeare was obliged to forge a language and a means of representation that would satisfy a heterogeneous audience representing diverse loci of power and support. Like any other royal subject, he had to satisfy – or at least not displease – the sovereign and her court; the Queen, for good reason, was sensitive to any challenge to the legitimacy of the monarchy, and her word could put an end to Shakespeare's career, if not his life.[8] He had also to avoid the censure of the London authorities, whose Puritanism militated against any dramatic production as decadent, superstitious frivolity, and who sought excuses to close the theatres. As a new kind of ideological entrepreneur still working within traditional patronage relations of literary production, Shakespeare had to keep favour with his court patron – in this case the powerful Lord Chamberlain – who afforded the company political protection, and, literally, licence to work; at the same time, he had to hold the interest of a broad public drawn from London's mercantile, artisanal and working classes. This audience, in fact a lucrative market, was the company's main economic support, and was hungry for concrete, even sensationalistic, representations that could not help but touch on politically sensitive subjects.

Modern students, who learn that works are literary in inverse proportion to the degree that they are political, might note that such a distinction – let alone such an opposition – would have been unimaginable in such a conjuncture, where any topic was potentially sensitive, and the very act of putting on a play was a charged political statement. Neither the social life nor the language gave room for the kinds of distinctions we make among the political, the religious, the sexual, the scientific and the aesthetic. The Elizabethan subject's lived relation to the real, unlike ours, presented all these elements as immediately and inextricably unified, such that questions or transformations in any one instance reverberated in all the others. If the discourse of religion – that is, of a theologized cosmological and social theory – tended to be the master-language in which all of these subjects were discussed, at stake in it were not obstinately held *ideas* or *opinions* (as the naive sense of ideology would have it), but the very order of the real. 'Sedition' and 'heresy' did not designate abstract 'ideas' that listeners/spectators might or might not file away in the religious or political compartment of the mind, but impossible, destructive schemes for overturning immutable natural/social laws.

Shakespeare's language intervenes in this context to produce what Pierre Macherey and Etienne Balibar call a 'linguistic compromise formation' which takes up *'an unequal and contradictory relation to the same ideology* – the dominant one' (Macherey and Balibar 1980, p. 48). Shakespeare's is a self-effacing but active work that forges from disparate ideological raw materials:

> [an] imaginary solution of implacable contradictions . . . in the sense of providing a *'mise en scène'*, a *'presentation as solution'* of the very terms of an insurmountable contradiction, by means of complex displacements and substitutions.
>
> (Macherey and Balibar 1980, p. 50)

II

As an appropriate vehicle for understanding how 'displacements and substitutions' generate the kind of overdetermined compromise ideological formation so far discussed, we will provide a critique of some of the strong *turns* in the discursive and rhetorical strategies of a Shakespearean romance and a tragedy, where apparently non-political concerns predominate. We will then attempt to show how Shakespearean ideological work is transformatively subsumed in critical languages whose ostensible theme is the literary appreciation of Shakespearean discourse itself.

A Midsummer Night's Dream nicely illustrates the textual and linguistic management of significant ideological contradictions in a work whose concerns seem politically innocent. Though framed as comic romance,

A Midsummer Night's Dream has a profoundly threatening and threatened aspect; it is a play formed around questions of desire and obedience, representation and class-power, and it is haunted throughout by the threat of death. The play begins with Theseus, the Duke, admonishing Hermia, who wants to choose her own husband, and ordering her to yield to the command of her father, who 'should be as a god' (I. i. 47) to her. 'Question your desires' (I. i. 67), Theseus warns, or as Duke he will enforce the 'father's voice' (I. i. 54) in the Name of the Law, and Hermia will have 'Either to die the death, or to abjure / Forever the society of men' (I. i. 65–6).

Of course, Hermia 'consents not to give sovereignty' (I. i. 82) to the Father under any Name (even that of the Law), and with her escape to the forest, we see the consequences of a world in which everyone follows their own desires. Unlike Hippolyta, Theseus's intended (who learns properly to submit to the man who literally won her in conquest), Titania, the Queen of the Fairies, resists Oberon's 'forgeries of jealousy' (II. i. 81) and stubbornly refuses to yield to her husband/King over possession of the 'little changeling boy' (II. i. 120). In the ensuing battle for phallic and political power, Oberon's revenge gives us the sight of Titania chasing an ass, an all too apt image of a world in which, no longer ruled by the voice of the Father/King, one is all the more capriciously ruled by the power of one's passions.

Thus, *A Midsummer Night's Dream* sets up a familiar, even typical, Shakespearean theatrical landscape: desire – feminine, rebellious, deserving sympathy – challenges authority – patriarchal, hierarchical, somewhat too obsessive, but demanding and worthy of respect. At stake are the analogous orders – political *and* ontological – of the microcosm (family, father) and the macrocosm (state, sovereign; nature, reason). Then onto this stage steps yet a third group of people, from a social order rarely so active on the Shakespearean stage – a group of characters explicitly defined as artisans (a carpenter, a joiner, a weaver, a bellowsmender, a tinker and a tailor) These characters have a somewhat different problem (or is it the same?): the problem of producing an *appropriate* – that is, class-appropriate, and therefore politically acceptable – dramatic representation. For this acting company in this Shakespearean play, the issues of theatrical production are inextricably linked with the related exigencies of ideology, social class and political power:

BOTTOM Let me play the lion too. I will roar, that I will do any man's heart good to hear me. I will roar, that will make the Duke say: 'Let him roar again; let him roar again!'

QUINCE And you should do it too terribly, you would fright the Duchess and the ladies, that they would shriek: and that were enough to hang us all.

ALL That would hang us, every mother's son.

BOTTOM I grant you, friends, if you should fright the ladies out of their wits, they would have no more discretion but to hang us. But I will aggravate my voice so, that I will roar you as gently as any sucking dove; I will roar you an 'twere any nightingale.

(I. ii. 66–78)

This dialogue functions as a kind of internal commentary on Shakespearean ideological practice. The problematic of proto-professional ideological production denied autonomous political weight in a society struggling to preserve the hegemony of an aristocratic class-ideology is here displayed in order to be ridiculed. Shakespeare's artisans pose the issues quite clearly in their discussion: for us to assert an effective ability to manipulate their sense of reality, for us to disrupt their lived relation to the real, would be an unacceptable usurpation of ideological power, possibly punishable by death; we must temper our dramatic practice, restrain its effect, and inscribe in it the marks of our own submission. That the noble lords and ladies laugh at these players' fear only confirms the political and ideological conditions which make it possible. The anxious emergence of an increasingly sophisticated manipulation of the reality-effect, culminating in what we call bourgeois realism, is partly defined by this sense of the unforeseeable consequences of us making them scream, or of getting the 'gentle' ladies over-excited.

These workers attempt to solve their problem by inventing a strategy that will break the illusion of transparency, and display the conditions of active ideological production, in a first version of the estrangement-effect:

BOTTOM Masters, you ought to consider with yourself; to bring in (God shield us!) a lion among ladies is a most dreadful thing; for

> there is not a more fearful wild-fowl than your lion living; and we
> ought to look to't.
>
> SNOUT Therefore another prologue must tell he is not a lion.
>
> BOTTOM Nay, you must name his name, and half his face must be
> seen through the lion's neck; and he himself must speak through,
> saying thus, or to the same defect: 'Ladies', or 'Fair ladies, I would
> wish you,' or 'I would request you,' or 'I would entreat you, not to
> fear, not to tremble: my life for yours! If you think I come hither as a
> lion, it were pity of my life. No, I am no such thing; I am a man, as
> other men are': and there, indeed, let him name his name, and tell
> them plainly he is Snug the joiner.
>
> (III. i. 28–44)

This strategy, of course, is actually an inversion of the Brechtian alienation aesthetic, displaying the conditions of ideological production –
of dramatic effect and 'defect'[9] – not in order to enable a working-class
audience intelligently to assert its political power, but to enable this
workers' troupe to *escape* the political power of a ruling class. And while
Shakespeare's fortuitous choice of 'pre-working class' characters in *A
Midsummer Night's Dream* might foreshadow for us the more modern
contradictions on which later literary ideologies will work, in his context, the image of artisanal workers comically undercuts any sense of
real threat, precisely because they are so marginal and politically impo-
tent within the dominant *ideology* (if increasingly strong within the
changing *economy*) of his social formation (as were women and slaves
for Plato and Aristotle). Thus, we do not use these figures to invoke a
non-existent contemporaneous 'working-class', but a real, nascent
bourgeois ideological practice, emerging under the contradictory conditions of economic independence and political submission described
above. This scene serves as an emblem of how the play itself speaks, in a
more surreptitious voice, a double discourse to a fractured audience,
taking up an '*unequal and contradictoy relation to the same*' dominant
modified aristocratic ideology.

A Midsummer Night's Dream reconciles all of the heterogeneous subject
positions it addresses to each other, under the general domination of
the sovereign Subject. Drawing ideological raw materials from both
insurgent bourgeois-individualist and entrenched feudal-absolutist

discourses, the play explicitly acknowledges the precariousness of its situation and the potential subversive implications of its own ideological work. The play then continues that work, in the form of a submission to its aristocratic audience,[10] finally trivializing any threat with a comic resolution that magically reconciles rebellious 'feminine' and individualist desire to a rigid social hierarchy of aristocratic and patriarchal privilege. It is its supple capacity to achieve such a reconciliation effect that will make Shakespearean language, as suggested below, a prime constituent of the recognition pattern for what we call 'literature':

> For there to be literature, the very terms of [a social] contradiction . . . must be enunciated at the outset in a special language, . . . realizing *in advance* the fiction of their forthcoming conciliation – a language of 'compromise' which presents the conciliation as 'natural', and ultimately as necessary and inevitable.
>
> (Macherey and Balibar 1980, p. 50)

This compromise-effect is accentuated by the relatively 'closed' comic frame of a work like *A Midsummer Night's Dream*, where the conflicting projects of desire and authority are reconciled in the plot by Puck's literally magical deflection of Demetrius's interest from Hermia to Helena. But, as Macherey and Balibar suggest (and as Bottom and Snug worry), it is not in a work's plot, but in its language and means of representation, that the primary conditions of an ideological unifying effect are forged. The tragic structure, with its more discomfiting dénouement, does tend to relatively 'open' and ambivalent resolutions of action; but even in the gloomiest of Shakespearean tragedies, where the plot offers a seemingly unrelieved compendium of cruelty and loss, the language still works to produce this ideological compromise-effect.

In *King Lear*, for example, the microcosm and macrocosm are disrupted by another crisis of the patriarchal and political order, with the sovereign himself substituting stubborn vanity for the authority of his position. In the face of Lear's confusion of self-aggrandizement with respect for natural/social Order, Cordelia quietly asserts her love, 'According to my bond; no more nor less' (I. i. 93). Lear's related tyranny and incestuousness (marked by Cordelia's telling 'Sure I shall never marry like my sisters, / To love my father all' (I. i. 103–4)), Gloucester's weakness and adultery, and both fathers' misrecognition of real loyalty, are symptoms of an individualist ideology that lives the world as a field of calculation, self-gratification and perverse desire. This ideology passes from the sovereign/father to the subjects/children, and – the real danger! – returns intensified to destroy the patriarchal order itself, in a cycle that reaches its nadir with Regan and Goneril's debasement of Lear, and Edmund's symbolic castration of Gloucester. Counterposed to this is the hierarchical ideology of fealty, faith and restraint, which lives the world as a field of reciprocal obligation. This ideology recognizes the 'real' order of familial-social-natural relations, which Kent and Edgar work to restore with their unfailing service, and Cordelia upholds with her consistent and *appropriate* love. Indeed, Cordelia's 'Happily when I shall wed, / That lord whose hand must take my plight shall carry / Half my love with him, half my care and duty' (I. i. 100–2), is perhaps the most clear-sighted affirmation of the Order that underpins Sovereignty.

King Lear effectively *hurls* these two ideologies against each other, in what is here certainly no clash of mere opinions but of whole modes of living – what the play constantly defines as opposed 'Natures'.[11] As Lear is crushed between the two, he becomes the focus of sympathy and what Macherey and Balibar call, after Brecht, 'identification', the mechanism by which

> the ideological effects of literature (and the theatre . . .) materialize via an identification process between the reader or the audience and the hero or anti-hero – the simultaneous mutual constitution of the fictive 'consciousness' of the character and the ideological 'consciousness' of the reader.
>
> (Macherey and Balibar 1980, p. 51)

Lear, as character rather than king, becomes the vehicle for another kind of 'subjection', evoking an ideological subjectivity in which the reader/spectator can 'live' an imaginary resolution of irreconcilable class projects.

One pole of the position he occupies has – especially for the modern reader, who sees it differently than did Shakespeare's contemporaries –

a universal empathetic appeal; this is the position of the degraded old man cast into the elements, victim of and witness to a world in which cruelty and egotism reign. This aspect of Lear, echoed in the play by Gloucester, makes sharp criticism of the anarchic world of isolated, calculating egos that is the feudal ideology's image of a society ruled by greed and the minds of fallen men. And the play elicits identification with this attack on the spectre of a bourgeois ethic by reducing Lear to common humanity, the 'unaccommodated man . . . poor, bare, forked animal' (III. iv. 109–10), by making him learn the value of dispossession, of 'Nothing'.[12] This is a strikingly egalitarian ideological move, especially as negatively reinforced by Regan's vicious class invective and violence, directed against her rebellious servant: 'A peasant stand up thus. [*Takes a sword and runs at him behind*.]' (III. vii. 79, seconded by Cornwall's 'throw this slave / Upon the dunghill' in 95–6).

But egalitarianism is finally more at home within bourgeois republican than within aristocratic Christian humanism, and *King Lear* appropriates egalitarianism for the latter only in order to try to occupy and *control* – in a conjuncture that still allows such a manoeuvre – a strategically important ideological terrain. The play attempts to incorporate the strongest element of bourgeois ideology in its language and images as an unequal, dominated element of a transformed aristocratic ideology – one that is now stronger for its unprecedented unitary cast and universalized appeal, but one also now attached to a discourse which can only undermine that ideology's own legitimacy.

Lear's famous plea – certainly one of the play's most effective catalysts of identification, and, significantly, one of the most quoted – exemplifies this discursive strategy of ideological reconciliation through domination:

> O! reason not the need; our basest beggars
> Are in the poorest things superfluous:
> Allow not nature more than nature needs,
> Man's life is cheap as beast's. Thou art a lady;
> If only to go warm were gorgeous,
> Why, nature needs not what thou gorgeous wear'st,
> Which scarcely keeps thee warm.
>
> (II. iv. 266–72)

In this passage, Lear speaks in a language to which everyone can assent, but which has a different meaning for each. An adequate notion of human needs must go beyond the requirements of subsistence: everyone 'needs' more than she/he *needs*. The 'basest beggar's' 'need' for more than bread becomes an image of and thus a discursive 'production' of Lear's 'need' to retain his royal perquisites. The quite specific address to Regan as an aristocratic subject – 'Thou art a lady', where 'lady' means a woman of a certain *class* – is conflated with the universalized address to 'everyman' who wants a life better than the beast's. Every class subject finds an equally comfortable imaginary place in this discourse, a discourse that effaces the less comfortable real inequality of place that it assumes and confirms. Just as rich man and poor man are equally free to sleep under bridges, so king and beggar are equally deserving of more than they 'need'.

What could have been a discourse historicizing the concept of 'human need' and relating the aspirations of all social subjects to the given level of material and cultural development, becomes part of an argument for the specific privileges of a ruling class, seen as needs within the context of a necessarily hierarchical cosmological and social order. But of course, one has *either* a universal concept of need tied to the satisfaction of all human subjects, *or* a variable concept of need tied to specific classes within a natural hierarchy.[13] These discourses are really incompatible and are only made imaginarily compatible in ideology, as a result of ideological work. As Macherey and Balibar remark:

> The text is produced under conditions which represent it as a finished work, displaying an essential order, expressing either a subjective theme or the spirit of the age, according to whether the reading is a naive or sophisticated one. Yet, in itself, the text is none of these; on the contrary, it is materially incomplete, disparate and incoherent, since it is the conflicted, contradictory effect of superimposing real processes which cannot be abolished in it except in an imaginary way.
> (Macherey and Balibar 1980, pp. 49–50)

The staying power of *King Lear*, and of Shakespeare's work in general, is partly a result of its fearlessness in representing and giving discursive space to such opposed ideological elements. This also destabilizes the reconciliation effect that the text seeks to achieve within a given cultural ideology. The achievement of the appropriate effect with a text that opens itself so to insurgent ideological positions becomes more heavily reliant on the context of extra-textual ideological, political, and economic practices that surround and enmesh the text, and manage its consumption. The Christian-feudal 'skew' of *King Lear's* ideological effect is part of its relation to a contemporary audience that bathes in an atmosphere of discourses and tropes which still tend to refract all ideological light at this angle. For a modern audience, which bathes in an ideological atmosphere of post-existentialist discourses and images that render this skew invisible, the textual ensemble seems dominated by those elements that support a culturally familiar reductive humanism. The dramatic visibility of the contradictions on which *King Lear* works makes it a text that fixes an ideological position only tenuously, and that is susceptible to a critical embarrassment of its ideological *activity* – the kind of text that is certainly:

> not so much the *expression* of ideology (its 'putting into words' [*sa mise en mots*] as its *staging* [*mise en scène*], its display – an operation in which ideology turns against itself in a certain manner, since it cannot be thus displayed without revealing its *limits*, at the precise point where it proves itself unable to subsume a hostile ideology.
>
> (Macherey and Balibar 1980, p. 50)

III

In the late eighteenth and early nineteenth century, when 'literature' was invented, the English bourgeoisie may have secured economic, political *and* ideological hegemony, but it did so only at the price of its own appropriation of aristocratic elements in all these practices. In a sense, the Elizabethan situation was reversed: aristocratic ideology now became the 'unequal, dominated' aspect of an ideology that helped to naturalize the bourgeois social order. The nascent ideological practice of literary criticism found in Shakespearean language a particularly appropriate raw material, which it eagerly worked into a virtual template for identifying and reproducing the literary. We can briefly look at how a few representative critical practices render the constituent contradictions and tensions of Shakespearean language invisible, and produce it as a truly author-itative voice for the needs of a developing literary ideology, supporting a remarkably analogous – but different![14] – social compromise, and a new kind of patriarchal aristocracy of discourse. In this sense, we are pursuing Macherey and Balibar's suggestive point that much critical commentary can be understood as 'resuming' or repeating, rather than analysing, the ideological work it addresses:

> it is possible (and necessary) when analyzing the literary effect . . . to treat as equivalents the 'reader' and the 'author'. Also equivalent are the 'intentions' of the author . . . and the interpretations, criticisms, and commentaries evoked from its more or less sophisticated readers.
>
> It is not important to know whether the interpretation 'really' identifies the author's intention (since the latter is not the cause of literary effects but is one of the effects). Interpretations and commentaries reveal the literary aesthetic effect precisely in full view.
>
> Freud was the first to follow this procedure in his account of the dream-work and . . . in his method of analyzing the compromise formations of the unconscious; he defined what must be understood by the 'text' of the dream. He gave no importance to . . . a careful isolated reconstruction of the 'real' dream. Or at least he accedes to it only through the intermediary of an 'account of the dream' which is *already* a transposition through which (via condensation, displacement and dream symbolism) the repressed material continues to work itself out. He also considered as the text of the dream – simultaneously the object for analysis and explanation, and, through its very contradictions, the means of its own explanation – not just the initial manifest text, the account of the dreamer, but also *all* the 'free' associations (i.e. the forced associations imposed by the psychic conflicts of the unconscious), the 'latent thoughts' for which the dream-account (or symptom) can serve as a pretext and which it arouses.
>
> In the same way, critical discourse – the discourse of literary ideology, an endless commentary of the 'beauty' and 'truth' of literary texts – is a train of 'free' associations (in actuality, forced and predetermined) which develops and realizes the ideological effects of a literary text. In a materialist account of the text, such a discourse must be

taken not as located *above* the text, as the beginnings of its explication, but as *at the same* level as the text, or, more precisely, at the same level as the 'surface' narrative. . . . Such a criticism constitutes the tendential prolongation of this facade. Regardless of any question of the *individuality* of the 'writer', the 'reader' or the 'critic', it is the same ideological conflicts, resulting in the last instance from the same historical contradictions, or from their transformations, that produce the form of the text and its commentaries.

(Macherey and Balibar 1980, p. 57)

Samuel Johnson's *Preface to Shakespeare* certainly occupies an important place as part of a corpus of writing that almost forms a Preface to English literary criticism itself. In one sense, Johnson's critical practice takes up where Shakespeare's dramatic practice left off – at a point when an ethic of propriety and order in criticism is in conflictual balance with the ethic of intense creativity that will ultimately displace it. As Johnson is still very much committed to the neo-classical rules of literary decorum, and more interested in preserving established aesthetic order than in promoting individualist expressive genius, he has a decidedly less 'enthusiastic' view of Shakespeare than later critics who want to enlist him as a founding father of post-Romantic authorial creativity. For Johnson, Shakespeare has 'faults sufficient to obscure and overwhelm any other merit' (Johnson 1977, p. 307), but has, among other 'excellencies', the distinction of being 'one of the original masters of the language' (ibid.). This virtue derives from Shakespeare's knack for reproducing what for Johnson is the common or natural language of men, 'a certain mode of phraseology so consonant and congenial to the analogy and principles of its respective language as to remain settled and unaltered' (Johnson 1977, p. 306). Johnson's Shakespeare catches a pitch of discourse 'above grossness and below refinement' that 'is probably to be sought in the common intercourse of life, among those who speak only to be understood, without ambition of elegance' (ibid.).

Johnson thus appropriates Shakespearean language as an aspect of a distinctly middle-class discursive (and social) order, one concerning which Johnson seems to have many ambivalences; and Johnson's 'Shakespeare' becomes an ideological vehicle for working these tensions through to a tenuous resolution in Johnson's own discourse. This critical 'Shakespeare' lacks decorum, flouts the unities, and must be given 'some allowance for his ignorance' (Johnson 1977, p. 314); but he also 'always makes nature predominate over accident' (Johnson 1977, p. 303), and 'holds up to his readers a faithful mirror of language and life' (Johnson 1977, p. 301). In Johnsonian critical discourse, then, Shakespearean language resumes its function as a vehicle for reconciling different class-affiliated ideologies, with dominance increasingly, if grudgingly, ceded to that which is now recognized to regulate efficiently 'the common intercourse of life'.

Coleridge's critical attitude to Shakespeare seems the very opposite of Johnson's. Coleridge does not want 'to oppose genius to rules' (Coleridge 1951, p. 432), but to insist on the intrinsic lawfulness of 'true' genius: 'No work of true genius dares want its appropriate form. . . . As it must not, so genius can not, be lawless' (p. 432). For Coleridge, 'that criticism of Shakespeare will alone be genial'[15] which is reverential' (p. 430), since Shakespearean poetry is the perfect exemplar of 'organic form', that 'innate' form which 'shapes, as it develops, itself from within, and the fulness of [whose] development is one and the same with the perfection of its outside form' (pp. 432–3). Shakespearean poetry is like Nature itself, where 'each exterior is the physiognomy of the being within', and Shakespeare is 'himself a nature humanized, a genial understanding directly self-consciously a power and an implicit wisdom deeper even than our consciousness'[16] (p. 433).

Of course, Coleridge's critical discourse is the paradigm of Romantic, expressivist aesthetic ideology. But his 'true' (genius), 'organic' (form), adding up finally to 'legitimate' poem, (Coleridge 1983, II, p. 13), legislate fully as much as Johnson's 'rules', although it is now the 'synthetic and magical power . . . of imagination' found in the 'poetic genius itself' (II, pp. 15–6) that guarantees a work's poeticity. This power of imagination is 'magical' because it is no less than a 'repetition in the finite mind of the eternal act of creation' (I, p. 304); it is 'synthetic' because it 'struggles to idealize and unify' (I, p. 304), 'fusing' disparate poetic faculties 'according to their relative worth and dignity' (II, p. 16), 'subordinat[ing] art to nature' (II, p. 17), and 'reveal[ing] itself in the balance or reconciliation of opposite or discordant qualities' (II, p. 16). For Coleridge, then, Shakespeare's work is the instantiation of this synthetic imaginative power, the perfect outward form manifesting the inner nature of poetry.

But Coleridge's discussion of Shakespeare as the literary model of organic form is part of an ongoing ideological work, producing an empiricist-idealist[17] discourse that finally has a political point – namely to assert the 'organic' rationality-reality of a specific 'fusion' of *social classes*. As Shakespeare's language is the perfect manifestation in English of the 'fusing', 'organic' imagination, so for Coleridge, the English Constitution is the perfect manifestation of the 'idea' of a state, 'so connatural and essential to the genius and innate disposition of this nation, it being formed (silk-worm like) as that no other law can possibly regulate it' (Coleridge 1976, p. 22). Just as the power of poetic imagination 'reveals itself in the balance or reconciliation of opposite or discordant qualities', so the state's 'principle of unity within itself' (p. 23) is manifested in a Constitution that balances 'the two antagonistic powers or opposite interests of the state . . . those of PERMANENCE AND PROGRESSION' (p. 24) – that is, the landed and bourgeois classes with their respective dependents (pp. 25–6). In Coleridge, then, 'Shakespeare' becomes the ideological condition of yet another discourse of ruling-class compromise and political stability.

By the twentieth century, literary and dramatic ideological practices have the task of effectively representing, under generalized conditions of more liberally-regulated (i.e. market- rather than court-dominated) 'free' competition among ideological entrepreneurs, the contradictions of a capitalist society to mass audiences without arousing radical ideological disaffection or the suppressed political power of the dominated working classes. Under these changing conditions of ideological production, the task of managing the accelerated dispersal of ideological power and effect becomes increasingly subtle, and almost completely divorced from discourses of explicit hierarchical order. 'Genius' entirely replaces 'rules' as the criterion and imaginary ground of aesthetic value, and literary ideology increasingly needs to reconcile an arbitrary authorial agent's/text's ability intensely to manipulate the real and our perceptions of it, with the same agent's/text's ability finally to stabilize heterogeneous social subjects in a fixed relation to an eternal, natural *and* transcendent, cultural reality. It is in such a conjuncture that we can find a statement like Northrop Frye's provocative remark that 'Shakespeare has no opinions, no values, no philosophy, no principles of anything except dramatic structure' (Frye 1965, p. 39).

One might say that the last thing Shakespeare had any opinions about was 'dramatic structure' in the sense that Northrop Frye uses the notion, invested as it now is with two hundred years of a discourse on the literary and the aesthetic whose most basic terms could not be uttered until two hundred years after Shakespeare wrote-acted-staged-made money – and thought about all those things. 'Dramatic structure' in Frye's sentence is unutterable and unreadable, and the concept it evokes unimaginable, by any Shakespeare but Frye's own. But what is most interesting is the way Frye himself tells us this, and the extra-literary point that is on display, but unnoticed, in his discourse. In preparation for making the above statement, Frye insists that 'His [Shakespeare's] chief motive in writing, apparently, was to make money'; this motive Frye goes on to treat as having no effect at all, other than to provide transparent access to the literary, as he continues the sentence: 'which is the best motive for writing yet discovered, as it creates exactly the right blend of detachment and concern' (Frye 1965, p. 38).

Frye's Shakespeare thus becomes a celebratory icon of a modern notion of the literary as governed at once by detachment and commerce (as if these were 'naturally' congruent). In this discourse, 'Shakespeare' is a discursive operator for reconciling autonomy with realism (in both text and author) within a modern ideology of the literary. Thus, Frye also says that 'It is consistent with Shakespeare's perfect objectivity that he should show no signs of wanting to improve his audience's tastes, or to address the more instructed members of it with a particular intimacy' (Frye 1965, p. 38). This certainly describes a real and important characteristic of Shakespearean dramatic practice. It is not, however, a characteristic that marks Shakespeare as a 'perfectly object-ive' 'great poet' (p. 39) but one that marks him as not at all implicated in the 'Literature' which is reproduced by such terms precisely as a practice that addresses its more sophisticated audience 'with a particu-lar intimacy'. Frye's Shakespeare is subsumed within an imaginary order of virtually perfect 'authors' and 'texts', two 'necessary illusions inscribed in the ideology of literature that accompanies all literary production' (Macherey and Balibar 1980, p. 49).

As Shakespearean practice uneasily produced a discourse of 'man' within a unified social order that echoed a necessary order of Nature, modern critical practice unfailingly produces a discourse of 'Shakespeare' as the origin of a coherence grounded in fidelity to an equally peculiar nature and its natural language – even if now the ironic motive of such faith is 'to make money'. Shakespeare is, as he always was, in ideology.

8

DISRUPTING SEXUAL DIFFERENCE

Meaning and gender in the comedies

Catherine Belsey

I

Meaning, Saussure argued, is an effect of difference. And if post-structuralism has moved beyond Saussure's diagrams, which seemed to imply a single meaning for every unit of language, every signifier, it has not abandoned the most radical principle of Saussurean theory, that meaning depends not on the referent, not on intention, but only on the relations of difference between one term and another within the language. Subsequently we have come to see meaning as unfixed, always in process, always plural. This is a result first of the analysis of language itself as the location of distinct discourses (or knowledges), sets of terms and relations between terms in which a specific understanding of the world is inscribed. And secondly it takes account of the argument that meaning is never fully present in an individual utterance but is always deferred, always provisional, precisely because it is dependent on the relations of difference between this term and all the other terms which constitute the language and which are by definition absent.

The problem with the meanings that we learn – and learn to produce – is that they seem to define and delimit what is thinkable, imaginable, possible. To fix meaning, to arrest its process and deny its plurality, is in effect to confine what is possible to what is. Conversely, to disrupt this fixity is to glimpse alternative possibilities. A conservative criticism reads in quest of familiar, obvious, common-sense meanings, and thus reaffirms what we already know. A radical criticism, however, is concerned to produce readings which challenge that knowledge by revealing alternative meanings, disrupting the system of differences which legitimates the perpetuation of things as they are. The project of such a criticism is not to replace one authoritative interpretation of a text with another, but to suggest a plurality of ways in which texts might be read in the interests of extending the reach of what is thinkable, imaginable or possible.

I want to suggest that Shakespearean comedy can be read as disrupting sexual difference, calling in question that set of relations between terms which proposes as inevitable an antithesis between masculine and feminine, men and women. But in order to do so I need first to draw attention to the context of this disruption, the opposition in the sixteenth and seventeenth centuries between two distinct meanings of the family. Women, then as now, were defined in relation to men and in terms of their relations with men. A challenge to the meaning of the family is a challenge to these relations and in consequence to the meaning of what it is to be a woman.

II

The setting is a domestic interior. On the back wall is a handsome clock. There are dishes on a carved sideboard and a ewer stands beside a couple of books on the window sill. On the floor in the foreground there are three or four more books and a low stool. The drawing shows Sir Thomas More, Chancellor of England, surrounded by his family. The artist gave it to Erasmus, who wrote to More, 'I cannot put into words the deep pleasure I felt when the painter Holbein gave me the picture of your whole family, which is so completely successful that I

should scarcely be able to see you better if I were with you'
(Pope-Hennessy 1966, pp. 99–100).

The drawing was a sketch for (or perhaps of) a painting, eight feet
high and thirteen feet wide, executed in 1527 and now lost (Morison
1963, pp. 18–28). Its mode, as Erasmus indicates, is realist – which is
to say illusionist. As the names and ages recorded below the drawing
make clear, it seems to portray a specific moment in the More house-
hold, probably Sir Thomas's fiftieth birthday. The family are in various
positions of relative informality. Margaret Giggs, More's adopted
daughter, shows old Judge More something in a book. Margaret Roper,
the Chancellor's eldest, most devoted and most learned daughter, sits
on the floor with a book open on her lap. She looks towards her sister,
Elizabeth, who returns her gaze. Young John, More's heir, is absorbed
in his reading. Dame Alice, Sir Thomas's second wife, and not the
mother of the children, kneels at a prie-dieu on the extreme right.
Cecily, holding a book and a rosary, looks towards her. None of the
figures, with the possible exception of the Fool, Henry Pattenson,
meets the spectator's gaze. We occupy a position outside the self-
contained world of the picture: the family are not aware of us and do
not address themselves to us.

Thomas More's family is an intimate, informal, affective unit. The
picture shows it inhabiting a private world of domesticity, piety and
learning. It is also a dynastic unit. Sir Thomas More, wearing his chain
of office, sits at the centre with his father on his right and his only son,
John, on his left. In the background is Anne Cresacre, who was to
marry John, thus ensuring the continuity of the line. In the sixteenth
and early seventeenth centuries these two meanings of the family – as
dynasty and as private realm of warmth and virtue – are both in play
and indeed in contest. In 1527 and for many years to come it was the
dynastic meaning which was dominant. Holbein's drawing, like so
many of the productions of the Sir Thomas More circle, seems to
anticipate the meanings of a later period.

In 1593 Thomas More II, grandson of the Chancellor, commissioned
Rowland Lockey to produce a painting modelled on Holbein's. In
Lockey's picture the domestic arrangements have been brought up to
date. The clock remains in position, but green hangings cover the
panelling. Lutes and flower arrangements replace the jugs and basins.

Figure 1 Hans Holbein the Younger, *Sir Thomas More, 1478–1535, and his family,* 1527

More, his father, his children and his daughter-in-law have been moved to the left of the picture. They are copied from the original, though Elizabeth now sits behind Margaret so that both of them, instead of looking at each other, gaze vacantly into space. Margaret Giggs, Alice More and the Fool have been eliminated. On the wall is a portrait of Anne Cresacre, More's daughter-in-law, painted in about 1560. She thus appears twice in Lockey's painting, aged 15 and 48. On either side of her portrait are coats of arms, and below them in a stiff little group sit her son, Thomas More II, his wife Mary, and two of their sons, John and Cresacre. They hold missals. All four of them stare challengingly back at the spectator. They make an odd contrast with the previous three generations copied from Holbein, because although the rearrangement of the figures and the elimination of those who played no genealogical part in the history of the Mores have removed the sense of intimacy and relationship, the early members of the family remain apparently unaware that they are being watched, while their descendants are clearly sitting to have their portraits painted. There is no interaction between them, or between the two groups.

They sit, what is more, with a certain defiance. The Mores had remained staunchly but quietly Catholic throughout the religious upheavals of the sixteenth century. In 1582 Thomas II had been imprisoned for four years. He was released in 1586 but remained under surveillance. The More family in the painting he commissioned is a dynastic and ideological unit. The illusion of a private moment of informality has given way to a declaration of unbroken allegiance to Catholicism through five generations. There is no identifiable moment of this painting. Sir Thomas More had been dead for nearly sixty years when the dynastic meaning of the family was thus invoked by the threatened Catholic descendants of a Catholic martyr.

The Lockey painting is an interesting variant on a familiar theme of the sixteenth century. Thomas More I is shown surrounded by his daughters, with Margaret very much in the foreground of the drawing. Thomas More II did not allocate any space in the picture for his daughters, though their names and ages were recorded on the inscription in the bottom left-hand corner. Sitters for portraits in sixteenth-century England were most commonly men, of course – men of property, or their heirs, or men of property and their heirs (the picture of Sir Walter

Figure 2 Rowland Lockey, partly after Holbein, *Sir Thomas More, 1478–1535, with his family and Descendants*, 1593

Raleigh and his eldest son in the National Portrait Gallery is a charming instance: the child, aged about nine, precisely replicates the pose of his father). Women are important when they are sovereigns, as the many portraits of Elizabeth testify. Otherwise they are significant mainly as wives who guarantee the continuity of the dynasty. Anne Cresacre features twice in Lockey's painting, though in neither case is she anywhere near the foreground.

Holbein's mural of Henry VIII and his family, completed ten years after the original More picture, showed Henry massive, legs astride, 'a fantastic amalgam of the static and the swaggering' (Strong 1967, p. 39), standing in front of the altogether more ethereal figure of his father, Henry VII. The body of the reigning prince is identified as the location and evidence of his power. According to a seventeenth-century copy which has survived, on the other side of a stone altar Jane Seymour, hands clasped demurely before her, stood in front of Henry's mother, Elizabeth of York. Jane has no dynasty. Her presence is authorized by her part in the occasion of the painting, the birth of the heir to the throne. He is not represented, since it is what he is to be and not the affection between parents and child which signifies. (Contrast Princes William and Harry, loved, petted and dandled in twentieth-century royal photographs.) Indeed, Jane herself may have been dead by the time the mural was installed in the Privy Chamber at Whitehall. It wouldn't have mattered. Henry VII and Elizabeth of York were dead too. All three had done their work in ensuring the continuity of the Tudors. In another portrait of Henry VIII's family, probably painted in 1545, Prince Edward sits on the king's right, Jane Seymour, now dead for about eight years, and succeeded by three subsequent wives, is shown on his left (Millar 1963, Text vol., p. 64). She, not the current queen Catherine Parr, was the mother of the heir.

In Holbein's mural Henry VIII meets the spectator's gaze – requiring obedience. Henry VII stares into the distance, perhaps visualizing his descendants in a line stretching out to the crack of doom. The two queens look at their husbands. Both sexually and politically the body of the prince exacts submission. Henry VIII, the image of absolute monarchy, is also the image of absolute patriarchy.

The place of the woman in the dynastic family is clear and well known, and is perfectly defined in Katherine's final speech in *The Taming* of the Shrew: 'Such duty as the subject owes the prince / Even such a woman oweth to her husband' (V. ii. 156–7). Sovereignty in marriage precisely resembles sovereignty in the state, and both are absolute. Men, Luciana explains in The Comedy of Errors, 'are masters to their females, and their lords' (II. i. 24). Wives 'are bound to serve, love, and obey' (The Taming of the Shrew, V. ii. 165). The perfect wife is 'meek and patient', 'pliant and duteous' as in Heywood's A Woman Killed with Kindness, I. 37–41. Her model is the silent and uncomplaining Griselda, whose story was retold several times in the sixteenth and early seventeenth centuries,[1] and was perhaps reworked in The Winter's Tale, where Hermione too loses both her children through her husband's tyranny, bears it patiently and is finally reunited with her family, though in this case Florizel stands in for Mamillius.

But there begins to be, as Holbein's drawing of the More family indicates, an alternative meaning for the family in the sixteenth century. In the intimate, affective realm which comes into being with the emergence of a set of differences between work and leisure, public and private, political and domestic, the place of both women and children is newly defined. The home comes to be seen as a self-contained unit, a little world of retreat from the conflicts of the market-place, and at the same time a seminary of good subjects, where the wife enters into partnership with her husband in the inculcation of love, courtesy and virtue in their children. The affective marriage is necessarily founded on consent and harmony. As one of the guests tells the happy bridegroom of A Woman Killed with Kindness, 'There's music in this sympathy, it carries/Consort and expectation of much joy' (I. 69–70).

A painting of 1628 shows something of the meaning of the new family. In a not very clearly defined natural setting, perhaps a leafy glade, the Duke of Buckingham sits beside his wife. From the positions of their shoulders we can judge that their hands would touch, if it were not for the fact that hers are occupied with the child on her lap. One-year-old George smiles as he leans towards his sister, Mary, who holds out to him the flowers in her apron. Katharine, wife and mother, dressed in yellow silk, is at the glowing centre of the canvas, though the Duke is nearer to us, and taller. The Duchess's literary models are not Griselda and Hermione, but Lady Macduff and the Duchess of Malfi, loving mothers of families whose innocence and affection constitute

Figure 3 Painting after Gerard Honthorst, *George Villiers, 1st Duke of Buckingham, 1592–1628, and his Family*, 1628

evidence for the audience of the wanton tyranny of those who destroy them. If it were not that both parents look out of the canvas at the spectator, this family could belong equally to the nineteenth century, the great age of the naturalized affective family, or indeed to the twentieth, where the family is once again a site of struggle, this time between conservatives and feminists.

The picture constitutes evidence that the new meaning of the family was neither exclusively 'Puritan' nor exclusively bourgeois: the Duke of Buckingham's worst enemies could hardly have accused him of belonging to either category. I do not intend to imply that the emergence of another meaning for the family has nothing to do with the Reformation or the rise of mercantile capitalism. On the contrary. But textual history, the history of meanings, is more complex, more contradictory, more deeply interwoven with the history of the whole social formation than traditional studies in the history of ideas or traditional Marxist economism would seem to imply. My primary concern in this essay is to attempt to trace the complexity and the implications of these meanings themselves rather than to locate their origins. Or perhaps one of these meanings. The new definition of the family entails a new definition of the relationship between husband and wife, a new understanding of the woman's place.

The new meaning of the family needs even less elaboration than the old, since it is familiar to us from countless nineteenth-century novels and twentieth-century breakfast-cereal advertisements. It is the meaning of the family which most of us have lived, or guiltily failed to live. It involves marriage based on romantic love and co-operation between parents to bring up their children as happy, productive and responsible members of society. The place of the woman in the affective family is now, therefore, that of a partner and companion to her husband, joined with him in 'a communion of life' (Smith 1591, p. 9), a source, as Milton was to put it, of 'apt and cheerfull conversation' (Milton 1959, p. 235). In the absolutist, dynastic meaning of marriage women were everything that men were not: silent, submissive, powerless. But in the marriage of true minds, where romantic love is not simply an adolescent aberration but the cement of a life-long relationship, men and women are alike – 'not always', as Donne explained in a marriage sermon, 'like in complexion, nor like in years, nor like in fortune, nor like in birth, but like in minde, like in disposition, like in the love of God, and of one another' (Donne 1957, p. 247).

A new polarity was, of course, to emerge. In about 1640 Cornelius Johnson painted Arthur, first Baron Capel, and his family, in front of an open window through which we can glimpse the extent of their property. The picture closely resembles the Buckingham painting in certain respects: the hands of the Baron and his wife would meet, but hers are holding the child on her lap; one of the little girls is offering the baby a flower from the basket she is carrying. But whereas the Baron faces the spectator, his wife, Elizabeth, looks at him. Patriarchy reasserts itself within the affective family. Perhaps the marriage of true minds had never implied equality for women, but only, as Thomas Taylor argued, a new kind of pliability:

> The wife must frame herself in all lawful things to helpfulnesse, to shew the likenesse of her minde to his minde. . . . A wife, as a wife, is to no end, but to frame her selfe to her husbands minde and manners.
> (Halkett 1970, p. 46)

Gradually the set of oppositions we recognize established the new meaning of sexual difference. Women were once again everything that men were not – this time caring, nurturing, intuitive, irrational – and their sphere of influence was precisely the newly defined place of retreat from the public world of work and politics. 'Hearth and home', 'the bosom of the family': the phrases evoke warmth and affection. They also have the effect of isolating women in a private realm of domesticity which is seen as outside politics and therefore outside the operations of power.

III

Meaning depends on difference, and the fixing of meaning is the fixing of difference as opposition. It is precisely this identification of difference as polarity which Derrida defines as *metaphysical*. In conjunction with the common-sense belief that language is a nomenclature, a set of labels for what is irrevocably and inevitably there – whether in the world or in our heads – this process of fixing meaning provides us with

Figure 4 Cornelius Johnson, *Arthur, 1st Baron Capel, 1604–49, and his Family,* c. 1640

a series of polarities which define what is. These definitions are also values. In the oppositions 'I/you', 'individual/society', 'truth/fiction', 'masculine/feminine' one term is always privileged, and one is always other, always what is not the thing itself.

The insistence on meaning as single, fixed and given is thus a way of reaffirming existing values. Conversely, those moments when the plurality of meaning is most insistent are also moments of crisis in the order of existing values. A contest for meaning disrupts the system of differences which we take for granted, throwing into disarray the oppositions and the values which structure understanding. The contest for the meaning of the family which took place in the sixteenth and seventeenth centuries disrupted sexual difference, and in the space between the two sets of meanings, the old and the new polarities, there appear in the fiction of the period shapes, phantasms perhaps, that unsettle the opposition defining the feminine as that which is not masculine – not, that is to say, active, muscular, rational, authoritative . . . powerful. Women are defined precisely as the *opposite* sex, and the 'evidence', the location of this antithesis, is the process of reproduction. The family as the proper source of that process, the place of reproduction, is thus among the major determinants of the meaning of sexual difference itself. A radical discontinuity in the meaning of the family, which is not in any sense an evolution, produces a gap in which definitions of other modes of being for women are momentarily visible. The period of Shakespeare's plays is also the period of an explosion of interest in Amazons, female warriors, roaring girls (Shepherd 1981) and women disguised as pages.

An interest in female transvestism is not, of course, confined to the Renaissance. It stretches at least from Ovid's story of Iphis and Ianthe (*Metamorphoses*, IX, lines 666–797) to twentieth-century pantomime. But it is hard to think of any period when the motif is so recurrent. It appears in five of Shakespeare's comedies of love and marriage. And in turn Rosalind and Viola, Portia, Julia and Imogen are the direct descendants of a long line of English and European Renaissance heroines of prose and drama, Neronis, Silla and Gallathea, Lelia, Ginevra, Violetta and Felismena, who are disguised as men in order to escape the constraints and the vulnerability of the feminine.

The great majority of these fictions are romances, narratives of the relations between women and men. It was the love stories of Hippolyta and Penthesilea, rather than their battles, which were commonly recounted. In *The Faerie Queene* romantic love leading to Christian marriage is personified in Britomart, the female knight, who does physical battle with Radigund for possession of Artegall. Julia in *Two Gentlemen of Verona*, Lelia, Silla and Violetta disguise themselves specifically to follow the men they love. Perhaps the most remarkable instance is the story of *Frederyke of Jennen*, known in Germany and the Netherlands in the fifteenth century and translated into English in 1518. Another edition appeared soon after this, and a third in 1560, testifying to the story's English popularity (Bullough 1975, pp. 15–16). A merchant's wife whose husband mistakenly believes that she has been unfaithful to him flees from Genoa to Cairo in male disguise. There she is made in rapid succession the king's falconer, a knight and then a lord. Left to govern the realm in the king's absence, she leads the army in a great victory against an invading force, and finally becomes protector of the realm until, twelve years later, in possession of evidence of her innocence, she reveals the truth of her identity and is reunited with her husband. Love and marriage are saved by the transgression of the opposition they are based on.

The redefinition of marriage entails a redefiniton of the feminine. It is not easy to imagine Griselda as a source of apt and cheerful conversation. She is the antithesis of her husband, not his like in disposition. It is as if in order to find a way of identifying women as partners for men, the romances of the sixteenth century draw on the old heroic and chivalric tradition of friendship between men – Palamon and Arcite, Damon and Pithias, Titus and Gisippus. Diguised as boys, Julia, Rosalind and Viola become the daily companions of the men they love and, paradoxically, their allies against love's cruelty. Portia fights Bassanio's legal battle for him – and wins. The two conventions of love and friendship appear side by side in *Two Gentlemen of Verona*, where by loving Silvia Proteus betrays both his friend, Valentine, and his mistress, Julia (II. vi). If the symmetry between love and friendship is disturbed when Julia disguises herself as Sebastian, it is thrown momentarily into crisis when Valentine offers Silvia to his friend as a token of reconciliation between them. But Julia's presence, possible only because she is disguised as a boy, and her swoon, which simultaneously reaffirms her femininity, are the means to the full repentance of Proteus and the reinstatement of both love and friendship, leading to closure in the promise of a double marriage (V. iv. 170–1).

The effect of this motif of women disguised as men is hard to define. In the first place, of course, it throws into relief the patriarchal assumptions of the period. 'Beauty provoketh thieves sooner than gold' (*As You Like It*, I. iii. 106): that women are vulnerable is seen as obvious and natural. It is not, on the other hand, seen as essential or inevitable, hut as a matter of appearance. Rape is a consequence not of what women are but of what men believe they are. Rosalind tells Celia,

> We'll have a swashing and a martial outside,
> As many other mannish cowards have
> That do outface it with their semblances.
>
> (*As You Like It*, I. iii. 116–18)

Not all men are equally courageous, but they are all less vulnerable then women because they look as if they can defend themselves. Similarly, Portia's right to exercise her authority depends on her lawyer's robes, and the episode can be seen as making visible the injustice which allows women authority only on condition that they seem to be men. Even while it reaffirms patriarchy, the tradition of female transvestism challenges it precisely by unsettling the categories which legitimate it.

IV

But I want to propose that a close reading of the texts can generate a more radical challenge to patriarchal values by disrupting sexual difference itself. Of course, the male disguise of these female heroines allows for plenty of dramatic ironies and double meanings, and thus offers the audience the pleasures of a knowingness which depends on a knowledge of sexual difference. But it can also be read as undermining that knowledge from time to time, calling it in question by indicating that it is possible, at least in fiction, to speak from a position which is not that of a full, unified, gendered subject. In other words, the plays can be read as posing at certain critical moments the simple, but in comedy unexpected, question, 'Who is speaking?'

As she steps forward at the end of *As You Like It*, Rosalind says to the audience, 'It is not the fashion to see the lady the epilogue' (V. iv. 198), and a little later, 'If I were a woman, I would kiss as many of you as had beards that pleased me' (lines 214–16). The lady is not a woman. In a footnote to the second of these observations the Arden edition reminds modern readers of the answer to the implied riddle: 'a boy-player is speaking'. Here in the margins of the play, when one of the characters addresses the audience directly and, by acknowledging that what has gone before is a performance, partly resumes the role of actor (though only partly, of course: the epilogue is a speech written by the dramatist for the actor to perform), the uncertainty about the gender of the speaker in a period when women's parts are played by male actors is part of the comedy. A male actor is speaking, but the joke is that he is simultaneously visually identifiable as a woman, the lady, dressed for her wedding ('not furnished like a beggar', as she insists, line 207), and that he/she will curtsey to acknowledge the audience's applause (line 220). A male actor *and* a female character is speaking.

The comedy of uncertainty about whether a character is speaking from inside or outside the fiction is evident as early as Medwall's *Fulgens and Lucres* (c.1500), where the servants, A and B, come out of the audience at the beginning of the play and assure each other that they are not actors. The epilogue of *As You Like It* simply compounds the uncertainty and therefore the comedy by confusing the gender roles, so that the question 'Who is speaking?' elicits no single or simple answer. But the comedy of the epilogue owes its resonance in its context to the play's recurrent probing of the question, 'Who is speaking when the protagonist speaks?' And here the uncertainty depends not only on the fact that a male actor plays a woman. Even in the most illusionist of modern theatre, members of the audience live perfectly comfortably with the knowledge that the actor is not *really* the character, that they have seen the actor in other roles and the character played by other actors. The convention that female parts are played by male actors is presumably equally taken for granted on the Renaissance stage. Within the fictional world of the play, the question 'Who is speaking?' is complicated not so much by the extra-textual sex of the actor as by the gender of the protagonist.

It is not that Rosalind-as-Ganymede becomes a man or forgets that she is in love with Orlando. On the contrary, the text repeatedly, if ironically, insists on her feminine identity: 'I should have been a woman by right' (IV. iii.175); 'Alas the day, what shall I do with my doublet and hose?' (III. ii. 215); 'I would cure you, if you would but call me Rosalind and come every day to my cote and woo me' (III. ii. 414–15). But at other moments the voice is not so palpably feminine and the pleasure of the audience is not a product of irony. When they arrive in the Forest of Arden, Celia-as-Aliena is too exhausted to go any further (II. iv. 61). It is Rosalind-as-Ganymede, therefore, who negotiates with Corin for accommodation:' 'Here's a young maid with travel much oppress'd, / And faints for succour' (II. iv. 72–3). We have seen the psychological transformation of Rosalind into Ganymede earlier in the same scene: 'I could find in my heart to disgrace my man's apparel and to cry like a woman. But I must comfort the weaker vessel, as doublet and hose ought to show itself courageous to petticoat; therefore courage, good Aliena' (lines 3–7). The audience's pleasure in the comedy here is the effect of Ganymede's escape from the limitations of Rosalind's femininity.

In *Cymbeline* when Imogen disguises herself as Fidele, Pisanio tells her,

> You must forget to be a woman: change
> Command into obedience [she is a princess]: fear, and niceness
> (The handmaids of all women, or, more truly,
> Woman it pretty self) into a waggish courage
>
> (III. iv. 156–9)

Fear and niceness (fastidiousness, daintiness) are the essence of the feminine, the text insists, 'Woman it pretty self', her identity. But the verbs contradict the notion of a fixed essence of womanhood: 'You must forget to be a woman; change. . . .' It is the mobility implied by the verbs which characterizes Imogen's reply: 'I see into thy end, and am almost / A man already' (lines 168–9). The scene is not comic; there are no distancing dramatic ironies to point to the absurdity of the claim. To be a woman, the text proposes, means to be nice and fearful; but it also means, as the play demonstrates, to be capable of a radical discontinuity which repudiates those defining characteristics. Imogen concludes: 'This attempt /I am soldier to, and will abide it with / A prince's courage' (lines 184–6). The context in which Imogen takes on the characteristics of a soldier and a prince is a journey which is to lead her to her husband.

Rosalind-as-Ganymede reproduces the conventional invective against women for Orlando, and shocks Celia:

> You have simply misused our sex in your love-prate. We must have your doublet and hose plucked over your head, and show the world what the bird hath done to her own nest.
>
> (IV. i. 191–4)

Who is speaking when the protagonist mocks women? The question is more or less eliminated in the process of reading the text by the speech prefixes, which identity the speaker as Rosalind throughout, and in modern performances, where Rosalind-as-Ganymede is played by a woman. No wonder that most of the standard twentieth-century criticism treats the disguise as transparent and stresses Rosalind's femininity (Wilson 1962, pp. 161–2; Barber 1959, pp. 231–3; Shakespeare 1975a, p. lxxiii). But if we imagine the part played by a male actor it becomes possible to attribute a certain autonomy to the voice of Ganymede here, and in this limited sense the extra-textual sex of the actor may be seen as significant. Visually and aurally the actor does not insist on the femininity of Rosalind-as-Ganymede, but holds the issue unresolved, releasing for the audience the possibility of glimpsing a disruption of sexual difference.

The sixteenth-century narrative source, Lodge's *Rosalynde*, is illuminating in this context. The third-person narrative, compelled, as drama is not, to find appropriate names and pronouns to recount the story, normally identifies the disguised heroine as Ganimede and uses the masculine pronoun. This leads to a good deal of comedy which depends on our acceptance of the discontinuity of identity:

> You may see (quoth Ganimede) what mad catell you women be, whose hearts sometimes are made of Adamant that will touch with no impression; and sometime of waxe that is fit for everie forme: they delight to be courted, and then they glorie to seeme coy . . . And I pray

> you (quoth Aliena) if your roabes were off, what metall are you made of that you are so satyricall against women? Is it not a foule bird defiles [his] owne nest? . . . Thus (quoth Ganimede) I keepe decorum, I speake now as I am *Alienas* page, not as I am Gerismonds daughter: for put me but into a peticoate, and I will stand in defiance to the uttermost that women are courteous, constant, vertuous, and what not.
>
> (Bullough 1958, p. 181)

Of course this is as absurd as it is delightful, but the delight stems from the facility with which Rosalynde-Ganimede can speak from anti-thetical positions, transgress the norms of sexual difference. What is delightful is that, in becoming Ganimede, Rosalynde escapes the con-finement of a single position, a single perspective, a single voice. The narrative calls its central figure a 'Girle-boye' (Bullough 1958, p. 233), and celebrates the plurality it thus releases.

In *As You Like It* Rosalind is so firmly in control of her disguise that the emphasis is on the pleasures rather than the dangers implicit in the transgression of sexual difference. Other heroines are not so fortunate. In *The Famous History of Parismus* by Emanuel Forde (1598) Violetta dis-guised as Adonius disrupts the story's pronouns when she spends the night sleeping between Parismus, whom she loves, and Pollipus, who loves her:

> the poore soule lay close at Parismus back, the very sweet touch of whose body seemed to ravish her with joy: and on the other side not acquainted with such bedfellowes, she seemed (as it were) meta-morphosed, with a kind of delightful feare . . . early in the morning Adonius was up, being afraid to uncover her delicate body, but with speed soone araid himself & had so neatly provided al things against these two knights should rise, that both of them admired his behaviour . . .
>
> (Bullough 1958, p. 367)

Barnabe Riche's Silla, disguised as Silvio, is compelled to reveal the truth when she is accused of being the father of Julina's child. The double danger implicit in concealment and exposure similarly unsettles the narrative:

And here with all loosing his garmentes doune to his stomacke, and shewed Julina his breastes and pretie teates, surmountyng farre the whitenesse of snowe itself saiyng: Loe, Madame! beholde here the partie whom you have chalenged to bee the father of your childe. See, I am a woman . . .

(Bullough 1958, p. 361)

What happens in these instances is not like the case Barthes identifies in Balzac's 'Sarrasine', where the narrative is compelled to equivocate each time it uses a pronoun to identify the castrato. Nor is it that the reader does not know what is 'true', as in a modernist text. It is rather that the unified subjectivity of the protagonist is not the focal point of the narrative. It is not so important that we concentrate on the truth of identity as that we derive pleasure (in these cases a certain titillation) from the dangers which follow from the disruption of sexual difference.

In *Twelfth Night* these dangers, here romantic rather than erotic,[2] constitute the plot itself – which means for the spectators a certain suspense and the promise of resolution. Viola, addressing the audience, formulates both the enigma and the promise of closure:

What will become of this? As I am man,
My state is desperate for my master's love:
As I am woman (now alas the day!)
What thriftless sighs shall poor Olivia breathe?
O time, thou must untangle this, not I,
It is too hard a knot for me t' untie.

(II. ii. 35–40)

Of all Shakespeare's comedies it is perhaps *Twelfth Night* which takes the most remarkable risks with the identity of its central figure. Viola is just as feminine as Rosalind, as the text constantly insists (I. iv. 30–4; III. i. 160–2), and Cesario is as witty a saucy lackey as Ganymede. But it is only in *Twelfth Night* that the protagonist specifically says, 'I am not what I am' (III. i. 143) where 'seem' would have scanned just as well and preserved the unity of the subject.

The standard criticism has had few difficulties with the 'Patience on a monument' speech, identifying the pining figure it defines as Viola herself, and so in *a sense* she is.[3] But it is by no means an unproblematic sense. The problems may be brought out by comparison with a parallel episode in *Two Gentlemen of Verona* (IV. iv. 108 ff). Julia disguised as Sebastian is wooing Silvia on behalf of Proteus. The ironies are clear, sharp and delightful. Sebastian asks Silvia for her picture for Proteus: Silvia says a picture of the neglected Julia would be more appropriate. Sebastian offers a ring: Silvia refuses it, since it was Julia's, and Sebastian, to her surprise, says, 'She thanks you'. Is Julia not 'passing fair'?, Silvia asks. She was, Sebastian replies, until, neglected by Proteus, she in turn neglected her beauty, 'that now she is become as black as I'. 'How tall was she?' asks Silvia, and Sebastian replies:

> About my stature: for at Pentecost,
> When all our pageants of delight were play'd,
> Our youth got me to play the woman's part,
> And I was trimm'd in Madam Julia's gown,
> Which served me as fit, by all men's judgments,
> As if the garment had been made for me;
> Therefore I know she is about my height.
> And at that time I made her weep agood,
> For I did play a lamentable part.
> Madam, 'twas Ariadne, passioning
> For Theseus' perjury, and unjust flight;
> Which I so lively acted with my tears,
> That my poor mistress, moved therewithal,
> Wept bitterly; and would I might be dead,
> If I in thought felt not her very sorrow.

(IV. iv. 56–70)

In these exchanges the irony depends on the series of identifications available to the audience which are not available to Silvia. Julia looks like Sebastian, her clothes fit Sebastian, Sebastian plays Ariadne lamenting betrayal in love so convincingly, and Sebastian feels Julia's own sorrow, because Sebastian is Julia and Julia is betrayed. The audience's pleasure here consists in recognizing the single speaker who momentarily occupies each of these identities as Julia, and the speeches as an elaborate invention rehearsing what we know to be true within the fictional world of the play.

But this is not so clearly the case in the (roughly) corresponding episode in *Twelfth Night*. Orsino is telling Cesario that men's love is more profound than women's:

VIOLA	Ay, but I know –
DUKE	What dost thou know?
VIOLA	Too well what love women to men may owe:
	In faith, they are as true of heart as we.
	My father had a daughter lov'd a man,
	As it might be perhaps, were I a woman,
	I should your lordship.
DUKE	And what's her history?
VIOLA	A blank, my lord: she never told her love,
	But let concealment like a worm i' th' bud
	Feed on her damask cheek: she pin'd in thought,
	And with a green and yellow melancholy
	She sat like Patience on a monument,
	Smiling at grief. Was not this love indeed?

(II. iv. 104–16)

How do the identifications work in this instance? Cesario is Viola and Cesario's father's daughter is Patience who is also Viola. But the equations break down almost at once with, 'what's her history?' 'A blank'. Viola's history is the play we are watching, which is certainly not a blank but packed with events. Nor is it true that she never told her love. She has already told it once in this scene (lines 26–8), and she is here telling it again in hints so broad that even Orsino is able to pick them up once he has one more clue (V. i. 265–6). In the play as a whole Viola is neither pining nor sitting, but is to be seen busily composing speeches to Olivia and exchanging jokes with Feste; and far from smiling at grief, she is here lamenting the melancholy which is the effect of unrequited love.

How then do we understand these fictions as telling a kind of truth? By recognizing that the Viola who speaks is not identical to the Viola she speaks of. If Viola is Patience, silent like Patient Griselda, it is not

Viola who speaks here. Viola-as-Cesario repudiates the dynastic mean-ing of the feminine as patience, and yet that meaning is as present in Cesario's speech as the other, the difference which simultaneously defines Cesario as Orsino's companion and partner in suffering, and Viola as a woman.

In reply to Orsino's question, 'But died thy sister of her love?', the exchange ends with a riddle. 'I am all the daughters of my father's house, / And all the brothers too: and yet I know not' (lines 120–2). At the level of the plot the answer to the riddle is deferred to the end of the play: Viola doesn't die; she marries Orsino. But to an attentive audience another riddle presents itself: who tells the blank history of Viola's father's pining daughter? The answer is neither Viola nor Cesario, but a speaker who at this moment occupies a place which is not precisely masculine or feminine, where the notion of identity itself is disrupted to display a difference within subjectivity, and the singularity which resides in this difference.

It cannot, of course, be sustained. At the end of each story the heroine abandons her disguise and dwindles into a wife. Closure depends on closing off the glimpsed transgression and reinstating a clearly defined sexual difference. But the plays are more than their endings, and the heroines become wives only after they have been shown to be something altogether more singular – because more plural.

V

In an article first published in French in 1979 Julia Kristeva dis-tinguishes between two 'generations' (though the term does not necessarily imply that they are chronologically consecutive) of femi-nism (Kristeva 1981). The first generation has been concerned with public and political equality for women (votes, equal opportunities, equal pay). The danger here, she argues, is that feminists who succeed in these terms come to identify with the dominant values and take up positions as guardians of the existing order. The second generation has insisted on an irreducible feminine identity, the opposite of what is masculine, accepting the theoretical and ideological structure of patriarchy but reversing its values. This leads to a radical, separatist feminism. The distinction does not, I suspect, stand up to historical analysis, but it does offer models of two kinds of feminist commitment from which Kristeva distinguishes a third generation, or perhaps a third possibility which, she says, 'I strongly advocate, which I imagine?', in which 'the very dichotomy man / woman as an opposition between two rival entities may be understood as belonging to metaphysics' (Kristeva 1981, p. 33). There can be no specifically feminine identity if identity itself does not exist. In the post-structuralist analysis subjectivity is not a single, unified presence but the point of intersection of a range of discourses, produced and re-produced as the subject occupies a series of places in the signifying system, takes on the multiplicity of meanings language offers. Kristeva's third possibility proposes the internalization of 'the founding separation of the sociosymbolic contract', difference itself as the ground of meaning, within identity, including sexual identity (p. 34). The effect will be to bring out 'the multiplicity of every person's possible identifications' and the relativity of his or her sociosymbolic and biological existence (p. 35).

The fragmentation of sexual identity in favour of this fluidity, this plurality, deconstructs all the possible metaphysical polarities between men and women. It is not a question of bisexuality, though the heterosexual 'norms' based on the metaphysics of sexual difference lose their status in the unfixing of sexual disposition. Nor is it a balance between extremes which is proposed, the 'poise' or 'complexity' which criticism has often found characteristic of Rosalind and Viola (Barber 1959, pp. 234–5, 258; Leggatt 1974, pp. 202 ff). The point is not to create some third, unified, androgynous identity which eliminates all distinctions. Nor indeed is it to repudiate sexuality itself. It is rather to define through the internalization of difference a plurality of places, of possible beings, for each person in the margins of sexual difference, those margins which a metaphysical sexual polarity obliterates.

One final instance may suggest something of the fluidity which is proposed. A Midsummer Night's Dream gives us on the periphery of the action a marriage between a warrior and an Amazon: 'Hippolyta, I woo'd thee with my sword, / And won thy love doing thee injuries' (I. i. 16–17). The text here proposes a parallel where we might expect an antithesis. None the less, apart from their shared commitment to blood sports, Theseus and Hippolyta take up distinct positions on all the issues they discuss. Where Theseus is cynical about the moon, Hippolyta invokes conventional poetic imagery (I. i. 4–11); when Theseus sceptically supposes that the young lovers have been deluded, Hippolyta counters cool reason with wonder (V. i. 2–27); but when Hippolyta finds the mechanicals' play 'the silliest stuff that ever I heard', it is Theseus who invokes imagination: 'The best in this kind are but shadows; and the worst are no worse if imagination amend them' (V. i. 207–9). A criticism in quest of character, of fixed identities, might have difficulty here, since the stereotypes of masculine rationality and feminine imagination are now preserved, now reversed. As a kind of chorus on the edges of a play about love, which in many ways relies on stereotypes, Theseus and Hippolyta present a 'musical discord' which undermines fixity without blurring distinctions. Difference coexists with multiplicity and with love.

VI

My concern in this essay has been with meanings and glimpses of possible meanings. Fictional texts neither reflect a real world nor prescribe an ideal one. But they do offer definitions and redefinitions which make it possible to reinterpret a world we have taken for granted. Post-structuralist theory liberates meaning from 'truth', 'the facts', but it implies a relationship between meaning and practice. New meanings release the possibility of new practices.

It is not obvious from a feminist point of view that, in so far as they seem finally to re-affirm sexual polarity, Shakespeare's comedies have happy endings. It is certain from the same point of view that the contest for the meaning of the family in the sixteenth and seventeenth centuries did not, though on this there is a good deal more to be said. What I have been arguing is that that contest momentarily unfixed the existing system of differences, and in the gap thus produced we are able to glimpse a possible meaning, an image of a mode of being, which is not a-sexual, nor bisexual, but which disrupts the system of differences on which sexual stereotyping depends.

Whether the remainder of the story of the relations between men and women ultimately has a happy ending is, I suppose, for us to decide.

9

NYMPHS AND REAPERS HEAVILY VANISH

The discursive con-texts of *The Tempest*

Francis Barker and *Peter Hulme*

I

No one who has witnessed the phenomenon of midsummer tourism at Stratford-upon-Avon can fail to be aware of the way in which 'Shakespeare' functions today in the construction of an English past: a past which is picturesque, familiar and untroubled. Modern scholarly editions of Shakespeare, amongst which the Arden is probably the most influential, have seemed to take their distance from such mythologizing by carefully locating the plays against their historical background. Unfortunately such a move always serves, paradoxically, only to highlight in the foregrounded text preoccupations and values which turn out to be not historical at all, but eternal. History is thus recognized and abolished at one and the same time. One of the aims of this essay is to give a closer account of this mystificatory negotiation of 'history', along with an examination of the ways in which the relationship between text and historical context can be more adequately formulated. Particular reference will be made to the way in which, in recent years, traditional notions of the historical sources of the text have been challenged by newer analyses which employ such terms as 'intertextuality' and 'discourse'. To illustrate these, a brief exemplary reading will be offered of *The Tempest*. But to begin with, the new analyses themselves need setting in context.

II

The dominant approach within literary study has conceived of the text as autotelic, 'an entity which always remains the same from one moment to the next' (Hirsch 1967; p. 46); in other words a text that is fixed in history and, at the same time, curiously free of historical limitation. The text is acknowledged as having been produced at a certain moment in history; but that history itself is reduced to being no more than a background from which the single and irreducible meaning of the text is isolated. The text is designated as the legitimate object of literary criticism, *over against* its contexts, whether they be arrived at through the literary-historical account of the development of particular traditions and genres or, as more frequently happens with Shakespeare's plays, the study of 'sources'. In either case the text has been separated from a surrounding ambit of other texts over which it is given a special pre-eminence.

In recent years, however, an alternative criticism, often referred to as 'structuralist' and 'post-structuralist', has sought to displace radically the primacy of the autotelic text by arguing that a text indeed 'cannot be limited by or to . . . the originating moment of its production, anchored in the intentionality of its author'.[1] For these kinds of criticism exclusive study of the moment of production is defined as narrowly 'historicist' and replaced by attention to successive *inscriptions* of a text during the course of its history.[2] And the contextual background – which previously had served merely to highlight the profile of the individual text – gives way to the notion of *intertextuality*, according to which, in keeping with the Saussurean model of language, no text is intelligible except in its differential relations with other texts.[3]

The break with the moment of textual production can easily be presented as liberatory; certainly much work of importance has stemmed from the study of inscription. It has shown for example that texts can never simply be *encountered* but are, on the contrary, repeatedly constructed under definite conditions: *The Tempest* read by Sir Walter Raleigh in 1914 as the work of England's national poet is very different from *The Tempest* constructed with full textual apparatus by an editor/ critic such as Frank Kermode, and from the 'same' text inscribed institutionally in that major formation of 'English Literature' which is the school or university syllabus and its supporting practices of teaching and examination.[4]

If the study of the inscription and reinscription of texts has led to important work of historical description, it has also led to the formulation of a political strategy in respect of literary texts, expressed here by Tony Bennett when he calls for texts to be 'articulated with new texts, socially and politically mobilized in different ways within different class practices' (Bennett 1982, p. 224). This strategy also depends, therefore, on a form of intertextuality which identifies in all texts a potential for new linkages to be made and thus for new political meanings to be constructed. Rather than attempting to derive the text's significance from the moment of its production, this politicized intertextuality emphasizes the present *use* to which texts can now be put. This approach undercuts itself, however, when, in the passage from historical description to contemporary rearticulation, it claims for itself a radicalism which it cannot then deliver. Despite speaking of texts as always being 'installed in a field of struggle' (Bennett 1982, p. 229), it denies to itself the very possibility of combating the dominant orthodoxies. For if, as the logic of Bennett's argument implies, 'the text' were wholly dissolved into an indeterminate miscellany of inscriptions, then how could any confrontation between different but contemporaneous inscriptions take place: what would be the ground of such a contestation?[5] While a genuine difficulty in theorizing 'the text' does exist, this should not lead inescapably to the point where the only option becomes the voluntaristic ascription to the text of meanings and articulations derived simply from one's own ideological preferences. This is a procedure only too vulnerable to pluralistic incorporation, a recipe for peaceful co-existence with the dominant readings, not for a contestation of those readings themselves. Struggle can only occur if two positions attempt to occupy the same space, to appropriate the 'same' text; 'alternative' readings condemn themselves to mere irrelevance.

Our criticism of this politicized intertextuality does not however seek to reinstate the autotelic text with its single fixed meaning. Texts are certainly not available for innocent, unhistorical readings. Any reading must be made from a particular position, but is not reducible to that position (not least because texts are not infinitely malleable or interpretable, but offer certain constraints and resistances to readings made of them). Rather, different readings struggle with each other on the site of the text, and all that can count, however provisionally, as knowledge of a text, is achieved through this discursive conflict. In other words, the onus on new readings, especially radical readings aware of their own theoretical and political positioning, should be to proceed by means of a critique of the dominant readings of a text.

We say critique rather than simply criticism, in reference to a powerful radical tradition which aims not merely to disagree with its rivals but to read their readings: that is, to identify their inadequacies and to explain why such readings come about and what ideological role they play.[6] Critique operates in a number of ways, adopting various strategies and lines of attack as it engages with the current ideological formations, but one aspect of its campaign is likely to have to remain constant. Capitalist societies have always presupposed the naturalness and universality of their own structures and modes of perception, so, at least for the foreseeable future, critiques will need to include an historical moment, countering capitalism's self-universalization by reasserting the rootedness of texts in the contingency of history. It is this particular ground that what we have been referring to as alternative criticism runs the risk of surrendering unnecessarily. As we emphasized earlier, the study of successive textual inscriptions continues to be genuinely important, but it must be recognized that attention to such inscriptions is not logically dependent on the frequent presupposition that all accounts of the moment of production are either crudely historicist or have recourse to claims concerning authorial intentionality. A properly political intertextuality would attend to successive inscriptions without abandoning that no longer privileged but still crucially important first inscription of the text. After all, only by maintaining our right to make statements that we can call 'historical' can we avoid handing over the very notion of history to those people who are only too willing to tell us 'what really happened'.

III

In order to speak of the Shakespearean text as an historical utterance, it is necessary to read it with and within series of con-texts.[7] These contexts are the precondition of the plays' historical and political signification, although literary criticism has operated systematically to close down that signification by a continual process of occlusion. This may seem a strange thing to say about the most notoriously bloated of all critical enterprises, but in fact 'Shakespeare' has been force-fed behind a high wall called Literature, built out of the dismantled pieces of other seventeenth-century discourses. Two particular examples of the occlusive process might be noted here. First, the process of occlusion is accomplished in the production of critical meaning, as is well illustrated by the case of Caliban. The occlusion of his political claims – one of the subjects of the present essay – is achieved by installing him at the very centre of the play, but only as the ground of a nature/art confrontation, itself of undoubted importance for the Renaissance, but here, in Kermode's account, totally without the historical contextualization that would locate it among the early universalizing forms of incipient bourgeois hegemony (Shakespeare 1964, pp. xxxiv–lxiii). Secondly, source criticism, which might *seem* to militate against autotelic unity by relating the text in question to other texts, in fact only obscures such relationships. Kermode's paragraphs on 'The New World' embody the hesitancy with which Shakespearean scholarship has approached the problem. Resemblances between the *language* of the Bermuda pamphlets and that of *The Tempest* are brought forward as evidence that Shakespeare 'has these documents in mind' but, since this must remain 'inference' rather than 'fact', it can only have subsidiary importance, 'of the greatest interest and usefulness', while clearly not 'fundamental to [the play's] structure of ideas'. Such 'sources' are then reprinted in an appendix so 'the reader may judge of the verbal parallels for himself', and the matter closed (Shakespeare 1964, pp. xxvii–xxviii).

And yet such closure proves premature since, strangely, source criticism comes to play an interestingly crucial role in Kermode's production of a site for *The Tempest's* meaning. In general, the fullness of the play's unity needs protecting from con-textual contamination, so 'sources' are kept at bay except for the odd verbal parallel. But occasionally, and on a strictly *singular* basis, that unity can only be protected by recourse to a notion of source as explanatory of a feature otherwise aberrant to that posited unity. One example of this would be Prospero's well-known irascibility, peculiarly at odds with Kermode's picture of a self-disciplined, reconciliatory white magician, and therefore to be 'in the last analysis, explained by the fact that [he] descend[s] from a bad-tempered giant-magician' (Shakespeare 1964, p. lxiii). Another would be Prospero's strange perturbation which brings the celebratory masque of Act IV to such an abrupt conclusion, in one reading (as we will demonstrate shortly) the most important scene in the play, but here explained as 'a point at which an oddly pedantic concern for classical structure causes it to force its way through the surface of the play (Shakespeare 1964, p. lxxv).' In other words the play's unity is constructed only by shearing off some of its 'surface' complexities and explaining them away as irrelevant survivals or unfortunate academicisms.

Intertextuality, or con-textualization, differs most importantly from source criticism when it establishes the necessity of reading *The Tempest* alongside congruent texts, irrespective of Shakespeare's putative knowledge of them, and when it holds that such congruency will become apparent from the constitution of discursive networks to be traced independently of authorial 'intentionality'.

IV

Essential to the historico-political critique which we are proposing here are the analytic strategies made possible by the concept of *discourse*. Intertextuality has usefully directed attention to the relationship *between* texts: discourse moves us towards a clarification of just what kinds of relationship are involved.[8]

Traditionally *The Tempest* has been related to other texts by reference to a variety of notions: *source*, as we have seen, holds that Shakespeare was influenced by his reading of the Bermuda pamphlets. But the play is also described as belonging to the *genre* of pastoral romance and is seen as occupying a particular place in the *canon* of Shakespeare's works. Intertextuality has sought to displace work done within this earlier paradigm, but has itself been unable to break out of the practice of connecting text with text, of assuming that single texts are the ultimate objects of study and the principal units of meaning.[9] Discourse, on the other hand, refers to the *field* in and through which texts are produced. As a concept wider than 'text' but narrower than language itself (Saussure's *langue*), it operates at the level of the enablement of texts. It is thus not an easy concept to grasp because discourses are never simply observable but only approachable through their effects just as, in a similar way, grammar can be said to be *at work* in particular sentences (even those that are ungrammatical), governing their construction but never fully present 'in' them. The operation of discourse is implicit in the regulation of what statements can and cannot be made and the forms that they can legitimately take. Attention to discourse therefore moves the focus from the interpretative problem of meaning to questions of instrumentality and function. Instead of *having* meaning, statements should be seen as *performative of* meaning; not as possessing some portable and 'universal' content but, rather, as instrumental in the organization and legitimation of power-relations – which of course involves, as one of its components, control over the constitution of meaning. As the author of one of the first modern grammars said, appropriately enough in 1492, 'language is the perfect instrument of empire'.[10] Yet, unlike grammar, discourse functions effectively precisely because the question of codifying its rules and protocols can never arise: the utterances it silently governs speak what appears to be the 'natural language of the age'. Therefore, from within a given discursive formation no general rules for its operation will be drawn up except against the ideological grain; so the constitution of the discursive fields of the past will, to some degree, need comprehending through the excavatory work of historical study.

To initiate such excavation is of course to confront massive problems. According to what we have said above, each individual text, rather than a meaningful unit in itself, lies at the intersection of different discourses which are related to each other in a complex but ultimately hierarchical way. Strictly speaking, then, it would be meaningless to talk about the unity of any given text – supposedly the intrinsic quality of all 'works of art'. And yet, because literary texts *are* presented to us as characterized precisely by their unity, the text must still be taken as a point of purchase on the discursive field – but in order to demonstrate that, athwart its alleged unity, the text is in fact marked and fissured by the interplay of the discourses that constitute it.

V

The ensemble of fictional and lived practices, which for convenience we will simply refer to here as 'English colonialism', provides *The Tempest*'s dominant discursive con-texts.[11] We have chosen here to concentrate specifically on the figure of usurpation as the nodal point of the play's imbrication into this discourse of colonialism. We shall look at the variety of forms under which usurpation appears in the text, and indicate briefly how it is active in organizing the text's actual diversity.'[12]

Of course conventional criticism has no difficulty in recognizing the importance of the themes of legitimacy and usurpation for *The Tempest*. Indeed, during the storm-scene with which the play opens, the issue of legitimate authority is brought immediately to the fore. The boatswain's peremptory dismissal of the nobles to their cabins, while not, according to the custom of the sea, strictly a mutinous act, none the less represents a disturbance in the normal hierarchy of power relations. The play then proceeds to recount or display a series of actual or attempted usurpations of authority: from Antonio's successful palace revolution against his brother, Prospero, and Caliban's attempted violation of the honour of Prospero's daughter – accounts of which we hear retrospectively; to the conspiracy of Antonio and Sebastian against the life of Alonso and, finally, Caliban's insurrection, with Stephano and Trinculo, against Prospero's domination of the island. In fact it could be argued that this series *is* the play, in so far as *The Tempest* is a dramatic action at all. However, these rebellions, treacheries, mutinies and conspiracies, referred to here collectively as usurpation, are not simply present in the text as extractable 'Themes of the Play'.[13] Rather, they are differentially embedded there, figural traces of the text's anxiety concerning the very matters of domination and resistance.

Take for example the play's famous *protasis*, Prospero's long exposition to Miranda of the significant events that predate the play. For Prospero, the real beginning of the story is his usurpation twelve years previously by Antonio, the opening scene of a drama which Prospero intends to play out during *The Tempest* as a comedy of restoration. Prospero's exposition seems unproblematically to take its place as the indispensable prologue to an understanding of the present moment of Act I, no more than a device for conveying essential information. But to see it simply as a neutral account of the play's prehistory would be to occlude the contestation that follows insistently throughout the rest of the first act, of Prospero's version of true beginnings. In this narration the crucial early days of the relationship between the Europeans and the island's inhabitants are covered by Prospero's laconic 'Here in this island we arriv'd' (I. ii. 171). And this is all we would have were it not for Ariel and Caliban. First Prospero is goaded by Ariel's demands for freedom into recounting at some length how his servitude began, when, at their first contact, Prospero freed him from the cloven pine in which he had earlier been confined by Sycorax. Caliban then offers his compelling and defiant counter to Prospero's single sentence when, in a powerful speech, he recalls the initial mutual trust which was broken by Prospero's assumption of the political control made possible by the power of his magic. Caliban, 'Which first was mine own King', now protests that 'here you sty me / In this hard rock, whiles you do keep from me / The rest o'th'island' (I. ii. 344–6).

It is remarkable that these contestations of 'true beginnings' have been so commonly occluded by an uncritical willingness to identify Prospero's voice as direct and reliable authorial statement, and therefore to ignore the lengths to which the play goes to dramatize its problems with the proper beginning of its own story. Such identification hears, as it were, only Prospero's play, follows only his stage directions, not noticing that Prospero's play and *The Tempest* are not necessarily the same thing.[14]

But although different beginnings are offered by different voices in the play, Prospero has the effective power to impose his construction of events on the others. While Ariel gets a threatening but nevertheless expansive answer, Caliban provokes an entirely different reaction. Prospero's words refuse engagement with Caliban's claim to original sovereignty ('This island's mine, by Sycorax my mother, / Which thou tak'st from me', I. ii. 333–4). Yet Prospero is clearly disconcerted. His sole – somewhat hysterical – response consists of an indirect denial ('Thou most lying slave', I. ii. 346) and a counter accusation of attempted rape ('thou didst seek to violate / The honour of my child', I. ii. 349–50), which together foreclose the exchange and serve in practice as Prospero's only justification for the arbitrary rule he exercises over the island and its inhabitants. At a stroke he erases from what we have called Prospero's play all trace of the moment of his reduction of Caliban to slavery and appropriation of his island. For, indeed, it could be argued that the series of usurpations listed earlier as constituting the dramatic action all belong to that play alone, which is systematically silent about Prospero's own act of usurpation: a silence which is curious, given his otherwise voluble preoccupation with the theme of legitimacy. But, despite his evasiveness, this moment ought to be of decisive *narrative* importance since it marks Prospero's self-installation as ruler, and his acquisition, through Caliban's enslavement, of the means of supplying the food and labour on which he and Miranda are completely dependent: 'We cannot miss him: he does make our fire, / Fetch in our wood, and serves in offices / That profit us' (I. ii. 313–5). Through its very occlusion of Caliban's version of proper beginnings, Prospero's disavowal is itself performative of the discourse of colonialism, since this particular reticulation of denial of dispossession with retrospective justification for it, is the characteristic trope by which European colonial regimes articulated their authority over land to which they could have no conceivable legitimate claim.[15]

The success of this trope is, as so often in these cases, proved by its subsequent invisibility. Caliban's 'I'll show thee every fertile inch o'th'-island' (II. ii. 148) is for example glossed by Kermode with 'The colonists were frequently received with this kindness, though treachery might follow', as if this were simply a 'fact' whose relevance to *The Tempest* we might want to consider, without seeing that to speak of 'treachery' is already to interpret, from the position of colonizing power, through a purported 'description'. A discursive analysis would indeed be alive to the use of the word 'treachery' in a colonial context in the early seventeenth century, but would be aware of how it functioned for the English to explain to themselves the *change* in native behaviour (from friendliness to hostility) that was in fact a *reaction* to their increasingly disruptive presence. That this was an explanatory trope rather than a description of behaviour is nicely caught in Gabriel Archer's slightly bemused comment: 'They are naturally given to trechery, howbeit we could not finde it in our travell up the river, but rather a most kind and loving people' (Archer 1979). Kermode's use of the word is of course by no means obviously contentious: its power to shape readings of the play stems from its continuity with the grain of unspoken colonialist assumptions.

So it is not just a matter of the occlusion of the play's initial colonial moment. Colonialist legitimation has always had then to go on to tell its own story, inevitably one of native violence: Prospero's play performs this task within *The Tempest*. The burden of Prospero's play is already deeply concerned with producing legitimacy. The purpose of Prospero's main plot is to secure recognition of his claim to the usurped duchy of Milan, a recognition sealed in the blessing given by Alonso to the prospective marriage of his own son to Prospero's daughter. As part of this, Prospero reduces Caliban to a role in the supporting sub-plot, as instigator of a mutiny that is programmed to fail, thereby forging an equivalence between Antonio's initial *putsch* and Caliban's revolt. This allows Prospero to annul the memory of his failure to prevent his expulsion from the dukedom, by repeating it as a mutiny that he will, this time, forestall. But, in addition, the playing out of the colonialist narrative is thereby completed: Caliban's attempt – tarred with the brush of Antonio's supposedly self-evident viciousness – is produced as final and irrevocable confirmation of the natural treachery of savages.

Prospero can plausibly be seen as a playwright only because of the control over the other characters given him by his magic. He can freeze Ferdinand in mid-thrust, immobilize the court party at will, and conjure a pack of hounds to chase the conspirators. Through this physical control he seeks with considerable success to manipulate the mind of Alonso. Curiously though, while the main part of Prospero's play runs according to plan, the sub-plot provides the only real moment of drama when Prospero calls a sudden halt to the celebratory masque, explaining, aside:

> I had forgot that foul conspiracy
> Of the beast Caliban and his confederates
> Against my life: the minute of their plot
> Is almost come.
>
> (IV. i. 139–42)

So while, on the face of it, Prospero has no difficulty in dealing with the various threats to his domination, Caliban's revolt proves uniquely disturbing to the smooth unfolding of Prospero's plot. The text is strangely emphatic about this moment of disturbance, insisting not only on Prospero's sudden vexation, but also on the 'strange hollow, and confused noise' with which the Nymphs and Reapers – two lines earlier gracefully dancing – now 'heavily vanish'; and the apprehension voiced by Ferdinand and Miranda:

> FERDINAND This is strange: your father's in some passion
> That works him strongly.
> MIRANDA   Never till this day
> Saw I him touch'd with anger, so distemper'd.
>
> (IV. i. 143–5)

For the first and last time Ferdinand and Miranda speak at a distance from Prospero and from his play. Although this disturbance is immediately glossed over, the hesitation, occasioned by the sudden remembering of Caliban's conspiracy, remains available as a site of potential fracture.

The interrupted masque has certainly troubled scholarship, introducing a jarring note into the harmony of this supposedly most highly structured of Shakespeare's late plays. Kermode speaks of the 'apparently inadequate motivation' for Prospero's perturbation (Shakespeare 1964, p. lxxv), since there is no obvious reason why he should so excite himself over an easily controllable insurrection.

What then is the meaning of this textual excess, this disproportion between apparent cause and effect? There are several possible answers, located at different levels of analysis. The excess obviously marks the recurrent difficulty that Caliban causes Prospero – a difficulty we have been concerned to trace in some detail. So, at the level of character, a psychoanalytic reading would want to suggest that Prospero's excessive reaction represents his disquiet at the irruption into consciousness of an unconscious anxiety concerning the grounding of his legitimacy, both as producer of his play and, *a fortiori*, as governor of the island. The by now urgent need for action forces upon Prospero the hitherto repressed contradiction between his dual roles as usurped and usurper. Of course the emergency is soon contained and the colonialist narrative quickly completed. But, none the less, if only for a moment, the effort invested in holding Prospero's play together as a unity is laid bare.

So, at the formal level, Prospero's difficulties in staging his play are themselves 'staged' by the play that we are watching, this moment presenting for the first time the possibility of distinguishing between Prospero's play and The Tempest itself.

Perhaps it could be said that what is staged here in The Tempest is Prospero's anxious determination to keep the sub-plot of his play in its place. One way of distinguishing Prospero's play from The Tempest might be to claim that Prospero's carefully established relationship between main and sub-plot is reversed in The Tempest, whose main plot concerns Prospero's anxiety over his sub-plot. A formal analysis would seem to bear this out. The climax of Prospero's play is his revelation to Alonso of Miranda and Ferdinand playing chess. This is certainly a true *anagnorisis* for Alonso, but for us a merely theatrical rather than truly dramatic moment. The Tempest's dramatic climax, in a way its only dramatic moment at all, is, after all, this sudden and strange disturbance of Prospero.

But to speak of Prospero's anxiety being staged by The Tempest would be, on its own, a recuperative move, preserving the text's unity by the familiar strategy of introducing an ironic distance between author and protagonist. After all, although Prospero's anxiety over his sub-plot may point up the *crucial* nature of that 'sub' plot, a generic analysis would have no difficulty in showing that The Tempest is ultimately complicit with Prospero's play in treating Caliban's conspiracy in the fully

comic mode. Even before it begins, Caliban's attempt to put his political claims into practice is arrested by its implication in the convention
of clownish vulgarity represented by the 'low-life' characters of Stephano and Trinculo, his conspiracy framed in a grotesquerie that ends
with the dubiously amusing sight of the conspirators being hunted by
dogs, a fate, incidentally, not unknown to natives of the New World.
The shakiness of Prospero's position is indeed staged, but in the end his
version of history remains *authoritative*, the larger play acceding as it
were to the containment of the conspirators in the safely comic mode,
Caliban allowed only his poignant and ultimately vain protests against
the venality of his co-conspirators.

That this comic closure is necessary to enable the European 'reconciliation' which follows hard on its heels – the patching up of a minor
dynastic dispute within the Italian nobility – is, however, itself symptomatic of the text's own anxiety about the threat posed to its decorum
by its New World materials. The lengths to which the play has to go to
achieve a legitimate ending may then be read as the quelling of a
fundamental disquiet concerning its own functions within the projects
of colonialist discourse.

No adequate reading of the play could afford not to comprehend both
the anxiety and the drive to closure it necessitates. Yet these aspects of
the play's 'rich complexity' have been signally ignored by European
and North American critics, who have tended to listen exclusively to
Prospero's voice: after all, he speaks their language. It has been left to
those who have suffered colonial usurpation to discover and map the
traces of that complexity by reading in full measure Caliban's
refractory place in both Prospero's play and The Tempest.[16]

VI

We have tried to show, within the limits of a brief textual analysis, how
an approach via a theory of discourse can recognize The Tempest as, in a
significant sense, a play imbricated within the discourse of colonialism;
and can, at the same time, offer an explanation of features of the play
either ignored or occluded by critical practices that have often been
complicit, whether consciously or not, with a colonialist ideology.

Three points remain to be clarified. To identify dominant discursive networks and their mode of operation within particular texts should by no means be seen as the end of the story. A more exhaustive analysis would go on to establish the precise articulation of discourses within texts: we have argued for the discourse of colonialism as the articulatory principle of The Tempest's diversity but have touched only briefly on what other discourses are articulated and where such linkages can be seen at work in the play.

Then again, each text is more than simply an instance of the operation of a discursive network. We have tried to show how much of The Tempest's complexity comes from its staging of the distinctive moves and figures of colonialist discourse. Discourse is always performative, active rather than ever merely contemplative; and, of course, the mode of the theatre will also inflect it in particular ways, tending, for example, through the inevitable (because structural) absence of any direct authorial comment, to create an effect of distantiation, which exists in a complex relationship with the countervailing (and equally structural) tendency for audiences to identify with characters presented – through the language and conventions of theatre – as heroes and heroines. Much work remains to be done on the articulation between discursive performance and mode of presentation.

Finally, we have been concerned to show how The Tempest has been severed from its discursive con-texts through being produced by criticism as an autotelic unity, and we have tried therefore to exemplify an approach that would engage with the fully dialectical relationship between the detail of the text and the larger discursive formations. But nor can theory and criticism be exempt from such relationships. Our essay too must engage in the discursive struggle that determines the history within which the Shakespearean texts will be located and read: it matters what kind of history that is.

10

HISTORY AND IDEOLOGY

The instance of *Henry V*
Jonathan Dollimore and *Alan Sinfield*

I

> Behind the disorder of history Shakespeare assumed some kind of
> order or degree on earth having its counterpart in heaven. Further, . . .
> in so assuming he was using the thought-idiom of his age and could
> have avoided doing so only by not thinking at all.
>
> (Tillyard 1944 (1962) p. 21)

The objections are familiar enough: the 'Elizabethan World Picture'
simplifies the Elizabethans and, still more, Shakespeare. Yet if we look
again at what Tillyard was opposing, his historicism seems less objec-
tionable – assertions, for example, that Shakespeare does not 'seem to
call for explanations beyond those which a whole heart and a free
mind abundantly supply'; that 'he betrays no bias in affairs of church
or state'; that 'No period of Enghsh literature has less to do with
politics than that during which English letters reached their zenith'

(Campbell 1964, pp. 3–4). All these quotations are taken by Lily B. Campbell from critics influential between the wars. She and Tillyard demonstrate unquestionably that there was an ideological position, something like 'the Elizabethan World picture', and that it is a significant presence in Shakespeare's plays. Unfortunately inadequacies in their theorizing of ideology have set the agenda for most subsequent work. We shall argue initially that even that criticism which has sought to oppose the idea that Shakespeare believed in and expresses a political hierarchy whose rightness is guaranteed by its reflection of a divine hierarchy, is trapped nevertheless in a problematic of order, one which stems from a long tradition of idealist philosophy.

Tillyard makes little of the fact that the writers he discusses were members of the class fraction of which the government of the country was constituted, or were sponsored by the government, or aspired to be. He seems not to notice that the *Homily Against Disobedience and Wilful Rebellion* is designed to preserve an oppressive regime – he admires the 'dramatic touch' at the start, 'a splendid picture of original obedience and order in the Garden of Eden' (Tillyard 1944 (1962), p. 69) His skills of critical analysis do not show him that the projection of an alleged human order onto an alleged divine order affords, in effect even if not intention, a mystifying confirmation of the *status quo*. On the contrary, he claims to show that Shakespeare was 'the voice of his own age first and only through being that, the voice of humanity' (ibid., p. 237). In similar fashion, Campbell speaks of 'the political philosophy of [Shakespeare's] age' as 'universal truth':

> If however, he is not merely a poet but a great poet, the particulars of his experience are linked in meaning to the universal of which they are a representative part ... a passion for universal truth ... takes his hatred and his love out of the realm of the petty and into the realm of the significant.
>
> (Campbell 1964, p. 6)

Of course, much critical energy has been spent on opposing Tillyard and Campbell; they were writing during the Second World War, and the idea that the great English writer propounded attitudes which tended to encourage acquiescence in government policy has come to seem less attractive subsequently. One point of view argues that Shakespeare saw through the Tudor Myth and, with it, all human aspirations and especially political aspirations. Shakespeare's plays are thus made to speak an absurdist or nihilist idea of the 'human condition' – a precise reversal of the divinely guaranteed harmony proclaimed by Tillyard. A second point of view again argues the limitations of the Tudor Myth and the futility of politics, but asserts over against these the possibility of individual integrity. This inhibits even more effectively specific consideration of how power works and how it may be challenged, since integrity may be exercised within – or, even better, over and against – any socio-political arrangements.

Anguish at the failure of the idea of order is represented most importantly by Jan Kott's *Shakespeare Our Contemporay* (1967). Kott sees that the Tudor Myth was always a political device, and he argues that the history plays disclose this. He sees also that the legitimacy or illegitimacy, the goodness or badness of the monarch, is not the real issue: 'there are no bad kings, or good kings; kings are only kings. Or let us put it in modern terms: there is only the king's situation, and the system' (p. 14). Kott has here the basis for a materialist analysis of power and ideology, but then takes the argument towards an inevitable, all-encompassing inversion of cosmic order: 'The implacable roller of history crushes everybody and everything. Man is determined by his situation, by the step of the grand staircase on which he happens to find himself' (p. 39). There seems to be no play in such a system – no scope for intervention, subversion, negotiation; analysis of specific historical process, with the enabling as well as the limiting possibilities within an ideological conjuncture, seems futile – the point being, precisely, that everything is pointless.

Kott does little more than invert the Elizabethan World Picture: the terms of the debate are not changed. As Derrida insists, a metaphysic of order is not radically undermined by invoking disorder; the two terms are necessary to each other, within the one problematic.[1] Order is predicated on the undesirability of disorder, and vice versa. 'Theatre of the Absurd', which Kott invokes in his chapter comparing *King Lear* to Beckett's *Endgame*, takes its whole structure from the absence of God, and therefore cannot but affirm the importance and desirability of God. Kott's approach has been influential, especially in the theatre, for it has chimed in with attention to modernist and existentialist writings which offer as profound studies of the human condition a critique of progressive ideals and an invocation of 'spiritual' alienation.[2]

The limitations of the Tudor Myth are pressed also by Wilbur Sanders in *The Dramatist and the Received Idea* (1968). Here the switch is not towards the futility of existence generally but towards the priority of personal integrity. Like Kott, he sees the plays as showing political action to be essentially futile, and that there is an inevitability in historical process before which 'even the best type of conservatism is ultimately powerless' (p. 157). But Sanders' next move is not into the absurd, but into a countervailing ideal order of individual integrity: the issue is how far any character 'has been able to find a mature, responsible, fully human way of preserving his integrity in face of the threatening realities of political life' (p. 166; cf. also p. 190). The selfish and inconsequential nature of this project, especially in so far as it is assigned to those who actually exercise power over others in their society, seems not to strike Sanders. Moreover, by refusing to discuss the political conditions within which integrity is to be exercised, he deprives his characters of knowledge which they would need to make meaningful choices; for instance, the decision York has to make between Richard II and Bolingbroke is structured by contradictions in the concept of monarchy and the position of regent, and York's integrity cannot be analysed sensibly without discussing those contradictions (cf Sanders 1968, pp. 183–5).

Sanders' position approaches the point where historical sequence, with all its injustice and suffering, may be regarded merely as a testing ground for the individual to mature upon. He seeks to fend off such anarchistic implications by declaring that 'In Shakespeare's imagination the ideal social order, the mutuality of fulfilled human society, is inseparably bound up with the sacredness of the individual' (p. 332). Literary critics have tended to place much stress on the sacredness, the redemptive power of the individual, especially in discussions of the tragedies. G. K. Hunter summarizes what he calls the 'modern' view of *King Lear*: it

> is seen as the greatest of tragedies because it not only strips and reduces and assaults human dignity, but because it also shows . . . the

> process of restoration by which humanity can recover from degrad-
> ation. . . . [Lear's] retreat into the isolated darkness of his own mind is
> also a descent into the seed-bed of a new life; for the individual mind
> is seen here as a place from which a man's most important qualities
> and relationships draw the whole of their potential.
>
> (Hunter 1978, pp. 251–2)

Sanders's recourse to the individual is less confident than this; in fact in places he remains poised uneasily between Kott and Tillyard, unable entirely to admit or repudiate the position of either. The characters he considers prove 'seriously defective' and he is driven to acknowledge the possibility that Shakespeare is expressing 'tragic cynicism' (p. 185). Thus he veers towards Kott. To protect himself from this, and to posit some final ground for the integrity he demands, he swerves back towards something very like Tillyard's Christian humanism, wonder-ing even 'whether we can receive [the Elizabethans'] humane wisdom without their belief in absolutes' (p. 333). The entrapment of the Shakespearean characters is thus reproduced for the modern reader, who is required similarly to quest for an elusive wholeness within conditions whose determinants are to be neither comprehended nor challenged.

Perhaps the most fundamental error in all these accounts of the role of ideology is falsely to unify history and/or the individual human subject. In one, history is unified by a teleological principle conferring meaningful order (Tillyard), in another by the inverse of this – Kott's 'implacable roller'. And Sanders's emphasis on moral or subjective integrity implies a different though related notion of unity: an experience of subjective autonomy, of an essential self uncontamin-ated by the corruption of worldly process; 'individual integrity' implies in the etymology of both words an ideal unity: the undivided, the integral.

Theories of the ultimate unity of both history and the human subject derive of course from a western philosophical tradition where, more-over, they have usually implied each other: the universal being seen as manifested through individual essences which in turn presuppose uni-versals. Often unawares, idealist literary criticism has worked within or in the shadow of this tradition, as can be seen for example in its insistence that the universal truths of great literature are embodied in coherent and consistent 'characters'.[3]

The alternative to this is not to become fixated on its negation – universal chaos and subjective fragmentation – but rather to understand history and the human subject in terms of social and political process. Crucial for such an understanding is a materialist account of ideology.

Ideology is composed of those beliefs, practices and institutions which work to legitimate the social order – especially by the process of representing sectional or class interests as universal ones.[4] This process presupposes that there are others, subordinate classes, who far from sharing the interests of the dominant class are in fact being exploited by that class. This is one reason why the dominant tend not only to 'speak for' subordinate classes but actively to repress them as well. This repression operates coercively but also ideologically (the two are in practice inseparable). So for example at the same time that the Elizabethan ruling fraction claimed to lead and speak for all, it persecuted those who did not fit in, even blaming them for the social instability which originated in its own policies. This is an instance of a process of displacement crucial then (and since) in the formation of dominant identities – class, cultural, racial and sexual.

Ideology is not just a set of ideas, it is material practice, woven into the fabric of everyday life. At the same time, the dominant ideology is realized specifically through the institutions of education, the family, the law, religion, journalism and culture. In the Elizabethan state all these institutions worked to achieve ideological unity – not always successfully, for conflicts and contradictions remained visible at all levels, even within the dominant class fraction and its institutions. The theatre was monitored closely by the state – both companies and plays had to be licensed – and yet its institutional position was complex. On the one hand, it was sometimes summoned to perform at Court and as such may seem a direct extension of royal power (see Orgel 1982); on the other hand, it was the mode of cultural production in which market forces were strongest, and as such it was especially exposed to the influence of subordinate and emergent classes. We should not, therefore, expect any straightforward relationship between plays and ideology: on the contrary, it is even likely that the topics which engaged writers and audiences alike were those where ideology was under strain. We will take as an instance for study *Henry V*, and it will appear that even in this play, which is often assumed to be the one where Shakespeare is closest to state propaganda, the construction of ideology is complex – even as it consolidates, it betrays inherent instability.

The principal strategy of ideology is to legitimate inequality and exploitation by representing the social order which perpetuates these things as immutable and unalterable – as decreed by God or simply natural. Since the Elizabethan period the ideological appeal to God has tended to give way to the equally powerful appeal to the natural. But in the earlier period both were crucial: the laws of degree and order inferred from nature were further construed as having been put there by God. One religious vision represented ultimate reality in terms of unity and stasis: human endeavour, governed by the laws of change and occupying the material domain, is ever thwarted in its aspiration, ever haunted by its loss of an absolute which can only be regained in transcendence, the move through death to eternal rest, to an ultimate unity inseparable from a full stasis, 'when no more *Change* shall be' and 'all shall rest eternally' (Spenser, *The Faerie Queene*, VII, ii). This metaphysical vision has its political uses, especially when aiding the process of subjection by encouraging renunciation of the material world and a disregard of its social aspects such that oppression is experienced as a fate rather than an alterable condition. Protestantism tended to encourage engagement in the world rather than withdrawal from it; most of *The Faerie Queene* is about the urgent questing of knights and ladies. The theological underpinning of this activist religion was the doctrine of callings: 'God bestows his gifts upon us . . . that they might be employed in his service and to his glory, and that in this life.'[5] This doctrine legitimated the expansive assertiveness of a social order which was bringing much of Britain under centralized control, colonizing parts of the New World and trading vigorously with most of the Old, and which was to experience revolutionary changes. At the same time, acquiescence in an unjust social order (like that encouraged by a fatalistic metaphysic of stasis) seemed to be effected, though less securely, by an insistence that 'whatsoever any man enterpriseth or doth, either in word or deed, he must do it by virtue of his calling, and he must keep himself within the compass, limits or precincts thereof' (Perkins 1970, p. 449). This ideology was none the less metaphysical.

Such an activist ideology is obviously appropriate for the legitim-ation of warfare, and so we find it offered by the Archbishop of Canter-bury in *Henry V* – as the Earl of Essex set off for Ireland in 1599 Lancelot Andrewes assured the Queen in a sermon that it was 'a war sanctified' (Andrewes 1841, I, p. 325). In the honeybees speech human endeavour is not denigrated but harnessed in an imaginary unity quite different from that afforded by stasis: 'So may a thousand actions, once afoot, / End in one purpose' (I. ii. 211–12). Like so many political ideologies, this one shares something essential with the overtly religious metaphysic it appears to replace, namely a teleological explanation of its own image of legitimate power – that is, an explan-ation which is justified through the assertion that such power derives from an inherent natural and human order encoded by God. Thus the 'one purpose' derives from an order rooted in 'a rule in nature' (I. ii. 188), itself a manifestation of 'heavenly' creation, God's regulative structuring of the universe. What this inherent structure guarantees above all is, predictably, obedience:

> Therefore doth heaven divide
> The state of man in divers functions,
> Setting endeavour in continual motion;
> To which is fixed, as an aim or butt,
> Obedience.

> (I. ii. 183–7)

And what in turn underpins obedience is the idea of one's job or calling – in effect one's bee-like function – as following naturally from a God-given identity: soldiers,

> armed in their stings,
> Make boot upon the summer's velvet buds;
> Which pillage they with merry march bring home
> To the tent-royal of their emperor.

> (I. ii. 193–6)

The activist ideology thus displaces the emphasis on stasis yet remains thoroughly metaphysical none the less. More generally: in this period, perhaps more than any since, we can see a secular appropriation of theological categories to the extent that it may be argued that Reformation theology actually contributed to secularization (see Sinfield 1983a, chapter 7); nevertheless, it was an appropriation which depended upon continuities, the most important of which, in ideological legitimation, is this appeal to teleology.

Not only the justification of the war but, more specifically, the heroic representation of Henry, works in such terms. His is a power rooted in nature – blood, lineage and breeding: 'The blood and courage that renowned them / Runs in your veins' (I. ii. 118–19) – but also deriving ultimately from God's law as it is encoded in nature and, by extension, society: France belongs to him 'by gift of heaven, / By law of nature and of nations' (II. iv. 79–80). Conversely the French king's power is construed in terms of 'borrow'd glories', 'custom'. and 'mettle . . . bred out' (II. iv. 79, 83; III. v. 29). With this theory of legitimate versus illegitimate power the responsibility for aggression is displaced onto its victims. Thus does war find its rationale, injustice its justification.

There are two levels of disturbance in the state and the ideology which legitimates it: contradiction and conflict.[6] Contradiction is the more fundamental, in the sense of being intrinsic to the social process as a whole – when for example the dominant order negates what it needs or, more generally, in perpetuating itself produces also its own negation. Thus, for example, in the seventeenth century monarchy legitimates itself in terms of religious attitudes which themselves come to afford a justification for opposition to monarchy. We shall be observing contradiction mainly as it manifests itself in the attempts of ideology to contain it. Conflict occurs between opposed interests, either as a state of disequilibrium or as active struggle; it occurs along the structural fault lines produced by contradictions. Ideology has always been challenged, not least by the exploited themselves, who have resisted its oppressive construction of them and its mystification of their disadvantaged social position. One concern of a materialist criticism is with the history of such resistance, with the attempt to recover the voices and cultures of the repressed and marginalized in history and writing. Moreover, ideology is destabilized not only from below, but by antagonisms within and among the dominant class or class fraction (high, as opposed to popular, literature will often manifest this kind of destabilization). Whereas idealist literary criticism has tended to emphasize the transcendence of conflict and contradiction, materialist criticism seeks to stay with them, wanting to understand them better.

Ideologies which represent society as a spurious unity must of necessity also efface conflict and contradiction. How successful they are in achieving this depends on a range of complex and interrelated factors, only a few of which we have space to identify here. One such will be the relative strength of emergent, subordinate and oppositional elements within society (see Raymond Williams 1977, pp. 121–7). The endless process of contest and negotiation between these elements and the dominant culture is often overlooked in the use of some structuralist perspectives within cultural analysis.

One other factor which militates against the success of ideological misrepresentation involves a contradiction fundamental to ideology itself (and this will prove specially relevant to *Henry V*): the more ideology (necessarily) engages with the conflict and contradiction which it is its *raison d'être* to occlude, the more it becomes susceptible to incorporating them within itself. It faces the contradictory situation whereby to silence dissent one must first give it a voice, to misrepresent it one must first present it.

These factors make for an inconsistency and indeterminacy in the representation of ideological harmony in writing: the divergencies have to be included if the insistence on unity is to have any purchase, yet at the same time their inclusion invites sceptical interrogation of the ideological appearance of unity, of the effacements of actual conflict. There may be no way of resolving whether one, or which one, of these tendencies (unity versus divergencies) overrides the other in a particular play, but in a sense it does not matter: there is here an indeterminacy which alerts us to the complex but always significant process of theatrical representation and, through that, of political and social process.

II

It is easy for us to assume, reading *Henry V*, that foreign war was a straightforward ground upon which to establish and celebrate national unity. In one sense this is so and it is the basic concern of the play. But in practice foreign war was the site of competing interests, material and ideological, and the assumption that the nation must unite against a common foe was shot through with conflict and contradiction. This was equally true for the hegemonic class fraction, though it was they who needed, urgently, to deny divisions and insist that everyone's purpose was the same. Queen Elizabeth feared foreign war because it was risky and expensive and threatened to disturb the fragile balance on which her power was founded. Members of the Privy Council favoured it – in some cases because it would strengthen their faction (puritans continually urged military support for continental protestants), in other cases because it would enhance their personal, military and hence political power. The Church resented the fact that it was expected to help finance foreign wars; but in 1588 Archbishop Whitgift encouraged his colleagues to contribute generously towards resistance to the Armada on the grounds – just as in *Henry V* – that it would head off criticism of the Church's wealth.[7]

For the lower orders, war meant increased taxation, which caused both hardship and resentment, as Francis Bacon testified in Parliament in 1593 (Neale 1957, pp. 309–10). On the other hand war profited some people, though in ways which hardly inspired national unity. Some officers took money in return for discharging mustered men and enlisting others instead – Essex complained in Star Chamber in 1596 that 'the liege and free people of this realm are sold like cattle in a market' (De Bruyn 1981, p. 36). In 1589 Sir John Smith overheard two gentlemen joking that the recent military expedition against Spain 'would be worth unto one of them above a thousand marks and to the other above £400 . . . by the death of so many of their tenants that died in the journey: that the new fines for other lives would be worth that or more' (Hunt 1983, p. 33). War, in these aspects, must have tended to discredit ideas of shared national purpose. Indeed, there are a number of reports of mutinous individuals asserting that poor people would do better under the King of Spain (Hunt 1983, pp. 60–1). This desperate inversion, whereby the demonized other of state propaganda was perceived as preferable, indicates the difficulty people have in envisaging alternatives to the existing power structure.

In fact, Henry V is only in one sense 'about' national unity: its obsessive preoccupation is insurrection. The King is faced with actual or threatened insurrection from almost every quarter: the Church, 'treacherous' fractions within the ruling class, slanderous subjects, and soldiers who undermine the war effort, either by exploiting it or by sceptically interrogating the King's motives. All these areas of possible resistance in the play had their counterparts in Elizabethan England and the play seems, in one aspect, committed to the aesthetic colonization of such elements in Elizabethan culture; systematically, antagonism is reworked as subordination or supportive alignment. It is not so much that these antagonisms are openly defeated but rather that they are represented as inherently submissive. Thus the Irish, Welsh and Scottish soldiers manifest not their countries' centrifugal relationship to England but an ideal subservience of margin to centre. Others in the play are seen to renounce resistance in favour of submission. Perhaps the most interesting instance of this is the full and public repentance of the traitors, Cambridge, Grey and Scroop. Personal confession becomes simultaneously a public acknowledgement of the rightness of that which was challenged. It is of course one of the most authoritative ideological legitimations available to the powerful: to be sincerely validated by former opponents – especially when their confessional self-abasement is in excess of what might be expected from the terms of their defeat.

Nevertheless, we should not assume inevitable success for such strategies of containment; otherwise how could there have been Catholic recusants, the Essex rebellion, enclosure riots? Henry V belongs to a period in which the ideological dimension of authority – that which helps effect the internalization rather than simply the coercion of obedience – is recognized as imperative and yet, by that self-same recognition, rendered vulnerable to demystification. For example, the very thought that the actual purpose of the war might be to distract from troubles at home would tend to undermine the purposed effect. The thought is voiced twice in 2 Henry IV: it is part of the advice given to Hal by his father (IV. v. 212–15) and John of Lancaster envisages it in the final speech. It is suppressed in *Henry V* – yet it twice surfaces obliquely (II. i. 90–2; IV. i. 228–9).

At the height of his own programme of self-legitimation Henry 'privately' declares his awareness of the ideological role of 'ceremony' (IV. i. 242–5). In the same soliloquy Henry speaks his fear of deceptive obedience – masking actual antagonism. It is a problem of rule which the play represses and resolves and yet reintroduces here in a half-rationalized form, as the 'hard condition! / Twin-born with greatness' is presented initially as the sheer burden of responsibility carried by the ruler, the loneliness of office, but then as a particular kind of fear. As the soliloquy develops its sub-text comes to the fore, and it is the same sub-text as that in the confrontation with Bates and Williams: the possibility, the danger of subjects who disobey. What really torments Henry is the inability to ensure obedience. His 'greatnesss' is 'subject to the breath / Of every fool', 'instead of homage sweet' he experiences 'poison'd flattery', and although he can coerce the beggar's knee he cannot fully control it (IV. i. 240–1, 256–7). Not surprisingly, he has bad dreams. The implication is that subjects are to be envied not because, as Henry suggests, they are more happy in fearing than (like him) being feared, but almost the reverse: because as subjects they cannot suffer the king's fear of being disobeyed and opposed. Henry indicates a paradox of power only to misrecognize its force by mystifying both kingship and subjection. His problem is structural, since the same ceremonies or role-playing which constitute kingship are the means by which real antagonisms can masquerade as obedience – 'poison'd flattery'. Hence, perhaps, the slippage at the end of the speech from relatively cool analysis of the situation of the labouring person (referred to initially as 'private men', lines 243–4) into an attack on him or her as 'wretched slave . . . vacant mind . . . like a lackey' (274–9), and finally 'slave' of 'gross brain' (287–8).

The play circles obsessively around the inseparable issues of unity and division, inclusion and exclusion. Before Agincourt the idea of idle and implicitly disaffected people at home is raised (IV. iii. 16–18), but this is converted into a pretext for the King to insist upon his army as a 'band of brothers' (IV. iii. 60). Conversely, unity of purpose may be alleged and then undercut. The Act III Chorus asks:

who is he, whose chin is but enrich'd
With one appearing hair, that will not follow
These cull'd and choice-drawn cavaliers to France?

(lines 22–4)

But within fifty lines Nym, the Boy and Pistol are wishing they were in London.

However, the threat of disunity did not involve only the common people. That the king and the aristocracy have more interest in foreign wars and in the area of 'England' produced by them than do the common people is easy enough for us to see now. But such a straight-forward polarization does not yield an adequate account of the divergent discourses which inform *Henry V*; on the contrary, it accepts uncritically a principal proposition of Elizabethan state ideology, namely that the ruling class was coherent, and unified in its purposes, a proposition necessary to the idea that the state could be relied upon to secure the peace of all its subjects. Evidence to the contrary was dangerous, helping to provoke the thought that most violence stemmed from the imposition of 'order' rather than its lack.

In practice, however, power was not coherently distributed. The Elizabethan state was in transition from a feudal to a bourgeois structure, and this had entailed and was to entail considerable violent disruption (see Anderson 1974, pp 16–59, 113–42). Whilst the aristocracy helped to sponsor the ideology of the monarch's supreme authority, it actually retained considerable power itself and the power of the crown probably decreased during Elizabeth's reign (MacCaffrey 1965). Elizabeth could maintain her position only through political adroitness, patronage and force – and all these, the latter especially, could be exercised only by and through the aristocracy itself. Elizabeth could oppose the Earl of Leicester if supported by Burghley, or vice versa, but she could not for long oppose them both. After the death of Leicester in 1589 the power struggle was not so symmetrical. The rise of the youthful, charismatic and militarily impressive Earl of Essex introduced a new element: he rivalled the Queen herself as Burghley and Leicester never did. The more service, especially military, Essex performed, the more he established a rival power base, and Elizabeth did not care for it (Harrison 1937, p. 102 and chapters 9–12). The Irish expedition was make or break for both; Essex would be away from court and vulnerable to schemes against him, but were he to return with spectacular success he would be unstoppable. In the event he was not successful, and thus found himself pushed into a corner where he could see no alternative but direct revolt. The exuberance of *Henry V* leads most commentators to link it with the early stages of the Irish expedition when the successful return could be anticipated; the Chorus of Act V (lines 29–35) actually compares Henry's return to England with it and there are indeed parallels between Henry and Essex. Both left dangers at home when they went to war, besieged Rouen, sacked foreign towns, were taken to represent a revival of chivalry and national purpose; Essex was already associated with Bolingbroke (Harrison 1937, pp. 214–15). The crucial difference of course is that Essex is not the monarch. That is why Henry must be welcomed 'much more, and much more cause'. Henry is both general and ruler, and therefore the structural problem of the over-mighty subject – the repeated theme of other plays – does not present itself.

The existence of such a profound structural flaw at the centre of state power affords a cardinal exemplification of why the representation of ideological containment so often proves complex and ambiguous. The pyramid of the Tudor Myth was under strain at its very apex, for the legitimate ruler was not the most powerful person – the same issue promotes the action of *Henry VI, Macbeth* and many other plays. *Henry V* was a powerful Elizabethan fantasy simply because it represented a single source of power in the state. Nothing is allowed to compete with the authority of the King. The noblemen are so lacking in distinctive qualities that they are commonly reorganized or cut in production. And the point where the issue might have presented itself – the plot of Cambridge, Scroop and Grey – is hardly allowed its actual historical significance. Holinshed makes it plain that Cambridge's purpose in conspiring against Henry was to exalt to the crown Edmund Mortimer and after that himself and his family; that he did not confess this because he did not want to incriminate Mortimer and cut off this possibility; that Cambridge's son was to claim the crown in the time of Henry VI and that this Yorkist claim was eventually successful (Bullough 1966, p. 386). Cambridge makes only an oblique reference to this structural fault in the state (II. ii. 155–7). The main impression we receive is that the conspirators were motivated by greed and incomprehensible evil – according to Henry, like 'Another fall of man' (line 142). Such arbitrary and general 'human' failings obscure the kind of instability in the ruling fraction to which the concurrent career of Essex bore witness.

That the idea of a single source of power in the state was, if not a fantasy, a rare and precarious achievement is admitted in the Epilogue. The infant Henry VI succeeded, 'Whose state so many had the managing, / That they lost France and made his England bleed' (lines 11–12). Many managers disperse power and unity falls apart.

The aristocracy is the most briskly handled of the various agents of disruption. Whether this is because it was the least or the most problematic is a fascinating question, but one upon which we can only speculate. *Henry V* far more readily admits of problems in the role of the Church, though the main effect of this is again to concentrate power, now spiritual as well as secular, upon the King. The Archbishop's readiness to use the claim to France to protect the Church's interests tends to discredit him and the Church, but this allows the King to appropriate their spiritual authority. Thus power which, in actuality, was distributed unevenly across an unstable fraction of the hegemonic class is drawn into the person of the monarch; he becomes its sole source of expression, the site and guarantee of ideological unity. This is a crucial effect of a process already identified, namely a complex, secular appropriation of the religious metaphysic in the legitimation of war:

> his wildness, mortified in him,
> Seem'd to die too; yea, at that very moment,
> Consideration like an angel came,
> And whipp'd th'offending Adam out of him,

> (I. i. 26–9)

The language is that of the Prayer Book service of Baptism: Henry takes over from the Church sacramental imagery which seems to transcend all worldly authority. Thus he is protected at once from any imputation of irreligion which might seem to arise from a preparedness to seize Church property, and he becomes the representative of the personal piety which adhered only doubtfully to the bishops. In him contradictions are resolved or transcended. This presumably is why the clerics are not needed after Act I. From the beginning and increasingly, Henry's appeals to God, culminating in the insistence that 'God fought for us' (IV. viii. 122), enact the priestly role as Andrewes in his sermon on the Essex expedition identified it. He observed that in successful Old Testament wars 'a captain and a Prophet sorted together' (Andrewes 1841, I, p. 326): the two roles are drawn into the single figure of Henry V.

On the eve of Agincourt Henry gives spiritual counsel to his soldiers:

> Every subject's duty is the king's; but every subject's soul is his own. Therefore should every soldier in the wars do as every sick man in his bed, wash every mote out of his conscience; and dying so, death is to him advantage; or not dying, the time was blessedly lost wherein such preparation was gained
>
> (IV. i. 182–9)

It is the high point of Henry's priestly function, the point at which the legitimation which religion could afford to the state is most fully incorporated into a single ideological effect. Yet Henry is defensive and troubled by the exchange and Williams is not satisfied. What has happened, surely, is that the concentration of ideological power upon Henry seems to amount also to concentration of responsibility:

> Upon the king! let us our lives, our souls,
> Our debts, our careful wives,
> Our children, and our sins lay on the king!
>
> (IV. i. 236–8)

In the play the drive for ideological coherence has systematically displaced the roles of Church and aristocracy and nothing seems to stand between the king and the souls of his subjects who are to die in battle.

The issue is handled in two main ways by Henry. First, he reduces it to the question of soldiers who have committed serious crimes, for which Henry can then refuse responsibility; initial questions about widows and orphans (IV. i. 141–3) slip out of sight. Second, the distinction between him and his subjects is effaced by his insistence that 'the king is but a man' (IV. i. 101–2) and that he himself gains nothing, indeed loses from the power structure:

> O ceremony, show me but thy worth!
> What is thy soul of adoration?
> Art thou aught else but place, degree, and form,
> Creating awe and fear in other men?
> Wherein thou art less happy, being fear'd,
> Than they in fearing.
>
> (IV. i. 250–5):

Here the king himself is collapsed, syntactically, into the mere shows of ceremony: 'thou' in the third line quoted refers to 'ceremony', in the fifth to Henry, and he slips from one to the other without the customary formal signals.[8] The effect, if we credit it, is to leave 'place, degree, and form', 'awe and fear' standing without the apparent support of human agency: Henry engrosses in himself the ideological coherence of the state and then, asked to take responsibility for the likely defeat of Agincourt, claims to be an effect of the structure which he seemed to guarantee.

The Act II Chorus wants to proclaim unity: 'honour's thought / Reigns solely in the breast of every man' – but is rapidly obliged to admit treachery: 'O England! . . . Were all thy children kind and natural!' (lines 3–4, 16, 19). The following scene is not however about Cambridge, Scroop and Grey, but Nym, Bardolph and Pistol. This disputatious faction proves much more difficult to incorporate than the rebel nobility. Increasingly, since 2 Henry IV, sympathy for these characters has been withdrawn; from this point on there seems to be nothing positive about them. It is here that Fluellen enters, offering an alternative to Falstaff among the lesser gentry and an issue – the control of England over the British Isles – easier to cope with. Fluellen may be funny, old-fashioned and pedantic, but he is totally committed to the King and his purposes, as the King recognizes (IV. i. 83–4). The low characters are condemned not only to death but to exclusion from national unity; it is as if they have had their chance and squandered it. Gower describes Pistol as 'a gull, a fool, a rogue, that now and then goes to the wars to grace himself at his return into London under the form of a soldier' (III. vi. 68–70) and Bardolph endorses the identification:

> Well, bawd I'll turn,
> And something lean to cut-purse of quick hand.
> To England will I steal, and there I'll steal:
> And patches will I get unto these cudgell'd scars,
> And swear I got them in the Gallia wars.
>
> (V. i. 89–93).

This group, disbanded soldiers, was a persistent danger and worry in Elizabethan society; William Hunt suggests that 'embittered veterans and deserters brought back from the Low Countries the incendiary myth of an army of avengers'.[9] Two proclamations were issued in 1589 against 'the great outrages that have been, and are daily committed by soldiers, mariners and others that pretend to have served as soldiers, upon her Highness' good and loving subjects'; martial law was instigated to hang offenders (De Bruyn 1981, p. 62). The Elizabethan state was prepared to exclude from its tender care such persons, perhaps exemplifying the principle whereby dominant groups identify themselves by excluding or expelling others; not only are the virtues necessary for membership identified by contrast with the vices of the excluded, but, often, the vices of the dominant are displaced onto the excluded. That Pistol has this degree of significance is suggested by the play's reluctance to let him go. He is made to discredit himself once more at Agincourt (IV. iv) and in his final confrontation with Fluellen he is clumsily humiliated (V. I).

Despite the thorough dismissal of Bardolph, Nym and Pistol, Henry V does not leave the issue of lower-class disaffection. If those characters must be abandoned because unworthy or incapable of being incorporated into the unified nation, yet others must be introduced who will prove more tractable.

The issue of the English domination of Wales, Scotland and Ireland appears in the play to be more containable, though over the centuries it may have caused more suffering and injustice than the subjection of the lower classes. The scene of the four captains (III. iii) seems to effect an effortless incorporation, one in which, as Philip Edwards has pointed out, the Irish Macmorris is even made to protest that he does not belong to a distinct nation.[10] The English captain, of course, is more sensible than the others. Most attention is given to Fluellen – Wales must have seemed the most tractable issue, for it had been annexed in 1536 and the English church and legal system had been imposed; Henry V and the Tudors could indeed claim to be Welsh. The jokes about the way Fluellen pronounces the English language are, apparently, for the Elizabethan audience and many since, an adequate way of handling the repression of the Welsh language and culture; the annexation of 1536 permitted only English speakers to hold administrative office in Wales (D. Williams 1977, chapter 3).

Ireland was the great problem – the one Essex was supposed to resolve. The population was overwhelmingly Catholic and liable to support a continental invader, and resistance to English rule proved irrepressible, despite or more probably because of the many atrocities committed against the people – such as the slaughter of all the six hundred inhabitants of Rathlin Island by John Norris and Francis Drake in 1575. The assumption that the Irish were a barbarous and inferior people was so ingrained in Elizabethan England that it seemed only a natural duty to subdue them and destroy their culture.[11] Indeed, at one level their ideological containment was continuous with the handling of the disaffected lower-class outgroup (a proclamation of 1594 dealt together with vagabonds who begged 'upon pretense of service in the wars without relief' and 'men of Ireland that have these late years unnaturally served as rebels against her majesty's forces beyond the seas').[12] But much more was at stake in the persistent Irish challenge to the power of the Elizabethan state, and it should be related to the most strenuous challenge to the English unity in *Henry V*: like Philip Edwards, we see the attempt to conquer France and the union in peace at the end of the play as re-presentation of the attempt to conquer Ireland and the hoped-for unity of Britain (Edwards 1979, pp. 74–86). The play offers a displaced, imaginary resolution of one of the state's most intractable problems.

Indeed, the play is fascinating precisely to the extent that it is implicated in and can be read to disclose both the struggles of its own historical moment and their ideological representation. To see the play in such terms is not at all to conclude that it is merely a deluded and mystifying ideological fantasy. We observed that the King finally has difficulty, on the eve of Agincourt, in sustaining the responsibility which seems to belong with the ideological power which he had engrossed to himself: thus the fantasy of establishing ideological unity in the sole figure of the monarch arrives at an impasse which it can handle only with difficulty. As we have argued, strategies of containment presuppose centrifugal tendencies, and how far any particular instance carries conviction cannot be resolved by literary criticism. If we attend to the play's different levels of signification rather than its implied containments, it becomes apparent that the question of conviction is finally a question about the diverse conditions of reception. How far the King's argument is to be credited is a standard question for conventional criticism, but a materialist analysis takes several steps back and reads real historical conflict in and through his ambiguities. Relative to such conflict, the question of Henry's integrity becomes less interesting.

If *Henry V* represents the fantasy of a successful Irish campaign it also offers, from the very perspective of that project, a disquietingly excessive evocation of suffering and violence:

> If not, why, in a moment look to see
> The blind and bloody soldier with foul hand
> Defile the locks of your shrill-shrieking daughters;
> Your fathers taken by the silver beards,
> And their most reverend heads dash'd to the walls;
> Your naked infants spitted upon pikes,
> Whiles the mad mothers with their howls confus'd
> Do break the clouds, as did the wives of Jewry
> At Herod's bloody-hunting slaughterman.
>
> (III. iii. 33–41)

This reversal of Henry's special claim to Christian imagery – now he is Herod against the Innocents – is not actualized in the play (contrary to the sources, in which Harfleur is sacked), but its rhetoric is powerful and at Agincourt the prisoners are killed (IV. vi. 37). Here and elsewhere, the play dwells upon imagery of slaughter to a degree which disrupts the harmonious unity towards which ideology strives. So it was with Ireland: even those who, like the poet Edmund Spenser, defended torture and murder expressed compunction at the effects of English policy:

> they were brought to such wretchedness, as that any stony heart would have rued the same. Out of every corner of the woods and glens they came creeping forth upon their hands, for their legs would not bear them. . . . They did eat of the dead carions . . .
>
> (Spenser 1970, p. 104)

The human cost of imperial ambition protruded through even its ideological justifications, and the government felt obliged to proclaim that its intentions was not 'an utter extirpation and rooting out of that nation' (Hughes and Larkin 1969, III, p. 201). The claim of the state to be the necessary agent of peace and justice was manifestly contradicted. Ireland was, and remains, its bad conscience.

Henry V can be read to reveal not only the strategies of power but also the anxieties informing both them and their ideological representation. In the Elizabethan theatre to foreground and even to promote such representations was not to foreclose on their interrogation. We might conclude from this that Shakespeare was indeed wonderfully impartial on the question of politics (as the quotations in our opening paragraph claim); alternatively, we might conclude that the ideology which saturates his texts, and their location in history, are the most interesting things about them.

AFTERWORD

Robert Weimann

Upon rereading *Alternative Shakespeares*, my first impulse is to congratulate the series editor and the editor of this volume on the publisher's decision to honour the 25th anniversary of the *New Accents* series by the republication of some of its most influential titles. The present volume, as many readers will agree, belongs to this category. As with perhaps no other in the series, its very title heralds the crucial aspect of the paradigm shift exemplified on its pages: after the end of consensus, the great classic, even Shakespeare, yields up its unity of meaning, identity and function in today's culture. The pluralized version of the Bard's *nomen*, abundantly vindicated since this volume's appearance, serves as a compelling *omen* of the cultural landslide affecting the larger premises on which, traditionally, Shakespeare criticism stood.

Perhaps only now, almost two decades after its first appearance, can we view in perspective the contestatory thrust that lies behind this pluralizing gesture. Let us for a moment recall that, over two centuries at least, Shakespeare critics tended to read him more or less in terms of Emerson's verdict, 'the poet is representative'. In so doing, they could derive an air of authority and security from an element of harmony or at least correspondence between the function of their criticism (usually on behalf of some national and educational design) and the functioning of its subject-matter. While the function of traditional Shakespeare criticism and what was taken to be the dramatist's own 'purpose of playing' were clearly not identical, they had a good deal in common. Identifying the poet's original meaning with what was meaningful in their own sense of the human condition, these critics tended, in Catherine Belsey's pregnant phrase, 'to fix meaning, to arrest its process and deny its plurality.' In doing so, they reduced or eliminated the difference between then and now, but also between what was represented and who was doing the representing. Since the representational type of closure ascribed to these texts could be assumed to be Shakespeare's own, representational form and representative function appeared permanently to complement and enhance one another. At the point of their conjunction, the sense of continuity must have been all the more overwhelming as long as a stable, near-authentic text could be cited in which to trace what between 'at the first and now, was and is' (Hamlet, III.ii.21) taken to be the Bard's meaning. Once these sites of difference and their dynamics and contingency were obliterated, the foremost critical task that remained was to seek, recover, and reproduce Shakespeare's universally valid meanings. Even in the midst of increasingly differentiated industrial societies, this untenable proposition was made to serve Shakespeare in the singular by somehow bracketing into one notion the word of the poet, the sentiment of characters, the voice (and interest) of actors, and the understanding and feeling of a rapidly expanding variety of readers.

In so far as this traditional state of affairs can be reduced to a brief formula, it helps to envision the consequence as well as the timeliness of the breach in this notion of a singular Shakespeare. At the same time, having exposed the massive weight and lingering burden of the critical past in its preoccupation with closure, singularity and universality as the criteria of literary value, *Alternative Shakespeares* makes it perfectly plain that the need for alternative readings will not go away. At this juncture, the recourse to theory is particularly needful; the potently combined impulse of semiotics, deconstruction, feminism, neo-Marxism, psychoanalysis, critique of ideology and whatever else has gone into the volume was (and continues to be) requisite for developing counterproposals to any singular model in Shakespeare studies. These critical proposals would wish to be vibrant with the tensions and discontents that result from an awareness of how living in contemporary societies would for better or worse pervade our most conscientious, most scrupulous reconstructions of historical circumstances and meanings.

It is all very well to complain these days about certain inflationary uses of theory in current critical discourses. Nor can it be denied that, in recent years, there has surfaced a certain critical arrogance, as if theoretically ambitious projects can offer convincing alternatives to the close study of the processes by which discursive meanings and, I maintain, poetic forms and functions were produced in social and cultural circumstances of the past. But as long as theory's suggestive claims and interventions are made to serve disciplinary insight (rather than demonstrated and evaluated at the level of theory itself) they turn out to be indispensable for revitalizing today's Shakespeare criticism.

The present volume is a case in point. To single out only one example, the first chapter remains to this day a *locus classicus* for the discussion of the uses and abuses of ideology in Shakespeare criticism. Solidly anchored in a study of cogently specified socio-historical circumstances, Terence Hawkes' critique of a representative, aggressively literary position, provides an eye-opening exemplar of how, and to what effect, a Shakespearean text can be harnessed to the most insufferable kind of reading. Illustrating the ineffable plurality of possible interpretations, the essay's trenchant drive is not without a disciplined elegance until, uproariously, the underlying sarcasm in the writing finally (and irresistibly) explodes in Rabelaisian laughter. Placed, for very good reasons, as the opening chapter, the essay's argument, like a powerful *leitmotif*, insists on the acute need for alternative readings. Revealing a particularly stark underside to the uses of Shakespeare's text, this writing points to a scandalous instability in the extraction of meaning, an instability that only theory – here a theoretical concept like ideology- can hope to deal with.

Thus, *Alternative Shakespeares* has its main referent in the acts of reception, not production. As John Drakakis notes in his Introduction, such forms of criticism are 'needed as a matter of extreme urgency' that 'will, in the final analysis, liberate these texts from the straitjacket of unexamined assumptions and traditions' and yet, for all that, will 'reject the notion that reading is itself *an exclusive effect of the text*' (pp. 24–5; my emphasis). No less commendable than either of these tasks is the necessary but ever so vulnerable conjuncture of the two. The editor's accomplishment is openly to confront both the enabling situation that requires the fullest range of contestation, and the textual constraints that limit it. Along these lines, there is his readiness not simply to contest the liberal bastions but to identify with 'a collective commitment to the principle of contestation of meaning': a principle that works 'both in relation to established views and *between* individual contributions' (p. 24).

This, indeed, is an admirable position to take, and it will stimulate future readers to share in or kindle afresh some of the excitement that the volume conveyed on the day of its first publication. With this position in view, a new generation of readers will have no problem recalling that the volume was originally addressed to, as it was written by, a younger group of people, who would now be in their fifties and sixties. Again, this only underlines the triumph when, upon republication, you discover that the majority of contributions read as freshly as if written yesterday. Still, what at the time must have appeared as an overdue articulation of rebellious critical energies cannot appear so two decades later. While, remarkably, the volume has stood the test of time, a congratulatory message culminating in the acknowledgement of its authority, even its position almost of dominance in terms of the current intellectual mainstream, might not be considered all that complimentary, at least to the subversive and deconstructive cast of mind that inspired this volume.

This may well have been the reason why the invitation to write this Afterword went to someone who is not himself a representative of Cultural Materialism, or at least finds himself at some remove from deconstruction. If, with some such premises in mind, I may conclude on a personal note (which to some extent is also an international one), my hope is the better to illustrate the ways in which enthusiasm and contestation, far from precluding one another, can come together in response to this volume.

'Enthusiasm' in critical matters is a strong word; but nothing less will do to convey recollections of my first encounter in the mid-eighties with the editor and a group of unorthodox academics associated with the present volume's critical directions. The occasion was, of all places, the annual gathering of the East German Shakespeare Society in Weimar. The intensely searching round table discussions, interspersed with brief prepared statements, extended over two or three days, during which our Anglo-American colleagues were greeted as thoroughly stimulating, warmly welcome harbingers of a new, provocatively contestatory paradigm in Shakespeare studies. The conference theme featured issues of power, discourse, and gender. At that time, there could hardly have been a more profoundly (and politically) challenging series of debates, considering the official orthodoxy of the *Einheit von Geist und Macht*, a forceful bracketing of discourse and power, *auctoritas* and *potestas*, bolstered up by unifying classical concepts of representation bridging the gap between Renaissance and socialist versions of what 'both at the first and now, was and is' realism and humanism. Even when strictly focused on Shakespeare, the counter-critical debates addressed a wide spectrum of problems, in fact too wide not to leave a number of desiderata behind. If, at this late date, these deserve at all to be recalled, the only reason is that even now, in contemplating future responses to *Alternative Shakespeares*, two of these desiderata may contain the seeds of contestatory positions that are potentially useful for stimulating further thought and discussion in and of the present volume.

First, there is the question of mimesis. In Anglo-American Shakespeare criticism, this concept is usually employed in a sense that is virtually synonymous with 'imitation', and even 'representation'. But today, is there not a stringent need to make distinctions that question the (neo)Aristotelian domestication of what mimesis stood for? In one of this volume's most thought-provoking, theoretically sophisticated contributions, Malcolm Evans' piece 'Deconstructing Shakespeare's Comedies' intriguingly portrays the 'mimetic sign' as problematically 'broken in the *signifier* released in the enactment of acting' (p. 70). But even though the editor provides a tempting enough cue, the concept is altogether either absent or reduced to what the socially distinct, and distinctly limited, cultural demands and interests of the dominant Renaissance poetics allowed. Even in a critique of critical aims and procedures, the provocative interface of semantic/semiotic perspectives on mimesis as a relevant tool of analysis is missing, as is an awareness of continental advances, from Hermann Koller to Philippe Lacoue-Labarthe, towards radically revising the Aristotelian version of the concept itself.

Second, there is the question of the text. It is surely not fortuitous that the desire to textualize cultural practice finds itself in complicity with the attempt to 'suspend mimesis in the Shakespearean text at large' (p. 95). But if 'Con-texts are themselves texts' (p. 246), does this mean that, say, pennies in a prentice's pocket, or the investment of an actor's finite wear and tear, exhaustion, recalcitrance or triumph, in short, all the non-discursive matter in a theatrical institution can be/ should be subsumed under a concept ultimately derived from writing? Certainly, it would be quite unfair to expect from this volume an anticipation of the current preoccupation with performance and the performative. But unless we are prepared hopelessly to homogenize the socially and culturally divisive site of the Elizabethan theatre, the arch-ives of writing cannot, metaphorically or methodologically, serve as the master key in massive social institutions for dealing with altogether vulnerable uses of orally delivered speech in its relation to bodies that do not represent what they perform. The question is, do we have the spirit, together with a socially anchored impulse, to think beyond the current scriptural universe of theory and thereby grasp the limits, without losing sight of the helpful uses, of deconstruction?

From the present writer's position, the greatest triumph of contest-ation is the capacity, if need be, for challenging some of its own decon-structionist directions, such as those impeding a dialectical approach to speech and the body. Those amongst us – surely a minority – who believe that Judith Butler has achieved a pioneering insight with her demonstration that the Derridean position in these matters has led to a confusion 'paralyzing the social analysis of utterance,' would as a matter of course wish to continue to applaud the present project. If the plural in Alternative Shakespeares, as its more recent sequel (1996) suggests, remains an open one, the strength of this project is such that in years to come it actually stands to gain from readings that follow up the vol-ume's invitation and in their own turn take a contestatory position, one with a difference, in Shakespeare studies.

NOTES

2 SWISSER-SWATTER: MAKING A MAN OF ENGLISH LETTERS

1 Hulme 1981. Compare Frank Kermode, introduction to the Arden edition of *The Tempest* (Shakespeare 1954), pp. xxxviii ff., and Hankins 1947.
2 See Palmer 1965, pp. 112 ff. There had been previous chairs of English at Oxford, but the main concern of their holders was philological. The new chair was not filled until the death of the Merton professor, John Earle, in 1904.
3 Raleigh 1926, I, pp. 253, 259. Aspects of Raleigh's career at Oxford are discussed in Baldick 1963, pp. 75–92.

4 DECONSTRUCTING SHAKESPEARE'S COMEDIES

1 See Puttenham 1589, p. I; *MND*, V. i. 16–17; Sidney 1966, p. 52; *Lear*, I. i. 89 and I. iv. 130; *Macb*, V. v. 26–8; *Ham*, III. ii. 116–17.
2 See Derrida 1976, pp. 62–7 and Norris 1982, pp. 32, 46–7.
3 *Poetics* 1448b. See also Derrida 1974, pp. 37–8.
4 As an 'arche-writing . . . which I continue to call writing only because it essentially communicates with the vulgar concept of writing' (Derrida 1976, p. 56).
5 'I have no other but a woman's reason: / I think him so, because I think him so' (*TGV*, I. ii., 23–4).

6 See *TN*, III. i. 143; IV. i. 8–9 and V. i. 20–1; *AYL*, V. iv. 214–15 and III. iii. 16–17; *Much Ado*, II. i. 311; *TN*, III. iv. 128–9; *AYL*, V. iv. 129.

7 See *MND*, I. i. 191; III. i. 114 and III. ii. 32; Puttenham 1589, pp. 128 ff.; Wilson 1909, pp. 172–3.

8 See Charlton 1938 and Long 1976, pp. 2–3.

9 Cf. *LLL*, I. i. 122, 129.

10 This phonocentric reading is developed at length in Evans 1975.

11 'To get at the form and meaning of the play . . . is my first and last interest' (Barber 1959, p. 4).

12 Hymen's tautology incorporates plays on 'truth' (which also connotes 'fidelity'); 'holds' ('sustains' and 'impedes'); 'true' (also 'chaste'); and 'contents' ('joys' or 'pleasures', 'contented people' and 'that which is contained'). For the 168 permutations of this line and their bearing on the play as a whole, see Evans 1985.

13 Cf. Brown 1957.

14 'Nothing odd will do long. *Tristram Shandy* did not last' (Johnson in Howes 1974, p. 219). '. . . . irresponsible (and nasty) trifling' (Leavis 1948, p. 2, on Sterne). Cf. Howes 1974, pp. 29–30.

15 The *Newbolt Report* describes books as being not ends in themselves but 'instruments through which we hear the voices of those who have known life better than ourselves' (1921, p. 14).

16 Cf. Weimann 1978, pp. 176–7, 241, 251.

17 Macherey 1977, p. 7. See also Bennett 1979, pp. 135–7.

18 'The traditional belief that study of great literature releases us from the debased myths of the present, that it ennobles and civilises, needs to be fought for . . .' (Cox 1971, p. 197).

19 See Pêcheux 1982, p. 180 and Eagleton 1976, p. 168. Cf. Gasché 1979.

20 See Belsey 1983, pp. 17–27 and Montrose 1981.

21 Cf. Belsey 1981, pp. 171–81; Morton 1970, pp. 91–7; Hill 1972.

5 SEXUALITY IN THE READING OF SHAKESPEARE: *HAMLET* AND *MEASURE FOR MEASURE*

1 See also on this image of the text as seducer and threat, Shoshana Felman's important psychoanalytic reading of responses to, and movement of, Henry James's *The Turn of the Screw* (Felman 1977).

2 All page references to Freud are to *The Standard Edition of the Complete Psychological Works of Sigmund Freud*, edited by James Strachey, with references to *The Pelican Freud*, where available, in italics.

3 See also C. K. Hunter's introduction to the Arden edition of *All's Well*

That Ends Well (Shakespeare 1967) which again traces the problem of interpretation to the woman: 'To fit Helena into the play or adapt the play to Helena is obviously the central problem of interpretation in *All's Well*' (p. xlviii), and makes explicit reference to Eliot's aesthetic concept: 'Her role is a complex one, but there is an absence of adequate external correlatives to justify this complexity' (p. xlix).

4   See Mulhern 1979 for a full discussion of the socio-political context of *Scrutiny* from 1932 to 1953 and its significance for British literary culture.

5   See also Harold Brooks's judgement on Titania in the introduction to the Arden edition of *A Midsummer Night's Dream* (Shakespeare 1979): 'it is of course she who is principally at fault' (p. cvi), 'her obstinacy has to be overcome' (p. cviii), a judgement which gives moral legitimation to, and even cancels out, the sinister and disturbing aspects of fairyland and of Oberon's actions: 'his ill-feeling does not grate so much as it would without this context. As a rule, the context is a complete control when anything sinister is introduced' (p. cviii) (as if control could not be sinister . . .).

6   Lever in the Arden edition (Shakespeare 1965) annotates the line and L. C. Knights's commentary by stating that there is no confusion since the 'thirsty evil' refers, not to lechery, but to the 'liberty' of the preceding lines (I. ii. 118–20), although he does acknowledge the sexual connotation of ratsbane (p. 15 n.); for Lever's relegation, or diminishing, of the sexual, see also the note on the meaning of 'torches' (I. i. 32, pp. 5–6 n.).

7   André Green gives an important discussion in psychoanalytic terms of the division of stage space (1969, pp. 11–29). See also note 9 below.

8   The concept of femininity in relation to Hamlet's character appears again in French 1982, p. 149, and in Leverenz 1980.

9   In *Hamlet et HAMLET* (1982), André Green continues the work he began in *Un Oeil en trop (The Tragic Effect)* (1969) on the psychoanalytic concept of representation in relation to dramatic form, and argues that, while the explicit themes of *Hamlet* (incest, parricide, madness) have the clearest links with the concerns of psychoanalysis, the play's central preoccupation with theatrical space and performance also fall within the psychoanalytic domain through the concept of psychic representation and fantasy. Green examines the way that theatricality, or show, and femininity, are constantly assimilated throughout the play (I. ii. 76 ff.; II. ii. 581 ff.; III. i. 50 ff.); in the remarks which follow I concentrate on the concept of femininity which he sets against

this negative assimilation in his final section on Shakespeare's creative art (pp. 255–62).

10 See especially Irigaray 1974 and 1977; Montrelay 1970.

11 Winnicott first presented this paper to the British Psycho-Analytic Society in 1966 under the title 'Split-off male and female elements found clinically in men and women: Theoretical inferences' (Winnicott, 1972). In the discussion which followed, which was not reprinted in the final publication, one objection raised to the definition 'Masculinity does, femininity is' pointed to its literary affinity, if not source, by referring to Winnicott's recent interest in Robert Graves's writings on Greek mythology and, specifically, the poem 'Woman Is, Man Does'. Winnicott's discussion of sexual difference in this paper is, however, far more complex and interesting than this final descent (ascent) into mythology although it is this concept of femininity, with its associated emphasis on mothering, which has recently been imported directly into psychoanalytic readings of Shakespeare (see especially Leverenz 1980 and the whole anthology in which the article appears, Schwarz and Kahn 1980).

6 READING THE SIGNS: TOWARDS A SEMIOTICS OF SHAKESPEAREAN DRAMA

1 For analyses of the sonnets see Levin 1962, Booth 1969a, Pagnini 1969, Jakobson and Jones 1970, Melchiori 1973, Serpieri 1975, Rutelli 1975, Hammond 1981. For structuralist and semiotic studies of the plays, see in particular Hawkes 1973; Pagnini 1976 on *King Lear* and *A Midsummer Night's Dream*; Gullì Pugliatti 1976 on *King Lear*; Serpieri 1978 on *Othello*; Dodd 1979 on *Measure for Measure*; Rutelli 1979 on *Romeo and Juliet*; A. Johnson 1979 on *Antony and Cleopatra* and *King Lear*; Corti 1983 on *Macbeth*; Mullini 1983 on the 'fool'; and the recent linguistic and dramatological study of the comedies by Elam (1984). These summary indications do not in any way exhaust the ample bibliography regarding structuralist-semiotic Shakespearean criticism, and furthermore they are largely limited to Italian contributions. This partiality is due in part to reasons of economy, in part to the cultural perspective from which the author writes.

2 By '*macro*textual allegiance' I mean the rapport that the single text entertains with other works within the (Shakespearean) canon; by '*inter*textual allegiance', the relationship of the text with other texts in general.

3 On the question of cultural models and systems within a pragmatic approach to literature and drama, see the important reflections of M. Pagnini (1980).

4 For an interesting approach to the problems of dramatic convention, with specific reference to – among others – Shakespeare, see the collective volume edited by Aston *et al. Interazione, dialogo, convenzioni: Il caso del testo drammatico* (1983).

5 See Elam 1980 for the best available account of the convergence of a semiotics of the dramatic text with a semiotics of the theatre.

6 See Eco 1976 for a further exposition of this concept.

7 See Gruppo 1970 for an analysis of 'metalogisms'.

8 See Styan 1971, Gullì Pugliatti 1976, Serpieri 1977 and Elam 1984.

7 SHAKESPEARE IN IDEOLOGY

1 This chapter incorporates revised portions of my earlier essay, 'To the same defect: Toward a critique of the ideology of the aesthetic', *The Bucknell Review* 27, no. 1 (Fall 1982)., pp. 102–23.

2 This essay will not attempt to review or critique the substantial body of previous marxist criticism of Shakespeare that assumes a traditional 'reflectionist' notion of ideology. One of the more important recent studies is surely Robert Weimann's *Shakespeare and the Popular Tradition in the Theatre: Studies in the Social Dimension of Dramatic Form and Function* (1978) which gives an excellent understanding of the disparate sources that nourished Shakespeare's work. I quote below from Paul Siegel's *Shakespearean Tragedy and the Elizabethan Compromise* (1957), which is too frequently overlooked; his *Shakespeare in His Time and Ours* (1968) collects a number of his other essays. Arnold Kettle's *Shakespeare in a Changing World* (1964) collects essays by Weimann, Kenneth Muir, David Craig, Charles Barber, and others. C. L. R. James's The *Old World and the New: Shakespeare, Melville and Others* (1971), is a provocative work that also deserves more attention than it gets. Annette Rubinstein's The *Great Tradition in English Literature from Shakespeare to Shaw*, vol.1 (1969) gives a useful traditional discussion. *The Shakespeare Jahrbuch* (Weimar, 1865–) is a continuing source of marxist work. For Marx's comments on Shakespeare, see Lee Baxandall and Stefan Morawski's anthology *Marx and Engels on Literature and Art: A Selection of Writings* (1973). For further bibliography, see Chris Bullock and David Peck, *Guide to Marxist Literary Criticism* (1980); Michael B. Folsom, *Shakespeare: A Marxist*

Bibliography (1971); and the special issue, 'Marxist Interpretations of Shakespeare', *The Shakespeare Newsletter*, 24 (September–November 1974).

3 For further reading on the Althusserian theory of ideology and its relation to literary studies, see, besides the work of Belsey, Bennett, Eagleton and Macherey and Balibar, cited herein, Macherey 1976, 1978 and Kavanagh 1980, 1982, and 1985.

4 Under the entry for 'ideology' in the most recent *MLA Bibliography*, one finds 'See also related terms: Doctrines' (Modern Languages Association (1983) *1981 MLA International Bibliography of Books and Articles on the Modern Languages and Literatures*, vol. 1. New York: Modern Languages Association, p. A168).

5 See, for example, Plato and Aristotle:

> Does not the latter – I mean the rebellious principle – furnish a great variety of materials for imitation. . . . The imitative poet implants an evil constitution, for he indulges the irrational nature . . . when any sorrow of our own happens to us, . . . we would fain be quiet and patient; this is the manly part, and the other which delighted us in the recitation is now deemed to be the part of woman . . . let us assure our sweet friend and the sister arts of imitation, that if she will only prove her title to exist in a well-ordered state we shall be delighted to receive her – we are very conscious of her charms.
>
> (Plato, *Republic*, 10, in Bate 1970, pp. 47–8)

> In respect of character there are four things to be aimed at. First and most important, it must be good. Now any speech or action that manifests moral purpose of any kind will be expressive of character: the character will be good if the purpose is good. This rule is relative to each class. Even a woman may be good, and also a slave; though the woman may be said to be an inferior being, and the slave quite worthless.
>
> (Aristotle, *Poetics*, 15, in Bate 1970, p. 28)

6 In the 'Catholic' versus 'Protestant' positions class-political divisions were, as Marx suggested, 'fought out in another language'. The Catholic position was associated with attempts to support a traditional conception of social hierarchy with the monarch representing the epitome of the social power of the aristocracy, in a system based on

qualification by blood, stable wealth in land, and rule by personal domination; while the Protestant position was associated with a 'levelling' tendency in which the sovereign was coming to represent a rational conception of necessary social order, in a system based on qualification by moral legitimacy, expanding wealth in money, and rule by popular recognition or even consent. King James's watchword, 'No bishops, no king', succinctly captured the fear of radical Protestantism, and the intensifying ideological-political bind in which the English monarchy found itself as a result of Henry VIII's actions in tying the fate of the institution to the developing Reformation – actions which, ironically, were meant to, and in the short run did, strengthen the power of the monarchy itself against the aristocracy and the Church.

7 As one critic remarked, Elizabeth had resisted executing Mary as 'setting an example of regicide . . . and . . . had sullenly assented only under the united pressure of her Council, Commons and the people of London' (Siegel 1957, p. 26), and the defeat of the Armada 'was a victory primarily for those classes which were later to conduct the war against Charles I' (p. 29). Elizabeth shrewdly finessed Essex; he was immensely popular as an anti-Spanish, anti-Papist militant, but the proximate cause of his rebellion – Elizabeth's revocation of his wine monopoly, a classically *feudal* privilege – failed to generate the broad support he needed among the London populace.

Essex's failure also throws into relief the contradictory position of the 'new aristocracy' itself: on the one hand, it constituted a truly 'enterprising' nobility, which did not hesitate to engage in capitalizing ventures and political blocs with the mercantile bourgeoisie; on the other hand, a great deal of its privileges and power still accrued from its aristocratic status, and from the concomitant 'patents' or monopolies granted by the Queen.

8 Essex's supporters tried to use a performance of *Richard II* on 7 February 1601 to incite rebellion against Elizabeth, thereby associating Shakespeare with their treason.

9 This word, which appears in the First and Second Quarto and the First Folio, seems clearly a pun, and not a mis-spelling. Polonius makes a similar pun in *Hamlet*: 'and now remains / That we find the cause of this effect / Or rather say the cause of this defect / For this effect defective comes by cause' (III. ii. 100–3).

10 *A Midsummer Night's Dream* was probably written (in 1595–6) as an epithalamium or wedding-masque, designed to be performed on a private stage in celebration of the marriage of an aristocratic couple,

though with the expectation that it would later be 'Sundry times pub-lickely acted', as the title page of the First Quarto edition puts it.

11 For some of the moments when the different senses of this word are put into play, see I. ii. 1–22; II. ii. 54–5; II. iv. 107–9 and 179–81; II. iv. 280; III. vi. 78–9 and 100; and IV. vi. 192–3.

12 For some of the play on this word, see I. i. 87 ff.; I. iv. 134 ff.; and II. 3. 21.

13 Or one has some other concept of need. This is not to rule out other possible concepts of need but to emphasize the incompatibility of the two that are conjuncturally in question.

14 Although this point cannot be developed here, neither the aristocracy nor the bourgeoisie of Johnson's and Coleridge's day were the same as that of Shakespeare's. Hill (1967) emphasizes this difference.

15 In Coleridge, this word functions as an adjectival form of 'genius'.

16 That is, for Coleridge, the power and wisdom of the 'imagination', which is in part unconscious.

17 'Idealist' because for Coleridge it is always an idea, of which material phenomena are *manifestations*, that is the essential structuring *principle* of the real; 'empiricist' because that idea is always contained, on virtually self-evident display, *in* a real phenomenon.

8 DISRUPTING SEXUAL DIFFERENCE: MEANING AND GENDER IN THE COMEDIES

1 See John Phillip, The *Play of Patient Grissell* (1558–61), ed. R. B. McKer-row and W. W. Greg, Oxford: Malone Society, 1909; Thomas Dekker, *Patient Grissill* (c. 1599), ed. Fredson Bowers, *The Dramatic Works of Thomas Dekker*, 4 vols, Cambridge: Cambridge University Press, 1953, vol. I; *The Ancient, True and Admirable Histoy of Patient Grisel* (1619), ed. J. P. Collier, *Early English Poetry*, London: Percy Society, vol. 3, 1842; Thomas Deloney, 'Of Patient Grissel and a Noble Marquesse' (printed 1631) and *The Pleasant and Sweet History of Patient Grissell* (printed c. 1630), *Works*, ed. F. O. Mann, Oxford: Clarendon Press, 1912.

2 I am not entirely persuaded by the argument that boy players are 'homoerotic' (Jardine 1983, pp. 9–36).

3 There are exceptions. C. L. Barber identifies the Patience figure as 'a sort of polarity within Viola' (Barber 1959, p. 247). In other cases a certain unease is evident in the identifications. Viola is describing 'her sister', but the image 'is drawn from her own experience' (Leggatt 1974, pp. 236–7). According to the Arden editor(s), the speech

describes 'Cesario's sister's love for a man to whom she never told it'. A footnote adds, 'I express it thus for brevity's sake. This is how it appears to Orsino: but everything Viola says is directly applicable to herself in her real person' (Shakespeare 1975b, p. lxviii). Kenneth Muir succeeds in evading any very specific identification of the speaker: 'Cesario tells the story of her imaginary sister. . . . But we know that Viola is too intelligent and too well-balanced to go the way of her "sister"' (Muir 1979, p. 98).

9 NYMPHS AND REAPERS HEAVILY VANISH: THE DISCURSIVE CON-TEXTS OF *THE TEMPEST*

1 Bennett 1982, p. 227; drawing on the argument of Derrida 1977.
2 For the theory behind the concept of inscription see Balibar 1974 and 1983; Macherey and Balibar 1978; and Davies 1978. For an accessible collection of essays which put this theory to work on the corpus of English literature, see Widdowson 1982.
3 Intertextuality is a term coined by Julia Kristeva 1970, from her reading of the seminal work of Mikhail Bakhtin, 1968, 1973, 1981.
4 For Raleigh's *Tempest* see Terence Hawkes, this volume, pp. 26–47; Kermode is editor of the Arden edition of *The Tempest* (Shakespeare 1964); on the formation of 'English' see Davies 1978.
5 Stanley Fish (1980, p. 165), whose general argument is similar to Bennett's, admits that in the last analysis he is unable to answer the question: what are his interpretative acts interpretations *of*?
6 Marx's work was developed out of his critique of the concepts of classical political economy that had dominated economic thought in the middle of the nineteenth century. We choose here to offer a critique of Kermode's introduction to the Arden *Tempest* (Shakespeare 1964) because of the *strengths* of his highly regarded and influential work.
7 Con-texts with a hyphen, to signify a break from the inequality of the usual text/context relationship. Con-texts are themselves *texts* and must be *read with*: they do not simply make up a background.
8 MacCabe 1979 offers a helpful guide through some of discourse's many usages. The concept of discourse at work in the present essay draws on Michel Foucault's investigation of the discursive realm. A useful introduction to his theorization of discourse is provided by Foucault's essays, 1978 and 1981. His most extended theoretical text is *The Archaeology of Knowledge*, 1972. However, a less formal and in many ways more suggestive treatment of discourse is practised and,

to a certain extent theorized, in his early work on 'madness' and in more recent studies of the prison and of sexuality, where discourse is linked with both the institutional locations in which it circulates and the power functions it performs: see Foucault 1967, 1977, 1979a. For a cognate approach to discourse see the theory of 'utterance' developed by Valentin Vološinov, 1973.

9 On the weakness of Kristeva's own work in this respect see Culler 1981, pp. 105–7.

10 Antonio de Nebrija, quoted in Hanke 1959, p. 8.

11 In other words we would shift the emphasis from the futile search for the texts Shakespeare 'had in mind' to the establishment of significant patterns within the larger discursive networks of the period. The notion of 'English colonialism' can itself be focused in different ways. The widest focus would include present con-texts, the narrowest would concentrate on the con-texts associated with the initial period of English colonization of Virginia, say 1585 to 1622. In the first instance many of the relevant texts would be found in the contemporary collections of Hakluyt (1903–5) and Purchas (1905–7). For congruent approaches see J. Smith 1974; Frey 1979; Greenblatt 1980, chapter 4; and Hulme 1981.

12 See Macherey 1978. Macherey characterizes the literary text not as unified but as plural and diverse. Usurpation should then be regarded not as the centre of a unity but as the principle of a diversity.

13 Kermode's second heading (Shakespeare 1964, p. xxiv).

14 This is a weak form of the critical fallacy that, more chronically, reads Prospero as an autobiographical surrogate for Shakespeare himself. On some of the theoretical issues involved here see Foucault 1979b.

15 This trope is studied in more detail in Hulme (forthcoming) chapters 3 and 4. See also Jennings 1976.

16 See for example Lamming 1960 and Fernández Retamar 1973. Aimé Césaire's rewriting of the play, *Une Tempête*, 1969, has Caliban as explicit hero. For an account of how Caliban remains refractory for contemporary productions of *The Tempest* see Griffiths 1983.

10 HISTORY AND IDEOLOGY: THE INSTANCE OF *HENRY V*

1 See Derrida 1978, p. 19; 1976, p. 315.

2 See Sinfield 1983b, pp. 94–105; and Dollimore and Sinfield (ed) 1985.

3 Here we are primarily concerned to offer a critique of the ideology which falsely unifies history; for a similar and fuller critique of

subjectivity see Dollimore 1984, especially chapters 1, 10 and 16.

4 A materialist criticism will be concerned with aspects of ideology additional to those dealt with here and our emphasis on ideology as legitimation, though crucial, should not be taken as an exhaustive definition of the concept. For a fuller discussion of ideology in the period see Dollimore 1984, especially chapters 1 and 16; Dollimore and Sinfield 1985, and, more generally, Wolff 1981, especially chapter 3.

5 Perkins 1970, p. 150. See Sinfield 1983a, pp. 37–8, 134–5.

6 This distinction derives (but also differs from) Giddens 1981, pp. 231–7.

7 Strype 1822, I, pp. 524–6. See further Heal 1980.

8 See Gary Taylor's note in Shakespeare 1982b.

9 Hunt 1983, p. 60; see for an instance, p. 50; and also De Bruyn 1981, pp. 26, 62.

10 P. Edwards 1979, pp. 75–8, referring to *Henry V*, III. ii. 125–7. Edwards shows how an Irish captain who had been in Essex's army made a similar protest.

11 Quinn 1966, chapters 4, 5 and 7. See also P. Edwards 1977.

12 Hughes and Larkin 1969, III, pp. 134–5.

BIBLIOGRAPHY

Althusser, Louis (1970) *For Marx*. New York: Vintage.
—— (1971) *Lenin and Philosophy*. New York: Monthly Review Press.
Anderson, Perry (1974) *Lineages of the Absolute State*. London: New Left Books.
—— (1983) *In the Tracks of Historical Materialism: The Wellek Library Lectures*. London: Verso Editions.
Andrewes, Lancelot (1841) *Works, II vols. Oxford: Clarendon Press.*
Archer, Gabriel (1979) 'The description of the now discovered river and county of Virginia . . .' [1607], in Quinn, D. *et al.* (eds) *New American World*, vol.5. London: Macmillan.
Aristotle (1938) *Aristotle's Organon*, trans. H. P. Cooke. Loeb Classical Library. London: Heinemann.
Arnold, Matthew (1962) *Culture and Anarchy*, ed. J. Dover Wilson, Cambridge: Cambridge University Press.
Aston *et al.* (1983) *Interazione dialogo convenzione: il caso del testo drammatico*. Bologna: CLUEB.
Bakhtin, Mikhail (1968) *Rabelais and His World*. Cambridge, Mass.: MIT Press.
—— (1973) *Problems of Dostoevsky's Poetics*. Ann Arbor, Mich.: Ardis.
—— (1981) The *Dialogic Imagination*. Austin: University of Texas Press.
Baldick, C. (1983) *The Social Mission of English Criticism*. London: Oxford University Press.

Balibar, Renée (1974) *Les Français fictifs: le rapport des styles littéraires au français national*. Paris: Hachette.

—— (1983) 'National language, education, literature', in Barker, F. *et al.* (eds) *The Politics of Theory*. Colchester: University of Essex, 79–99.

Barber, C. L. (1959) *Shakespeare's Festive Comedy*. Princeton, NJ: Princeton University Press.

Barker, Francis (1984) *The Tremulous Private Body*. London: Methuen.

Barthes, Roland (1970) *S/Z*. Paris: Seuil. In English: *S/Z*, trans. Richard Miller. New York: Hill & Wang, 1974.

—— (1971) 'La mythologie aujourd'hui', *Esprit*, April. In English: 'Change the object itself', in *Image-Music-Text*, trans. Stephen Heath. London: Fontana, 1977, 165–9.

—— (1972) *Mythologies*, trans. Annette Lavers. London: Jonathan Cape.

Bate, Walter Jackson (1970) *Criticism: The Major Texts*. New York: Harcourt.

Baxandall, L. and Morawski, S. (eds) (1973) *Marx and Engels on Literature and Art: A Selection of Writings*. St Louis, Mo.: Telos Press.

Bayley, John (1981) *Shakespeare and Tragedy*. London: Routledge & Kegan Paul.

Belsey, Catherine (1980) *Critical Practice*. London: Methuen.

—— (1981) 'Tragedy, justice and the subject', in Barker, F. *et al.* (eds) *1642: Literature and Power in the Seventeenth Centuy*. Colchester: University of Essex, 166–86.

—— (1983) 'Literature, history, politics', *Literature and Histoy*, 9, 17–27.

Benjamin, Walter (1970) *Illuminations*. London: Jonathan Cape.

Bennett, T. (1979) *Formalism and Marxism*. New Accents series. London: Methuen.

—— (1982) 'Text and history', in Widdowson, Peter (ed.) *Re-Reading English*. London: Methuen, 223–36.

Bethell, S. L. (1944) *Shakespeare and the Popular Dramatic Tradition*. Reprinted 1970, New York: Octagon Books.

Booth, Stephen (1969a) *An Essay on Shakespeare's Sonnets*. New Haven and London: Yale University Press.

—— (1969b) 'On the value of *Hamlet*', in Rabkin, Norman (ed.) *Reinterpretation of Elizbethan Drama*. New York and London: Columbia University Press, 137–76.

—— (ed.) (1977) *Shakespeare's Sonnets*, edited with an analytic commentary. New Haven and London: Yale University Press.

Bradbrook, M. C. (1935) *Themes and Conventions in Elizabethan Tragedy*. Cambridge: Cambridge University Press.

Bradley, A. C. (1904) *Shakespearean Tragedy*. Reprinted 1961, London: Macmillan.

—— (1909) *Oxford Lectures on Poetry*. Reprinted 1965, London: Macmillan.

Brooke-Rose, Christine (1981) ' "The Turn of the Screw" and its critics: an essay in non-methodology', in *A Rhetoric of the Unreal*. Cambridge: Cambridge University Press, 128–57.

Brooks, Cleanth (1947) 'The naked babe and the cloak of manliness', in *The Well Wrought Urn*. New York: Harcourt, Brace & World, 22–49.

Brown, J. R. (1957) *Shakespeare and his Comedies*. London: Methuen.

—— (1974) *Free Shakespeare*. London: Heinemann.

Bullock, C. and Peck, D. (1980) *Guide to Marxist Literary Criticism*. Bloomington, Ind.: Indiana University Press.

Bullough. G. (1958) *Narrative and Dramatic Sources of Shakespeare*, vol.2, *The Comedies*. London: Routledge & Kegan Paul.

—— (1966) *Narrative and Dramatic Sources of Shakespeare*, vol. 4, *Later English History Plays: King John, Henry IV, Henry V, Henry VIII*. London: Routledge & Kegan Paul.

—— (1975) *Narrative and Dramatic Sources of Shakespeare*, vol. 8, *Romances*. London: Routledge & Kegan Paul.

Calderwood, J. L. (1965) '*A Midsummer Night's Dream*: The illusion of drama', *Modern Language Quarterly*, 26, 506–22.

Campbell, Lily B. (1964) *Shakespeare's Histories*. London: Methuen.

Carlyle, T. (1841) *On Heroes, Hero-Worship and the Heroic in Histoy*. London: James Frazer.

Césaire, Aimé (1969) *Une Tempête*. Paris: Seuil.

Charlton, H. B. (1938) *Shakespearian Comedy*. London: Methuen.

Coleridge, Samuel Taylor (1951) *Selected Poety and Prose*, ed. Donald A. Stauffer. New York: Random House.

—— (1969) *Coleridge on Shakespeare*, ed. Terence Hawkes. Harmondsworth: Penguin.

—— (1976) *On the Constitution of the Church and State*, ed. John Colmer. Princeton, NJ: Princeton University Press.

—— (1983) *Biographia Literaria*, 2 vols, ed. James Engell and W. Jackson Bate. Princeton, NJ: Princeton University Press.

Cooke, Katharine (1972) *A. C. Bradly and His Influence in Twentieth-Century Shakespeare Criticism*. Oxford: Clarendon Press.

Corti, Claudia (1983). *Macbeth: la parola e l'immagine*, Pisa: Pacini.

Cox, C. B. (1971) Editorial, *Critical Quarterly*, 13.

Culler, J. (1979) 'Jacques Derrida', in Sturrock, J. (ed.) *Structuralism and Since*. London: Oxford University Press, 154–80.

—— (1981) *The Pursuit of Signs*. London: Roudedge & Kegan Paul.

Davies, Tony (1978) 'Education, ideology and literature', *Red Letters*, 7, 4–15.

Dawson, A. B. (1982) 'Much ado about signifying', *Studies in English Literature*, 22, 211–21.

De Bruyn, Lucy (1981) *Mob-Rule and Riots*. London: Regency.

Derrida, Jacques (1972) *La Dissemination*. Paris: Seuil. In English: *Dissemination*, trans. Barbara Johnson. London: Athlone, 1981.

—— (1974) 'White mythology: Metaphor in the text of philosophy', *New Literary History*, 6, 7–74.

—— (1976) *Of Grammatology*, trans. Gayatri Chakravorty Spivak. Baltimore, Md.: Johns Hopkins University Press.

—— (1977) 'Signature event context', *Glyph*, 1, 172–98.

—— (1978) *Writing and Difference*, trans. Alan Bass. London: Routledge & Kegan Paul.

—— (1979a) 'Living on: Border lines', in Bloom, H. *et al.* (eds) *Deconstruction and Criticism*. London: Routledge & Kegan Paul, 75–176.

—— (1979b) *Spurs: Nietzsche's Styles*, trans. Barbara Harlow. Chicago: University of Chicago Press.

Dodd, W. (1979) *Misura per misura: La trasparenza della commedia*. Milan: Il Formichieve.

Dollimore, Jonathan (1984) *Radical Tragedy: Religion, ideology and Power in the Drama of Shakespeare and his Contemporaries*. Brighton: Harvester Press; Chicago: University of Chicago Press.

—— and Sinfield, Alan (eds) (1985) *Political Shakespeare*. Manchester: Manchester University Press.

Donne, John (1957) *The Sermons*, 10 vols, ed. George R. Potter and Evelyn M. Simpson, vol. 3. Berkeley and Los Angeles: University of California Press.

Eagleton, Terry (1976) *Criticism and Ideology*. London: New Left Books.

—— (1981) *Walter Benjamin or Towards a Revolutionary Criticism*. London: Verso.

—— (1983) *Literary Theory: An Introduction*. Oxford: Blackwell.

Eco, U. (1976) *A Theory of Semiotics*. Bloomington Ind.: Macmillan.

Edwards, Philip (1979) *Threshold of a Nation*. Cambridge: Cambridge University Press.

Edwards, Philip, Ewbank, Inga-stina, Hunter, G. K. *et al.* (eds) (1980) *Shakespeare's Styles: Essays in Honour of Kenneth Muir*. Cambridge: Cambridge University Press.

Edwards, R. Dudley (1977) *Ireland in the Age of the Tudors: The Destruction of Hiberno-Norman Civilization*. London: Croom Helm.

Elam, K. (1980) *The Semiotics of Theatre and Drama*. London and New York: Methuen.

—— (1984) *Shakespeare's Universe of Discourse: Language Games in the Comedies*. Cambridge: Cambridge University Press.

Eliot, T. S. (1933) *The Use of Poetry and the Use of Criticism*. London: Faber & Faber.

—— (1951) *Selected Essays*. London: Faber & Faber.

—— (1975) *Selected Prose of T. S. Eliot*, ed. Frank Kermode. London: Faber & Faber.

Evans, M. (1975) 'Mercury versus Apollo: A reading of *Love's Labour's Lost*', *Shakespeare Quarterly*, 26, 113–27.

—— (1985) 'Asterion's door: Truth's true contents in Shakespeare, Nietzsche, Artaud, the Rev A. E. Sims . . .', *Glyph*, 9.

Felman, Shoshana (1977) 'Turning the screw of interpretation', in Felman, S. (ed.) *Literature and Psychoanalysis, The Question of Reading: Otherwise*. Yale French Studies 55/56. New Haven: Yale University Press, 94–207.

Fernández Retamar, Roberto (1973) *Caliban: Apuntes sobre la Cuitura de Nuestra América*. Buenos Aires: Editorial la Pleyade.

Fischer, Ernst (1963) *The Necessity of Art*, trans. Anna Bostock. Harmondsworth: Penguin.

Fish, Stanley (1980) *Is There a Text in this Class?: The Authority of Interpretive Communities*. Cambridge, Mass.: Harvard University Press.

Florio, John (trans.) (1885) *The Essays of Michael, Lord of Montaigne* [1603]. London and New York: Routledge & Sons.

Folsom, Michael B. (1971) *Shakespeare: A Marxist Bibliography*. New York: The American Institute for Marxist Studies.

Foucault, Michel (1967) *Madness and Civilization: A History of Insanity in the Age of Reason*. London: Tavistock Publications.

—— (1970) *The Order of Things*. London: Tavistock Publications.

—— (1972) *The Archaeology of Knowledge*. London: Tavistock Publications.

—— (1977) *Discipline and Punish: the Birth of the Prison*. London: Allen Lane.

—— (1978) 'Politics and the study of discourse', *Ideology and Consciousness*, 3, 7–26

—— (1979a) *The History of Sexuality*, vol. I. London: Allen Lane.

—— (1979b) 'What is an author?', in Harari, J. V. (ed.) *Textual Strategies: Perspectives in Post-structuralist Criticism*. London: Methuen, 141–60.

—— (1981) 'The order of discourse', in Young, Robert (ed.) *Untying the*

Text: A Post-structuralist Reader. London: Routledge & Kegan Paul, 48–78.

French, Marilyn (1982) *Shakespeare's Division of Experience*. London: Jonathan Cape.

Freud, Sigmund (1887–1902) *The Origins of Psychoanalysis*, letters to Wilhelm Fliess, Drafts and Notes, ed. by Marie Bonaparte, Anna Freud and Ernst Kris. Reprinted 1954, London: Imago.

—— (1900) *The Interpretation of Dreams*, in Strachey, James (ed.) *The Standard Edition of the Complete Psychological Works of Sigmund Freud*. Reprinted 1955–74, London: Hogarth, vols IV–V. Reprinted 1976, in *The Pelican Freud*, vol. 4. Harmondsworth: Penguin.

—— (1910) 'Leonardo da Vinci and a memory of his childhood', *Standard Edition*, vol. XI, 57–137.

—— (1917) [1915] 'Mourning and melancholia', *Standard Edition*, vol. XIV, 237–58. Reprinted in *The Pelican Freud*, vol. 2. 245–68.

—— (1924) 'The dissolution of the Oedipus complex', *Standard Edition*, vol. XIX, 173–9. Reprinted in The *Pelican Freud*, vol. 7, 313–22.

—— (1925) 'Some psychical consequences of the anatomical distinction between the sexes', *Standard Edition*, vol. XIX, 243–58. Reprinted in The *Pelican Freud*, vol. 7, 323–43.

—— (1931) 'Female sexuality', *Standard Edition*, vol. XXI, 223–43. Reprinted in The *Pelican Freud*, vol. 7, 367–92.

—— (1933) [1932] 'The dissection of the psychical personality', *New Introductory Lectures, Standard Edition*, vol. XXII, 57–80. Reprinted in *The Pelican Freud*, vol 2, 88–122.

—— (1942) [1905 or 1906] 'Psychopathic characters on the stage', *Standard Edition*, vol. VII, 303–10.

Frey, Charles (1979) '*The Tempest* and the New World', *Shakespeare Quarterly*, 30, 29–41.

Frye, N. (1965) *A Natural Perspective: The Development of Shakespearean Comedy and Romance*. New York: Columbia University Press.

Gardner, Helen (1959) *The Business of Criticism*. Oxford: Clarendon Press.

Gasché, R. (1979) 'Deconstruction as criticism', *Glyph*, 6, 177–215.

Giddens, Anthony (1981) *A Contemporary Critique of Historical Materialism*, vol. 1. London: Macmillan.

Girard, R. (1980) 'Myth and ritual in Shakespeare: *A Midsummer Night's Dream*', in Harari, J. V. (ed.) *Textual Strategies: Perspectives in Post-Structuralist Criticism*. London: Methuen, 189–212.

Goldberg, Jonathan (1983) *James I and the Politics of Literature: Jonson,*

Shakespeare, Donne and their Contemporaries. Baltimore Mds: Johns Hopkins University Press.

Goldmann, Lucien (1964) The *Hidden God*, trans. Philip Thody. Reprinted London: Routledge & Kegan Paul, 1977.

Gollancz, I. (1916) *Shakespeare Day 1916*. London: Geo W. Jones.

Green, André (1969) *Un Oeil en trop*. Paris: Minuit. In English: *The Tragic Effect: Oedipus Complex and Tragedy*, trans. Alan Sheridan. Cambridge: Cambridge University Press, 1979.

—— (1973) *Le discours vivant, le concept psychanalytique de l'affect*. Paris: Presses Universitaries de France.

—— (1982) *Hamlet et HAMLET, une interprétation psychanalytique de la répresentation*. Paris: Ballard.

Greenblatt, Stephen (1980) *Renaissance Self-Fashioning from More to Shakespeare*. Chicago: University of Chicago Press.

—— (ed.) (1982) *The Power of Forms in the English Renaissance*. Oklahoma: Pilgrim Books.

Griffiths, Trevor R. (1983) '"This island's mine": Caliban and colonialism', *The Yearbook of English Studies*, 13, 159–80.

Gross, John (1973) *The Rise and Fall of the Man of Letters*. Harmondsworth: Penguin. Orig. publ. 1969.

Gruppo, U. (1970) *Rhétorique générale*. Paris: Librerie Larousse.

Gullì Pugliatti, P. (1976) *I segni latenti: Scrittura come virtualitî scenica in 'King Lear'*. Florence and Messina: D'Anna.

Hakluyt, Richard (1903–5) *The Principle Navigations, Voyages Traffiques and Discoveries of the English Nation* [1589], 12 vols. Glasgow: James MacLehose and Sons.

Halkett, John (1970) *Milton and the Idea of Matrimony*. New Haven: Yale University Press.

Halliday, F. E. (1958) *Shakespeare and his Critics*. London: Duckworth.

Hammond, G. (1981) *The Reader and Shakespeare's Young Man Sonnets*. London: Macmillan.

Hanke, Lewis (1959) *Aristotle and the American Indians*. Bloomington, Ind.: Indiana University Press.

Hankins, J. E. (1947) 'Caliban the Bestial Man', *PMLA*, LXII, 793 ff.

Harbage, Alfred (1941) *Shakespeare's Audience*. Reprinted New York and London: Columbia University Press, 1969.

—— (1966) *Conceptions of Shakespeare*. Cambridge, Mass.: Harvard University Press.

Harrison, G. B. (1937) *The Life and Death of Robert Devereux Earl of Essex*. London: Cassell.

Hawkes, Terence (1973) *Shakespeare's Talking Animals: Language and Drama in Sociey*. London: Edward Arnold.

—— (1977) *Structuralism and Semiotics*. New Accents series. London: Methuen.

Hazlitt, William (1906) *Characters of Shakespeare's Plays*. London: J. M. Dent.

Heal, Felicity (1980) *Of Prelates and Princes*. Cambridge: Cambridge University Press.

Heywood, Thomas (1961) *A Woman Killed with Kindness*, ed. R. W. Van Fossen. The Revels Plays. London: Methuen.

Hill, C. (1965) *The Intellectual Origins of the English Revolution*. Oxford: Clarendon Press.

—— (1967) *Reformation to Industrial Revolution: A Social and Economic History of Britain, 1530–1780*. London: Weidenfeld & Nicolson. Reprinted Harmondsworth: Penguin, 1969.

—— (1972) *The World Turned Upside Down: Radical Ideas during the English Revolution*. London: Temple-Smith. Reprinted Harmondsworth: Penguin, 1975.

Hirsch, E. D. (1967) *Validity in Interpretation*. New Haven: Yale University Press.

Horkheimer, M. (1969) *Critical Theory*. Italian edition: *Teoria critica*. Turin: Einaudi.

Howes, A. B. (1974) *Sterne: The Critical Heritage*. London: Routledge & Kegan Paul.

Hughes, Paul L. and Larkin, James F. (1969) *Tudor Royal Proglamations*, 3 vols. New Haven: Yale University Press.

Hulme, Peter (1981) 'Hurricanes in the Caribbees: The constitution of the discourse of English colonialism', in Barker, F. *et al.* (eds) *1642: Literature and Power in the Seventeenth Century*. Colchester: University of Essex, 55–83.

—— ' "Of the caniballes": the discourse of European colonialism 1492–1797.' London: Methuen, forthcoming.

Hunt, William (1983) *The Puritan Moment*. Cambridge, Mass. and London: Harvard University Press.

Hunter, G. K. (1978) *Dramatic Identities and Cultural Tradition*. Liverpool: Liverpool University Press.

Irigaray, Luce (1974) *Speculum de l'autre femme*. Paris: Minuit. In English: *Speculum of the Other Woman*, trans. Gillian C. Gill. Ithaca, NY: Cornell University Press, 1985.

—— (1977) 'Women's exile: an interview with Luce Irigaray', *Ideology and Consciousness*, 1, 24–39.

Jakobson, R. and Jones, L. G. (1970) *Shakespeare's Verbal Art in 'The Expense of Spirit'*. The Hague: Mouton.

James, C. L. R. (1971) *The Old World and the New: Shakespeare, Melville and Others*. Detroit, Mich.: Facing Reality Publications.

Jardine, Lisa (1983) *Still Harping on Daughters: Women and Drama in the Age of Shakespeare*. Brighton: Harvester Press.

Jennings, Francis (1976) *The Invasion of America: Indians, Colonialism and the Cant of Conquest*. New York: Norton.

Johnson, A. (1979) *Readings of 'Antony and Cleopatra' and 'King Lear'*. Pisa: ETS.

Johnson, Samuel (1969) 'Preface to the Plays of William Shakespeare', in Wimsatt, W. K. (ed.) *Johnson On Shakespeare*. Harmondsworth: Penguin, 57–98.

Johnson, Samuel (1977) *Selected Poetry and Prose*, ed. Frank Brady and W. K. Wimsatt. Berkeley: University of California Press.

Jones, Ernest (1949) *Hamlet and Oedipus*. New York: Norton. Anchor edition 1954.

Kavanagh, James H. (1980) 'Marks of weakness: Ideology, science, and textual criticism', *Praxis*, 5, 23–38.

—— (1982) 'Marxism's Althusser: Toward a politics of literary theory', *Diacritics*, 12, 1, 25–45.

—— (1982) 'To the same defect: Toward a critique of the ideology of the aesthetic', *The Bucknell Review*, 27, 1, 102–23.

—— (1985) *Emily Brontë*. Oxford: Basil Blackwell.

Kermode, Frank (1975) *The Classic*. New York: Viking Press; London: Faber. Re-issued Cambridge, Mass. and London: Harvard University Press, 1983.

Kernan, Alvin (1982) 'Shakespeare's stage audiences: The playwright's reflections and control of audience response', in Highfill, Philip H., Jr (ed.) *Shakespeare's Craft*. Carbondale, Ill.: Southern Illinois University Press, 138–55.

Kettle, A. (1964) *Shakespeare in a Changing World*. London: Lawrence & Wishart.

Knight, G. Wilson (1930) *The Wheel of Fire*. Reprinted London: Methuen, 1964.

—— (1931) *The Imperial Theme*. Reprinted London: Methuen, 1965.

Knights, L. C., (1933) 'How many children had Lady Macbeth? An essay on the theory and practice of Shakespeare criticism', Cambridge: The Minority Press. Reprinted in *Explorations* London: Chatto & Windus, 1946; Harmondsworth: Peregrine Books, 1964.

—— (1937) *Drama and Society in the Age of Jonson*. London: Chatto & Windus.

—— (1942) 'The ambiguity of *Measure for Measure*', *Scrutiny*, X, 3, 222–33.

—— (1959) *Some Shakespearean Themes*. London: Chatto & Windus. Reprinted as *Some Shakespearean Themes and an Approach to 'Hamlet'*. Harmondsworth: Penguin, 1966.

Kott, Jan (1967) *Shakespeare Our Contemporary*, 2nd edn. London: Methuen.

Kristeva, Julia (1970) *Le Texte du roman*. The Hague: Mouton.

—— (1974) *La Révolution du langage poétique*. Paris: Seuil.

—— (1980) *Desire in Language, A Semiotic Approach to Literature and Art*, ed. Leon S. Roudiez, trans. Thomas Gora, Alice Jardine and Leon S. Roudiez. Oxford: Blackwell.

—— (1981) 'Women's time', *Signs* 7, 1, 13–35.

Lacan, Jacques (1957) 'L'instance de la lettre dans l'inconscient ou la raison depuis Freud', in *Ecrits*. Paris: Seuil, 1966, 493–528. In English: 'The agency of the letter in the unconscious', trans. Alan Sheridan, in *Ecrits, a Selection*. London: Tavistock Publications, 1977, 146–78.

—— (1957–8) 'Les formations de l'inconscient', *Bulletin de Psychologie*, II, 1–15.

—— (1958) 'Propos directifs pour un Congrès sur la sexualité feminine', in *Ecrits*. Paris: Seuil, 1966, 725–36. In English: 'Guiding remarks for a congress on feminine sexuality', trans. Jacqueline Rose, in Mithell, J. and Rose, J. (eds) *Feminine Sexuality, Jacques Lacan and the École Freudienne*. London: Macmillan, 1982, 86–98.

—— (1959) 'Desire and the interpretation of desire in *Hamlet*', in Felman, Shoshana (ed.) *Literature and Psychoanalysis, the Question of Reading: Otherwise*, Yale French Studies 55/56. New Haven: Yale University Press, 11–52.

Lamming, George (1960) *The Pleasures of Exile*. London: Michael Joseph.

Laslett, Peter (1965) *The World We Have Lost*. London: Methuen.

Lausberg, H. (1949) *Elemente der literarischen Rhetorik*. Munich: Max Hueber Verlag.

Leavis, F. R. (1942) 'The greatness of *Measure for Measure*', *Scrutiny*, X, 3, 234–47.

—— (1948) *The Great Tradition*. London: Chatto & Windus.

—— (1952) 'Diabolic intellect and the noble hero: Or the sentimentalist's Othello', in *The Common Pursuit*. London: Chatto & Windus, 136–59.

—— (1975) 'Thought and emotional quality' and 'Reality and sincerity', reprinted in *The Living Principle: 'English' as a Discipline of Thought*. London: Chatto & Windus, 71–93.

Lee, Sidney (1929) 'The American Indian in Elizabethan England', in *Elizabethan and Other Essays*, ed. F. S. Boas. London: Oxford University Press, 263–301.

Leggatt, Alexander (1974) *Shakespeare's Comedy of Love*. London: Methuen.

Lerner, L. (ed.) (1963) *Shakespeare's Tragedies, An Anthology of Modern Criticism*. Harmondsworth: Penguin.

—— (1967) *Shakespeare's Comedies: An Anthology of Modern Criticism*, Harmondsworth: Penguin.

Lever, J. W. (1976) 'Shakespeare and the ideas of his time', in Muir, K. (ed.) *Shakespeare Survey*, 29. Cambridge: Cambridge University Press, 79–81.

Leverenz, David (1980) 'The woman in Hamlet: An interpersonal view', in Schwarz, Murray M. and Kahn, Coppélia (eds) *Representing Shakespeare, New Psychoanalytic Essays*. Baltimore, Md. and London: Johns Hopkins University Press.

Levin, S. R. (1962) *Linguistic Structures in Poetry*. The Hague: Mouton.

Long, M. (1976) *The Unnatural Scene: A Study in Shakespearean Tragedy*. London: Methuen.

Lotman, Y. (1970) *Struktura Khudozhestvennogo teksta*. Moscow: Iskusstuo. In Italian: *La struttura del testo poetico*. Milan: Mursia, 1973. In English: *The Structure of the Artistic Text*, trans. Ronald Vroon. Ann Arbor: University of Michigan Press, 1977.

—— and Uspensky, B. (1973) *Semoticheskie isledovanija*. Moscow: In Italian *Ricerche semiotiche*. Turin: Einaudi, 1973.

Lukács, Georg (1974) *Soul and Form*. London: Merlin Press.

MacCabe, Colin (1979) 'On discourse', *Economy and Society*, 8, 4, 279–307.

MacCaffrey, W. T. (1965) 'England: The Crown and the New Aristocracy, 1540–1600', *Past and Present*, 30, 52–64.

McDonald, D. J. (1978) '*Hamlet* and the mimesis of absence: A post-structuralist analysis', *Educational Theatre Journal*, 30, 36–53.

Macherey, P. (1976) 'The problem of reflection', *Sub-stance*, 15, 6–20.

—— (1977) 'An interview', *Red Letters*, 5, 3–9.

—— (1978) *A Theory of Literary Production*, trans. Geoffrey Wall. Reprinted London: Routledge & Kegan Paul, 1980.

—— and Balibar, E. (1978) 'On literature as an ideological form: Some Marxist propositions', *Oxford Literary Review*, 3, 4–12.

—— (1980) 'Literature as an ideological form: Some Marxist hypotheses', *Praxis*, 5, 43–58.

Maxwell, J. C. (1947) '*Measure for Measure*: A footnote to recent criticism', *Downside Review*, 65, 45–59.

Melchiori, G. (1973) *L'uomo e il potere*. Turin: Einaudi. English edition: *Shakespeare's Dramatic Meditations*. Oxford: Clarendon Press, 1976.

Millar, Oliver (1963) *The Tudor, Stuart and Early Georgian Pictures in the Collection of H.M. the Queen*, 2 vols. London: Phaidon.

Milton, John (1959) *The Complete Prose Works*, vol. 2, ed. Ernest Sirluck. London: Oxford University Press.

Modern Languages Association (1983) *1981 MLA International Bibliography of Books and Articles on the Modern Languages and Literatures*, vol. 1. New York: Modern Languages Association.

Montrelay, Michèle (1970) 'Recherches sur la féminité, *Critique*, 26, 654–74; revised 'Inquiry into femininity', trans. and intro. by Parveen Adams, *m/f*, 65–101.

Montrose, L. A. (1981) '"The Place of a Brother" in *As You Like It*: Social process and comic form', *Shakespeare Quarterly*, 32, 28–54.

Morgann, Maurice (1903) 'Essay on the dramatic character of Sir John Falstaff' [1777], in Smith, D. Nichol (ed.) *Eighteenth-Century Essays on Shakespeare*. Glasgow: James MacLehose.

Morison, Stanley (1963) *The Likeness of Sir Thomas More*. London: Burns & Oates.

Morton, A. L. (1970) *The World of the Ranters*. London: Lawrence & Wishart.

Muir, Kenneth (1977) *The Singularity of Shakespeare and Other Essays*. Liverpool: Liverpool University Press.

—— (1979) *Shakespeare's Comic Sequence*. Liverpool: Liverpool University Press.

Mulhern, Francis (1979) *The Moment of 'Scrutiny'*. London: New Left Books. Reprinted Verso, 1981.

Mullini, R. (1983) *Corruttore di parole: il fool nel teatro di Shakespeare*. Bologna: CLUEB.

Murray, K. M. Elizabeth (1977) *Caught in the Web of Words*. New Haven and London: Yale University Press.

Neale, J. E. (1957) *Elizabeth I and Her Parliaments, 1584–1601*. London: Jonathan Cape.

Newbolt Report (1921) *The Teaching of English in England*, Report of the Board of Education. London: HMSO.

Norris, Christopher (1982) *Deconstruction: Theory and Practice*. London: Methuen.

Nowell-Smith, S. (ed.) (1967) *Letters to Macmillan*. London: Macmillan.

Nuttall, A. D. (1983) *A New Mimesis: Shakespeare and the Representation of Reality*. London: Methuen.

Ohmann, R. (1971) 'Speech, action and style', in Chatman, Seymour (ed.) *Literary Styles*. London: Oxford University Press.

—— (1973) 'Literature as act', in Chatman, Seymour (ed.) *Approaches to Poetics*. New York: Columbia University Press.

Orgel, Stephen (1975) *The Illusion of Power: Political Theatre in The English Renaissance*. Berkeley: University of California Press.

—— (1982) 'Making greatness familiar', in Greenblatt, Stephen (ed.) *The Power of Forms in the English Renaissance*. Oklahoma: Pilgrim Books.

Pagnini, M. (1969) 'Lettura critica (e metacritica) del sonetto 20 di Shakespeare.', *Strumenti critici*, III, 1.

—— (1976) *Shakespeare e il paradigma della specularità*. Pisa: Pacini.

—— (1980) *Pragmatica della lettereatura*. Palermo: Sellerio.

Palmer, D. J. (1965) *The Rise of English Studies*. Oxford and Hull: Oxford University Press.

Pêcheux, M. (1982) *Language, Semantics and Ideology*, trans. H. Nagpal. London: Macmillan. Orig. publ. in French, 1975.

Perkins, William (1970) *Works*, ed. Ian Breward. Abingdon: Sutton Country Press.

Pope-Hennessy, John (1966) *The Portrait in the Renaissance*. London: Phaidon.

Purchas, Samuel (1905–7) *Purchas His Pilgrimes* [1625], 20 vols. Glasgow: James MacLehose.

Puttenham, G. (1589) *The Arte of English Poesie*. London: Richard Field.

Quinn, David Beers (1966) *The Elizabethans and the Irish*. Ithaca, NY: Cornell University Press.

Raleigh, W. A. (1905) 'The English voyages of the sixteenth century', in Hakluyt, R. *The Principal Navigations, Voyages, Traffiques and Discoveries of the English Nation* [1589], 12 vols. Glasgow: James MacLehose, XII.

—— (1907) *William Shakespeare*. 'English Men of Letters' series. London: Macmillan.

—— (1918) *England and the War*. Oxford: Clarendon Press.

—— (1926) *Letters*, ed. Lady Raleigh, London: Methuen.

Rubinstein, A. (1969) *The Great Tradition in English Literature from Shakespeare to Shaw*, vol. I. New York: Monthly Review Press.

Rutelli, R. (1975) *Saggi sulla connotazione: tre sonetti di Shakespeare*. Torino: Giappichelli.

—— (1979) *Romeo e Giulietta: l'effabile*. Milan: Il Formichiere.

Ryan, M. (1982) *Marxism and Deconstruction*. Baltimore, Md. and London: Johns Hopkins University Press.

Salgádo, G. (1973) 'The middle comedies', in Wells, S. (ed.) *Shakespeare: Select Bibliographical Guides*. London: Oxford University Press, 74–93.

Sanders, Wilbur (1968) *The Dramatist and the Received Idea*. Cambridge: Cambridge University Press.

Saussure, Ferdinand de (1983) *A Course in General Linguistics*, trans. Roy Harris. London: Duckworth.

Scarman, Lord (1981) *The Brixton Disorders 10–12 April 1981* (The Scarman Report). London: HMSO.

Schücking, Levin L. (1922) *Character Problems in Shakespeare's Plays*. London: George Harrap.

Schwarz, Murray M. and Kahn, Coppélia (1980) *Representing Shakespeare, New Psychoanalytic Essays*. Baltimore, Md. and London: Johns Hopkins University Press.

Segre, C. (1979) 'Generi', *Enciclopedia Einaudi*, vol. 6. Turin: Einaudi.

Serpieri, A. (1975) *I sonetti dell'immortalitî*. Milan: Bompiani.

—— (1977) 'Ipotesi teorica di segementazione del testo teatrale', *Strumenti critici*, 32–3. Turin: Einaudi.

—— (1978) *Otello: l'Eros negato*. Milan: Il Folmchiere.

—— (1980) 'La retorica a teatro', *Strumenti critici*, 41.

—— (ed) (1978) *Come comunica il teatro: dal testo alla scena*. Milan: Il Folmchiere.

Shakespeare, William (1877) *Hamlet*. Variorum Edition, ed. H. H. Furness, 15th edn. Philadelphia: Lippincott.

—— (1954) *The Tempest*, ed. Frank Kermode. London: Methuen.

—— (1965) *Measure for Measure*, ed. J. W. Lever. London: Methuen.

—— (1966) *King Lear*, ed. Kenneth Muir. London: Methuen.

—— (1967) *All's Well That Ends Well*, ed. G. K. Hunter. London: Methuen.

—— (1975a) *As You Like It*, ed. A. Latham. London: Methuen.

—— (1975b) *Twelfth Night*, ed. J. M. Lothian and T. W. Craik. London: Methuen.

—— (1979) *A Midsummer Night's Dream*, ed. Harold F. Brooks. London: Methuen.

—— (1982a) *Hamlet*, ed. H. Jenkins. London: Methuen.

—— (1982b) *Henry V*, ed. Gary Taylor. London: Oxford University Press.

Shakespeare Newsletter (1974) 'Marxist Interpretations of Shakespeare'. Special issue. *Shakespeare Newsletter*, 24 (September–November).

Shepherd, Simon (1981) *Amazons and Warrior Women: Varieties of Feminism in Seventeenth-century Drama*. Brighton: Harvester Press.

Sidney, Sir Philip (1966) *A Defence of Poetry*. ed. J. A. Van Dorsten. London: Oxford University Press.

Siegel, P. (1957) *Shakespearean Tragedy and the Elizabethan Compromise*. New York: New York University Press.

—— (1968) *Shakespeare in His Time and Ours*. Notre Dame, Ind.: University of Notre Dame Press.

Sinfield, Alan (1983a) *Literature in Protestant England 1560–1660*. London: Croom Helm; Totowa, N.J.: Barnes and Noble.

—— (1983b) *Sociey and Literature 1945–1970*. London: Methuen.

Smith, James (1974) 'The Tempest', in *Shakespearian and Other Essays*. Cambridge: Cambridge University Press, 159–261.

Smith, Henry (1591) *A Preparative to Marriage*. London.

Smith, Robert M. (1950) 'Interpretations of *Measure for Measure*', *Shakespeare Quarterly*, I, 208–18.

Spencer, Theodore (1942) *Shakespeare and the Nature of Man*. London: Macmillan.

Spenser, Edmund (1970) *A View of the Present State of Ireland*. Oxford: Clarendon Press.

Stewart, J. I. M. (1949) *Character and Motive in Shakespeare*, ed. W. L. Renwick. London: Longmans.

Stoll, E. E. (1960) *Shakespeare Studies: Historical and Comparative in Method*. New York: Frederick Ungar. Orig. publ. 1927.

Stone, Lawrence (1965) *The Crisis of the Aristocracy 1558–1641*. Oxford: Clarendon Press.

—— (1972) *The Causes of the English Revolution 1529–1642*. London: Routledge & Kegan Paul.

—— (1977) *The Family, Sex and Marriage in England 1500–1800*, London: Weidenfeld & Nicholson.

Strong, Roy (1967) *Holbein and Henry VIII*. London: Routledge & Kegan Paul.

Strype, John (1822) *The Life and Acts of John Whitgift*, vol. 1. London: Oxford University Press.

Styan, J. (1971) *Shakespeare's Stagecraft*. Cambridge: Cambridge University Press.

Tillyard, E. M. W. (1943) *The Elizabethan World Picture*. London: Chatto & Windus'. Reprinted Harmondsworth: Penguin, 1960.

—— (1944) *Shakespeare's History Plays*. London: Chatto & Windus. Reprinted Harmondsworth, Penguin, 1962.

Trevelyan, G. M. (1942) *English Social History*. London: Longmans.

Vološinov, Valentin (1973) *Marxism and the Philosophy of Language*. New York: Seminar Press.

Weimann, R. (1978) *Shakespeare and the Popular Tradition in the Theater*, ed. R. Schwartz. Baltimore, Md, and London: Johns Hopkins University Press.

Widdowson, Peter (ed.) (1982) *Re-Reading English*. London: Methuen.

Williams, David (1977) *A History of Modern Wales*, 2nd edn. London: John Murray.

Williams, Raymond (1977) *Marxism and Literature*. London: Oxford University Press.

—— (1980) *Problems in Materialism and Culture*. London: Verso.

—— (1984) *Writing in Society*. London: Verso.

Wilson, John Dover (1962) *Shakespeare's Happy Comedies*. London: Faber & Faber.

Wilson, T. (1909) *The Arte of Rhetorique. 1560*, ed. G. H. Mair. Oxford: Clarendon Press.

Winnicott, D. W. (1971) *Playing and Reality*. London: Tavistock Publications.

—— (1972) [1966] 'Split-off male and female elements found clinically in men and women: theoretical inferences'. *Psychanalytic Forum*, 4, (ed.) J. Linden. New York: International Universities Press.

Wolff, Janet (1981) *The Social Production of Art*. London: Macmillan.

Woolf, C. and Moorcroft Wilson, J. (eds) (1982) *Authors Take Sides on the Falklands*. London: Woolf.

Young, Robert (ed.) (1981) *Untying the Text: A Post-Structuralist Reader*. London: Routledge & Kegan Paul.

INDEX